LONDON: HUMPHREY MILFORD
OXFORD UNIVERSITY PRESS

A Century of
Latin-American Thought

A Century of Latin-American Thought

BY

WILLIAM REX CRAWFORD
Cultural Attaché, United States Embassy, Rio de Janeiro

CAMBRIDGE · MASSACHUSETTS
HARVARD UNIVERSITY PRESS
1944

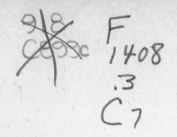
ACKNOWLEDGMENTS

THE AUTHOR gratefully acknowledges a grant from the Faculty Research Committee of the University of Pennsylvania which enabled him to do the research for this study. He is also indebted to his friends Dr. and Mrs. John M. Fogg, Jr., for reading the proof and seeing the book through the press, and to certain other colleagues at the University of Pennsylvania for their generous assistance.

Contents

A Century of Latin-American Thought

Noble deseo, pero grave error cuando se quiere hacer historia es el que pretende recordar a todos los héroes. En la historia literaria el error lleva a la confusión.

— Pedro Henríquez Ureña

Pero en la Argentina se ignora quién es Montalvo: el adolescente cansado de oír hablar de Alberdi y Sarmiento, apenas ha oído nunca el nombre de Rodó . . . y no sabe que haya existido la espléndida floración que fué el espíritu de José Martí. Las literaturas nacionales no tienen sentido en América. En cada país no hay sino figuras de un gran movimiento de pensamiento originado en Europa y sentido en forma americana. Es pues absurdo querer organizar literaturas nacionales.

— José Luis Romero

Los sistemas filosóficos no son toda la filosofía, ni siquiera toda la filosofía sistemática. Las ideas filosóficas revisten formas poéticas, históricas, políticas, religiosas, que no se formularon en enunciados rigurosamente sistemáticos.

— Antonio Caso

En lo principal, una recopilación y ordenación de los materiales contenidos en obras que por su extensión, su costo o el idioma en que están escritas, son inaccesibles a la generalidad de los estudiantes.

— Agustín Alvarez

Sólo del pensamiento derivan las formas más humildes y las más altas del progreso; sólo del pensamiento podemos esperar redención, entendiendo por pensamiento, es claro, no sólo el frío razonar, sino la noción integral mística, de la existencia, con todas sus angustias y deleites y claridades.

— José Vasconcelos

Maestro no significa sólo sabiduría; significa a la vez valor moral, belleza moral, aptitud innata para derramar por sobre todas las conciencias el milagro de una palabra de amor, de un signo de esperanza. Maestro es algo más: la evidencia de un equilibrio permanente de todas las facultades superiores de *hombre*.

— Rómulo Nano Lottero

CHAPTER I

Introduction

IN THE FLURRY of recent inter-American cultural developments our interest and our knowledge have remained
curiously spotty. The wisest observer of these developments
has remarked our deficiencies in the fields of economics and
sociology, and the scantiness of materials on Latin-American
art and music. To these we should like to add another. Not
to know the men of ideas of Latin America is particularly
unfortunate. Honest introspection will convince the average
educated North American — not the specialist, for whom this
book is not intended — that the names of Latin-American
thinkers are hardly even names to him.

No countries attach more importance to their intellectual
élite than do the Latin-American republics. It is as natural
for them to have confidence in the great figures in whom their
culture has flowered as it is for us to rely proudly on the
machine which is the symbol of our civilization. Even those
whose official Marxism would seem to require giving primacy
to the economic factor impress the outsider as being first of
all believers in the power of the idea. This statement does
not imply that the ideas we shall study have shaped practical
politics or that they are universally accepted — the wide differences among them would alone prevent that — or that
they are even continentally known.

There is no surer way to reach the heart and soul of a culture than to know the men whom it calls great, and to determine whether they represent something distinctive in
their culture.

As the generic name for those under discussion, the Latin Americans' own term *pensadores* is inevitable. It is a term as elastic as the eighteenth-century *philosophes*, which is as close to sociologist as to philosopher. Perhaps in a young country philosophy is bound to be social philosophy; such, at any rate, is the case with Latin America. The term *pensadores* includes men who have tried to interpret the whole social reality that lay about them, seeking its roots in the past and looking with grave concern for their country and for America into an unknown future. They are moralists, critics, publicists, political scientists, and sociologists — rarely philosophers. Those writers who are primarily men of action have been deliberately omitted from this study, together with those whose history writing is predominantly narrative rather than interpretative, and those whose names are linked only to some field of scientific specialization. Economists and statisticians do not bulk large here, for it is harder for them to achieve the status of *pensador* than for the Biblical camel to go through the eye of the needle.

While all parallels are dangerous, and no detailed comparison is intended, it may help the uninitiated to suppose that we are to meet the equivalent in Latin America of the English Bentham, Coleridge, Mill, Buckle, Lecky, T. H. Green, Carlyle, Ruskin, Bagehot, Newman, Arnold, Maine, Spencer, Hobhouse, Westermarck, Sidney and Beatrice Webb, Bertrand Russell, H. G. Wells, Laski, Toynbee; or the American Jefferson, Irving, Emerson, Lincoln, Pierce, Henry and Brooks Adams, Royce, William James, Santayana, F. J. Turner, Sumner, Ward, Cooley, Dewey, Whitehead, Veblen, Sorokin, Stuart Chase, Walter Lippmann, Lewis Mumford.

Such lists suggest variety to us. Yet there are central themes running through Latin-American thought, and all related to the historic situation of the Latin-American countries after the achievement of independence. In fact, it would be difficult to find a period of the world's thought which better illustrates the thesis that philosophy gets its new and urgent problems from the place and plight of the society in which it arises. Latin-American countries had accomplished that for which they had long fought — independence — and yet the promised Rousseauian Utopia was not theirs. There were still problems. Borrowed constitutions seemed impotent to solve these problems. Separation from Spain left the new nations with a legacy of Spain and the colonial régime; Spain was in their souls. The persistent problems that presented themselves were: Why are we different from the United States? What shall be our relation to the northern republic and to Europe? How did we get to be what we are, and what is our destiny as a people and as a continent? There is no exaggeration in proclaiming these to be the most constant preoccupations of the Latin-American thinkers for over a century.

The answers given by the *pensadores* exhaust the range of possibilities. Some, like Gálvez, lament the break with Hispanic tradition; others, like Alvarez, would not undo the revolution, but believe the necessary break with tradition is responsible for many problems. González pleads for admiration of or at the least for an accommodation with Spain, and points to Anglo-American coöperation. At the opposite extreme Lastarria and Bilbao help to found the Black Legend of Spanish cruelty, intolerance, and incompetence. Some thinkers look to the United States as the great example of successful development, to be copied in politics and economics; Lastarría and Sarmiento come to mind immediately. Others, and it will be noted that they are the more recent thinkers, like Ugarte, Vasconcelos, and Haya de la Torre, fear and resent the Colossus of the North even bearing gifts and Dwight Morrows. In their attitude toward the Catholic heritage, they range from the resolutely Catholic, like Gálvez, through the friendly attitude of Rodó or Vasconcelos and the criticism of Montalvo that earns him the undeserved label of heretic, to the virulent attacks of Mexico's Voltaire, Ramírez, or Peru's accusing voice, González Prada. Their position toward Positivism is nearly always an important part of their thought, difficult for us to grasp because our thought is so bounded by Positivism that only a few of us have glimpsed the possibility of any other attitude, and also because "positivist" and its opposites have become epithets incidental to a combat situation and often unfair to the shades of thought of an individual. Thus Dr. Mora, labeled a precursor of Positivism in Mexico,[1] can hardly be claimed as an adherent of a school that did not exist, and Varona, who is considered the great exponent of Positivism in Cuba, if not in all Latin America, displays in reality an independent and eclectic attitude; the anti-Positivistic elements in Antonio Caso, on the other hand, are explicit.

Some of the thinkers are thoroughly European in their culture, and give scant attention to the Indian and other disquieting aspects of the South American reality; Montalvo and Rodó are examples, although even they do not flee from America, and desire its salvation through European culture. Rojas stands for a fusion, Freyre for the importance of the Indian and Negro contribution; Vasconcelos glorifies the new race to emerge on this continent; and for Luis Alberto Sánchez, Mariátegui, and Haya de la Torre the question of America is the question of the Indian.

Not all Latin-American *pensadores* are as spiritual as Rodó; abundant attention is given to economic realities by Alberdi, Bulnes, and the Marxist Mariátegui. A few have impressed their fellow-countrymen as men *de mesure*, eminently well-balanced, self-controlled, like Bello, Hostos, Acosta, Varona. They are the same who have mediated to Latin America the

---

[1] Leopoldo Zea, *El positivismo en México* (Mexico, 1942), pp. 78–106.

spirit of the Anglo-Saxon civilization which they have known and admired. One is tempted to conclude that neither their restraint nor their "English" mentality do them any good with Latin-American society; the figures that win acclaim are those with the divine gift of passion, God's "men-in-a-hurry," in Gabriela Mistral's untranslatable phrase. These men have usually sought action as well as literary expression; Sarmiento and Martí are preëminently geniuses in organization and action as well as in the word, and are for that reason the supreme figures of the nineteenth century. Those who found it possible to live and serve without perpetual fighting, like Bello and Sierra, have suffered some neglect with the passing years.

Among peoples reputedly touchy and resentful of the truth when it is unpleasant, it is surprising to find how many thinkers have made most forthright and bitter attacks upon their country's political and economic institutions, and even upon the essential qualities of its population; no less flattering picture of the biological and cultural elements of a society could be found than that offered by Bunge, Bulnes, Bomfim, Alvarez, Arguedas, and even the placid but disillusioned Varona. Rodó's glorification of Hispanic America's essential qualities and unlimited possibilities, and the South American dream of many another, are very natural reactions in the opposite direction.

On the one hand, then, we North Americans must disabuse ourselves of the idea that Latin America speaks with one voice, has but one answer to the basic problem of her being and becoming. On the other hand, we need not forego the attempt at a generalization on the attitudes and character-istics of these thinkers, in contrast to our own. This is not to claim great philosophic originality for them, nor for our-selves for that matter; we have followed different masters. Francisco García Calderón, preparing a report on philo-

sophical tendencies in Latin America for a Congress at
Heidelberg in 1908,[2] found no original system of philosophy
in the hundred years since independence, but only the proof
of intellectual curiosity and power of assimilation in imita-
tions and adaptations of foreign thought. This thought, he
rightly maintained, was in major part French. Politically,
Latin America had followed Rousseau and the ideals of the
French Revolution. On the morrow of the wars of independence, the Saint-Simonian influence was strong, and it
was succeeded by the supremacy of Positivism, which in
turn provoked a reaction to French idealism. The great
teachers of Latin America were Leroux and Comte, Guyau,
Fouillée, Renan, and Taine, rather than the Kantian, He-
gelian, or pessimistic schools. There was some acceptance of
Spencer; to some thinkers Nietzsche is at least in part congenial; and recently there has been a turn to Kant, but still
the French influence is predominant. Latterly the influence
of Boutroux and Bergson has been notable. If in their
emphasis on the social aspects of philosophy the Latin
Americans are like ourselves, it is clear that in their choice
of foreign masters they have sat at the feet of men whose
following in the United States has not been large.

For the Spanish philosopher José Gaos, who writes a striking article on the philosophic significance of Hispanic American thought in *Cuadernos americanos*,[3] the essential trait of
this thinking is the emphasis on the personal. It is a Latin
American who speaks of the holy sacrament of conversation.
The thinker falls a prey to his own satisfaction with his
happy find in ideas and words. His first aim is esthetic.
Vasconcelos remarks with some astonishment [4] that "there

[2] Francisco García Calderón, "Las corrientes filosóficas en la América latina," in
his *Ideas e impresiones* (Madrid, 1919), pp. 56–57.
[3] José Gaos, "Significación filosófica del pensamiento hispano-americano,"
Cuadernos americanos (Mexico), II (1943), 63–86.
[4] José Vasconcelos, *Indología* (Barcelona, n.d.), p. 111.

are some of us who write badly, and still we are read; people pay attention to us." But this is new, and still unusual. Many of the *pensadores* were poets first, and nearly all wrote poetry. Even of a contemporary with a North American education, Gilberto Freyre, his admiring friend José Lins do Rego remarks that he is great not because he is a social scientist, but because he writes so poetically; and Freyre himself prefers to be called a writer rather than a sociologist. When the Latin-American thinker aims at a satisfaction more outgoing and social than the simple *Erlebnis* of his own creative thinking, it is notable how constantly he aims at impressing a small group of habitual listeners. If in actual life his personality does not lend itself to this Socratic method of public philosophizing, he imagines the scene of his success, as does Rodó in *Ariel*. This situation is recognized by the words in which Latin America expresses the relationship: on the one hand master, apostle, director of the minds of youth, and on the other hand, disciple. It is implicit in the appeal thinkers make to youth, so inseparable from their thought in Rodó, Ingenieros, González Prada, Vasconcelos, and others. It is reflected in the numerous biographies which disciples have written of their masters — lyrical, fervent works of devotion, frank eulogies even when, like Luis Alberto Sánchez' dissertation on González Prada, they are submitted to a university for the doctorate. Note also the immense amount of work which exists in the form of letters, and which cannot be disregarded when one seeks the doctrine of the man; Acosta, Martí, Ruy Barbosa, and many others were great letterwriters. As a second-best and less intimate relation between master and followers, the public oration plays an important part. Discourses to the nation or to America are prominent in the work of Sarmiento, Bilbao, the Mexicans, González Prada, Haya de la Torre, Varela, Varona, Ingenieros. There is little thought of the "absent, distant, unknown, anonymous, impersonal reader," and consequently little acceptance of the kind of scientific responsibility that accompanies addressing him, and perhaps an excessive tendency toward the esthetic and amethodical. Since the themes of Latin-American thought are chiefly ethical, pedagogical, social, and political, the test of effectiveness is the formation of a minority that in Toynbee's terms is "creative," that has a solution and attempts to make it operative in the national life. It is only a step from the themes of the *pensadores'* writing to action in the political arena, and most Latin-American writers have wished to take this step, even when like Gálvez they have failed to win an effective following. The logical end of this process is Haya de la Torre's confession that he is a man of action rather than of literature; books are incidental to the direct appeal to party and people. To the practical-minded, this closeness of relation to the cultural community and its problems here and now is a merit. To the philosopher Gaos it is disquieting, and he finds the themes circumstantial, and the thought itself of a type which gives the impression of dilettantism, volubility, lightness, superficiality, lack of principle and system. To him, the desire of the philosopher to be a politician, to engage in politics by forming or reforming the national life through beautiful ideas beautifully expressed to intimate groups of followers, casts doubt upon the value of his philosophy. The fusion of ethics, esthetics, and politics does not promise science, and the result is something that seems far from the monuments of European philosophy — Descartes, Spinoza, Kant, Hegel. Gaos even considers dismissing this type of writing as literature, although with the pat on the back of calling it good literature. Further reflection recalls to mind the ethical and social interests of Plato and Aristotle, and all the tradition of Hobbes, Locke, Condorcet, Comte, Marx, Nietzsche, Taine, and our own John Dewey. Would it not be wise to admit that philosophy

means different things in different cultures, that its definition
and its aims are themselves historic products, and because of
the meaning the word "philosopher" has for us, to deny that
name to Latin Americans who have chosen to be more like
the eighteenth-century *philosophe* than the early nineteenth-
century *Philosoph*?

CHAPTER II

Independence and Nationhood

Esteban Echeverría (1805–1851)

WE SHALL NOT begin by quarreling with history for having selected the names of Echeverría, Alberdi, and Sarmiento as the outstanding ones in the thought of the new nation of Argentina; she might have paid more attention to Juan María Gutiérrez or Vicente Fidel López or many another, but she has chosen not to do so. In any case, the ideas that agitated the minds of patriots and men of culture in the early days of the nation can be suggested in connection with the three names listed.

What was on the minds of these thinkers can best be expressed in their own words, with a minimum of that historical background which we take for granted, and no psychoanalysis at all.

"Let us weep, brothers: our country does not exist!" sang Echeverría, who was first of all a romantic poet. Certainly the country dreamed of by the patriots who had thrown off the heavy hand of Spain did not exist. The petty tyranny of *caudillos* from the pampas gave place to the massive and ubiquitous tyranny of Rosas, and young men with dangerous thoughts kept them quiet or indulged in them in exile. Statistics are not needed, but probably more than half of the *pensadores* experienced banishment. Echeverría was only the first of many to go into exile for a longer or shorter time. The disappointment he felt that his land was lagging behind the homeland of the French Revolution — failing to establish a republican society — could find an outlet only in drawing up plans against the day when tyranny should be no more. Thus he summarized all he had learned in France.[1] Orgaz, in his *Echeverría y el saintsimonismo* (1934), proves to the hilt that his theories, and even their verbal expression, are derived from French sources; if not from Saint-Simon, from Leroux and other Saint-Simonians of the period after the master's death. Saint-Simonian socialism was a theory impossible of application at the moment, and the contradictory Byronic poet was not the man to apply it; but his fiery words stabbed awake the spirits of others, including Alberdi and Sarmiento. In a later day what he said in the Association of May — that revolutionary brotherhood of young Argentine patriots which he helped to found — came to have the quality of a great historic event; there had been formed a nucleus of ideas and convictions which has played and still plays in these days of renewed revolution a vital part in Argentine thinking about freedom.[2] Echeverría's immortality is assured.

The spirit of the rebellious young poet and an adumbration of all his future work is contained in the words with which he saluted his coming of age and freedom from an unsympathetic guardian: "Now at last I am free, on the path of glory, struggling against fate!" He promised himself to triumph and to show men that they should not take the path of happiness, which enslaves and degrades them, but rather the road of honor and glory.[3] This is a road that for Latin Americans led through Paris and the cramped offices of successive little journals of opinion, wriggling and squirming to avoid sup-

[1] Jorge M. Furt, *Esteban Echeverría* (1936), p. 61.
[2] Argentina, formerly called the United Provinces of the Río de la Plata, had finally broken from Spain in 1816. The powerful city of Buenos Aires now expected to take the place of Spain and rule the upland provinces. Two main political parties contended on this issue, the unitarians supporting control by Buenos Aires, the federalists opposing. Rosas, powerful Gaucho chief, finally achieved unification of the country, but his tyrannical rule was one of persecution and bloodshed, admitting no government by law. Thus was called into being the young group known as the Asociación de Mayo, whose message of revolt and reform was contained in Echeverría's *Dogma Socialista*.   [3] Alberto Palcos, *Echeverría* (1941), p. 15.

pression by the censor and starting up again under new names. In Paris, as a relief from more serious studies, Echeverría read Shakespeare, Schiller, Goethe, and especially Byron, who moved him profoundly and opened up for him a new world. Under their influence he decided to write poetry, but, he explains, he had become so French that he felt ignorant of his own language, its versification and its classic authors.[4] On his return to Argentina, he wrote both prose and verse, and expounded the ideas of those European authors from whom his eclectic nature had derived inspiration, including Mazzini.

Less the man of action than Mazzini, and with less faith in the people, Echeverría sympathized with his aims; or perhaps both derived their goals from the same French sources. Both laid stress on what they called socialism, namely the supremacy of society and its interests over the individual and individual interests — over the machinations of classes and cliques. One student of Echeverría (Bogliolo) attempts to make of his socialism an anticipation of the Marxian, but does some violence to the ensemble of Echeverría's writing.

In a forerunner of the *Dogma Socialista*, the "Code" of 1839, Echeverría insisted on the irrevocable nature of the Argentine declaration of independence, designed to assure forever the rule of liberty, of happiness, and of law. The Code went further, preaching self-study for the country, and in the light of that self-examination the making of plans which should not be mere aping of foreign models or experience. If we are faithful to these principles, says Echeverría, there is no doubt that our country, and with it all of America, will achieve a notable synthesis between the opposing concepts of country and humanity and between those of individual and society.

[4] Gutiérrez, "Noticias Biográficas," in Echeverría, *Obras*, V, xviii, repr. in *Dogma Socialista* (ed. of 1940), pp. 14–15.

There is no mention in the Code of particular personalities that must be followed; Echeverría has raised the banner (which perpetually needs to be unfurled) of a politics based on principles — on issues and not on leaders. The greatest of all principles for him is that of democracy; he makes all the objections he can to it, and yet finds it the only acceptable and suitable form of government for his people. The criterion of democracy determines whether religions, philosophies, forms of art, findings of science, the results of business and industrial enterprise are to be welcomed or refused. Asked for a definition, Echeverría needs few words: democracy is the régime of liberty, founded on the equality of social classes. The immediate step in the direction of these never-quite-attained ideals is to attempt a reconciliation of the warring elements within the family of the nation, not to take sides. This same spirit lives in Echeverría's other work, and is transmitted to Alberdi and through him to the actual legal organization of the country.

It would be a serious error to think of Echeverría as being satisfied with legislative solutions alone to his country's problems. Indeed, while we North Americans have a tendency to associate such legerdemain with the countries of Latin America, there is scarcely one of the Latin-American thinkers who does not criticize it unsparingly and insist on getting behind the political organization and legislative enactments to the social order, and especially to the reform of education. This is true of Echeverría, who says roundly: "There is no health, no happy future, no solid progress for these countries without this condition: the education of the people, an education for democratic living, which must be the flag, the symbol, the social religion of intelligent men on both banks of the River Plate." [5] From such education we may hope for an increase in both talent and virtue, which

[5] Palcos, p. 137.

are the only forms of supremacy he recognizes. "And among the able and worthy, you will give respect to each man according to his capacity, and to each capacity according to its fruits." [6]

Men have, he believes, such innate love for justice that with a modicum of such education the spiritualized, cooperative socialism that is his ideal can be brought into being peacefully and progressively. He had a hope (which present-day socialism would call utopian), that all good citizens, all classes and interests, would coöperate loyally once matters were explained to them, and that each succeeding generation would by appropriate educational measures have its feet set on the path of virtue and duty.

In a writing of considerable importance entitled "A Glance Back over the Intellectual Movement in the Plata Region Since 1837," prefixed to the second edition (1846) of his *Dogma Socialista*, Echeverría raises his voice for religion, pointing out that religious questions generally have little interest for his people, who smile ironically at them; the revolution had nothing good to say for religion, and religious feeling has died out. Our proud self-sufficiency, he says, has thought it could do without the greatest incentive to morality and civilization, the most powerful restraint on evil passions; perhaps philosophers can do without religion, but the people never.[7]

It is the *Dogma Socialista de la Asociación Mayo*, however, which he directs to the youth of Argentina, that contains in least diffuse form Echeverría's political teaching. "Work in brotherhood; do not fall into the error of your fathers. We were lost, because we shouted liberty, liberty, and were not brothers: disunion made all our sacrifices of no avail." [8]

[6] *Id.* at 138.
[7] Echeverría, *Dogma Socialista* (ed. of 1940), pp. 88–89.
[8] *Id.* at 149. The *Dogma Socialista* was first published in 1839, in the *Iniciador*

He seeks great symbolic words to stand for the credenda of the movement. "Association, progress, liberty, equality, fraternity: these sum up the great social and humanitarian synthesis; these are the divine symbols of the happy future of nations and of humanity." [9] Of them all, perhaps equality is the ideal nearest to his heart. It consists "in the fact that rights and duties are equally admitted and declared for all, so that no one can make himself an exception to the law, but every man shares with equal right in an enjoyment proportional to his intelligence and his work." [10] And he proceeds to a damning list of infringements on this rule by privilege on the one hand and deprivation on the other.

Like Montesquieu, he relies upon a psychological principle to make the republic function. "Morality regulates the acts of man as a private individual; honor his acts as a public man." [11] Honor, however, needs to be supplemented by something more forward-looking. "The great thought of the revolution has not been carried out. We are independent, but we are not free. The arms of Spain do not oppress us; but its traditions still weigh us down. Out of anarchy has come counter-revolution" and the recrudescence of the old ideas, the Spanish ideas, "the stationary idea." [12]

After his glorification of liberty and majority rule, he attempts a statement that will harmonize them, put limits to what the majority may require, and safeguard the liberty of the individual. "The sovereignty of the people is unlimited in all that pertains to society — in politics, in philosophy, in religion; but the people is not sovereign in what pertains to the individual — his conscience, his property, his life, his liberty." [13]

---

of Montevideo; a second edition appeared in book form in Montevideo in 1846. All references here are to the critical edition of 1940.

[9] *Id.* at 157.
[10] *Id.* at 162–163.
[11] *Id.* at 173.
[12] *Id.* at 193.
[13] *Id.* at 200.

In other related writings Echeverría examines the state of culture and civilization in Argentina. "We have neither literature nor philosophy; our political ability has produced nothing stable and adequate in social organization; our legislation is uncodified; in science, we have scarcely the name; the education of the people has not made a beginning . . . in short, our intellectual culture is embryonic. . . . This embryonic state of our civilization is natural and normal; there is nothing in it to humiliate or discourage us." [14] He has the hope of a Condorcet for unlimited progress; the best race in the world can surely in so splendid a country march unafraid and confident into the future. For "man is perfectible, society is perfectible, the human race is perfectible." [15] The vision is not elaborated with detail, but who can deny that it is a vision?

Juan Bautista Alberdi (1810–1884)

Out of the somewhat nebulous idealism of Echeverría there rose the magnificent systematization of Alberdi, in his "Bases and Points of Departure for the Political Organization of the Argentine Republic" and other writings. Alberdi was no natural leader of the masses, hardly a successful practical politician, and more a man of the clear and rational page than of the moving oration. Great popularity is not built out of his qualities, but the solitary, silent work of the thinker has made him a revered figure in Argentine universities. There are those who maintain that his analysis of the central problem of his country is still the valid one; even those who disagree, disagree with Alberdi and take his "Bases" as their point of departure.

For Alberdi, action should follow prolonged thought, and the thought should take the form of an analysis of the con-

[14] *Id.* at 276–277.
[15] Echeverría, *La filosofía social.*

ditions under which the action is to take place, and of the
probable consequences of the proposed course. The revolution was not the result of established principles, nor was it
sufficiently subordinated to the peculiar conditions of time
and place. Argentina declared herself free without having
prepared herself for freedom. Inner freedom should come
first, as it did in France and the United States. The anoma-
lies of Argentine society sprang from its having jumped to
political freedom while it remained the slave of the old ideas
and traditions. The forms of freedom coexist with the most
primitive ignorance. At times, he admits that Argentina is
only a dismembered part of Europe, to which it owes all it
has that is good, including its racial stock, so superior to the
aborigines of America.[16]

In the fall of Rosas, Alberdi saw a great opportunity for a
fresh start for the nation, this time based on the careful consideration of the nature of its problems, and for this opportunity he worked out his most imperishable volume, the
"Bases" (1852), called by Sarmiento an Argentine Deca-
logue. Without denying that the problems he discusses are
common to all Latin America, Alberdi paints a picture of the
needs and peculiarities of his country, seeking the root of the
difficulties and the remedies that reason recommends. The
problem, as he sees it, is essentially economic, and the root
of all difficulties is "poverty, underpopulation, backwardness, and misery." The program that he advocates is one of
hard work and economic development, and he is not afraid
to admit that South America will need much help from outside to carry out the program.[17]

To the romanticism of Echeverría and Gutiérrez, who were
more to him than any of his regular professors, Alberdi

[16] García Merou, *Alberdi* (1916), p. 85.
[17] Later, in *Vida y trabajos industriales de William Wheelwright* (1876), he did
not hesitate to glorify the builder of railroads as the man who more than any other
fought Argentina's real enemies, the desert and lack of communication.

brought his own solid learning, his leanings toward philosophy, the Locke and Bentham he carried in his pocket, and his sense of the vast emptiness of his country. It is characteristic of him that his favorite books should be English; he left Geneva after only two or three days because there were not enough Englishmen there, and he professed a strong distaste for the Spanish language.

He had something to learn from life, too, for his earliest writings were abstract, lacking in contact with reality and bearing no urgent message to his fellow men. After his trip around the southern tip of the continent and his arrival at Valparaiso he entered a second and sadder part of his life in which these lacks were remedied. During these years Sarmiento, López, and other Argentinians sought refuge in Chile, and there argued endlessly about the state of their own country. The arguments were not always friendly; Sarmiento may have been irked by his own inferior education; certainly he and Alberdi were miles apart in temperament in spite of the essential agreement of their ideas. They were soon involved in recriminations, and Sarmiento, the ex-soldier, attempted to crush his rival with the remark, "I have been a commander of men, you have not." (The word "I" was so much in his mouth that he was called "Don Yo.") The bluster of Sarmiento did not disturb Alberdi too much, however. On one occasion his friends asked why he had not answered Sarmiento's abuse, and he replied that he had not even read it for fear it might upset the literary work on which he was engaged. When he did answer, it was with an exactitude and a brilliance that was final.

To observe Argentina from the other side of the Andes for a time was all very well, but a separation that was to cut off Alberdi from Argentina far too completely was in store for him. He spent almost all his last forty years in Europe, in quasi-exile, more and more the solitary figure to whom there came only scanty and distorted news. When, an old man, he returned to Argentina, he could not act with knowledge, and his triumph fell flat, although he had become almost a mythical figure.

We are concerned with Alberdi's ideas rather than with his life, but there are anecdotes connected with his trip to the United States in 1855 that both have local interest and reflect his ideas. Although he was enthusiastic about visiting the country of Franklin and Washington, the home of a political wisdom that he wished to see copied in his own country, he did not see much of the United States. Ten days in New York was enough, for its impact was crushing to his egotism. Baltimore pleased him more, for it reminded him of South American cities. Philadelphia was his Mecca, and he felt a deep emotion as he entered Independence Hall. His irony, nevertheless, had not deserted him, and when he came out and saw a magnificent carriage passing on Chestnut Street, with two Negro footmen in uniform, he asked his companion pointedly how it was possible to reconcile that with the republic.[18]

The central idea of his "Bases," expressed in the phrase "to govern is to populate," has been so generally misunderstood that a little explanation is in order:

"To govern is to populate in the sense that to populate is to educate, to improve, to civilize, to enrich and make great, spontaneously and rapidly, as has happened in the United States.

"But to civilize by means of population it is necessary to have civilized populations; to educate our America in liberty and industry it is necessary to populate it with people from Europe, which is farther advanced in liberty and industry, as is being done in the United States. The United States can very well take an abject and servile immigrant and make a

[18] Pablo Rojas Paz, *Alberdi* (Buenos Aires, 1941), pp. 173–174.

good free citizen out of him by the simple natural pressure of its freedom upon him." For South America, to govern is to populate, because this inclusive ideal implies strengthening and affirming the freedom of the country, giving it intelligence and the habit of governing itself.[19]

"To govern is to populate; well and good: but to populate is a science, and this science is none other than political economy, which looks upon population as an instrument by which to achieve wealth and as a factor in prosperity." [20] Such progress as South America has so far made, he said, is inextricably connected with the growth in its European population, doubling every twenty years.[21] An immigration policy worked out in friendly coöperation with European nations can insure further and even accelerated progress in the same direction. This policy and all other policies that achieve legislative status need to be based on a scientific study of the needs and interests of the nation at the present moment. Thirty years ago the need of the hour was independence, and naturally the constitutions adopted had liberty more in view than any other object. Today, he insisted, things have changed, and without forgetting liberty an America that is "more practical than theoretical, more given to reflection than to enthusiasm, as a result of maturity and experience, must think of things rather than of men, and turn its attention not so much to final goals as to the means for reaching them. Today we seek the practical reality of that which in other days we were content to proclaim in writing. This is the end of constitutions today; they must organize and bring into being the great practical measures which will lift an already emancipated America from its present obscure and secondary position. Such measures must come before all else in our constitutions." [22]

[19] Alberdi, *Bases y puntos de partida para la organización de la Confederación Argentina* (1852).   [20] *Id.* at 19.   [21] *Id.* at 34.   [22] *Id.* at 66–67.

Some of the practical measures he proposed were in the field of education. "The English language, the language of liberty, of industry, and of order, must be made more obligatory than Latin; no one should get a diploma or university degree without speaking and writing it. This change in itself would profoundly transform our youth. How can we follow the example of the civilization of the Anglo-Saxon race without knowing its language?" Moreover, "Our youth must be educated in industrial life, and to that end must be instructed in the arts and sciences that are the handmaids of industry"; they must be made into the kind of men who will conquer "the desert, the material retardation, the brute, primitive nature of our continent." [23] The moral effects of such education would be splendid, for "industry is the only means of directing our youth toward order. . . . Industry is the great tranquilizer. It leads mankind through prosperity and wealth to order, and through order to liberty: examples of this you may see in England and the United States." [24]

In addition to training her own, he held, Argentina can attract from Europe the kind of settlers she needs. "Every European who comes to our shores brings us more civilization in the habits which he spreads immediately to our people than many books of philosophy. We cannot understand the perfection we do not see and touch and feel. A hard-working man is the most edifying catechism. . . . Let us bring from abroad new population elements already trained and well prepared. . . . The government that does not double the census every ten years has wasted its time on trifles." [25]

This is to be accomplished not by going into the shipping business, by offering labor contracts, or by working through middle-men, but by making conditions such that immigration will come spontaneously, and the immigrant will find such

[23] *Id.* at 78.
[24] *Id.* at 79.   [25] *Id.* at 89–90.

liberty that a short stay will convince him that the new country is henceforth his homeland. The United States is again
the example to be followed. Its religious tolerance is a point
to be noticed. While no country wants irreligious or immoral immigrants, it cannot avoid them by insisting on one
exclusive type of religious belief; it must offer asylum and
freedom to all types of worship. Here is the dilemma:
"Either exclusively Catholic and underpopulated, or popu-
lated, prosperous, and tolerant in religion." [26]

That Alberdi did not confuse means with ends is indicated
by his own emphatic statement. "The fact is, that railroads
and telegraph lines are no ends, but only means, instruments
of civilization. The proof is that these instruments can be
also the instruments of barbarism. . . . These agents are the
auxiliaries of other more solid and useful things, such as commerce, industry, wealth and liberty; and when the latter do
not develop *pari passu*, they are pure charlatanism, just a
pretense of civilization and progress. True civilization grows
from within toward the surface, and ends in railroads and
telegraphs; an incipient and rudimentary civilization begins
at the surface, and ends with the essentials; it has still not
broken its ties with barbarism and only shows off its steam
and telegraph and gas — that is to say, the part that shines
and attracts notice; a garment that it wears outside." [27]

Certainly he was not blind to moral considerations, and
could be earnestly satirical. Speaking of the Spanish, he
said, "we accuse them of having been cruel with the Indian
savages. Are we any more humane than the Spaniards with
our fellow countrymen, the Indians who are left?" [28]

There is both social theory and humanitarianism in his
observations about the relation between geography and type
of economy and character. "With the physical description

[26] *Id.* at 92–93.
[27] Alberdi, *Obras selectas*, XVIII, 18–19.   [28] *Id.* at 78.

of a country, it is easy to picture to oneself what its people will be like. When I hear people talk of a country that produces gold, silver, silk, cotton, linseed, wheat, wool, cattle growing wild, I say at once: the chief product of that country is idle, lazy, unskilled, poor, irresponsible, wicked men. . . . The worst thing you can say about a country is that it does not require labor to produce sustenance for man. That is equivalent to proclaiming that it will always be a poor country, for riches do not spring from the earth, but from man." [29]

The basic reform that Alberdi sought to bring about can only be called moral; he wrote constitutions, but had little faith in them *per se*. What was needed, he held, was self-government; he was fond of the English word, and of the self-reliance he got from Emerson. "Personal government is the natural government of a country where people do not know how to rule themselves." [30] It was not the government in South America which called for reform: "It is society, the people, the way of living and thinking . . . their mentality, their literature, their point of view in social and political matters. . . . For the condition of the soldier, the politician, the *fonctionnaire*, of every one who lives like a true communist at public expense, we must substitute the industry which consists in individual productive labor, every man living on his own, and so the country achieving freedom. This is the granite foundation of all liberty." [31]

If these are hard sayings, he could defend himself as all moralists can, by asserting that a moralist is one who criticizes the thing he loves because of his greater love for perfection. Patriotism by adulation, which praises the defects and vices of the people, is their worst enemy.[32] For him, the unpalatable but salutary truth. Truth, by the way, has

[29] *Id.* at 88–89.
[30] *Id.* at 105.
[31] *Id.* at 129.
[32] *Id.* at 139.

little to do with that most popular form of literature, poetry. He would dispose of most South American poetry up to his time with the offhand judgment that "poetry in South America is found everywhere except in verses. The verses are the sepulchres of Spanish poetry . . . and that is the reason poetic works in South America are so sickening and sad." [33]

When Alberdi tries his own hand at imaginative literature, the candid critic must admit that the results are sad. There exists a curious performance called "The Light of Day in America," in which a lady with that most allegorical name, disgusted with the lack of truth in Europe, sets out to seek it in the Western Hemisphere. She has a variety of conversations and adventures, but, of course, does not find truth, and at last hires a hall to give people a piece of her mind. This is what the author has been uncomfortably waiting for; he *can* write speeches, but not novels. "America," the fleshless allegorical female tells her audience, "will not be free until it is free of liberators. . . . Its liberators are the chief obstacle to its achieving liberty. . . . With the best intentions, they are the very ones who keep it without liberty. No one is free in South America but its liberators. Their liberty is so immense that it knows no limits; it is so great, that it becomes confused with unlimited power." [34] The dilemma of a freedom-loving South America is that it must be "either exclusively Latin and then slave, or free, and so Anglo-Saxon, at the very least in education and temperament. Does South America want to have the constitution and liberties of North America? It cannot except through the cooperation of the same races that have educated North America and taught it self-government." For liberty is con-

[33] *Id.* at 195.
[34] Alberdi, *Peregrinación de Luz del día o Viaje y aventuras de la verdad en el nuevo mundo*, p. 259.

duct, a deep-rooted way of life.[35] Only if South America truly wishes to be the country of poetry instead of the country of liberty should it fill itself with immigrants from Latin countries.[36] For Latin liberty is imperial or dictatorial, that is, a contradiction in terms; the liberty of today and to-morrow is Anglo-American, which alone preserves some rights to the individual.[37] The rivers of Anglo-Saxon immigration have not flowed toward South America, but *canals* of immigration might, and the water that is in canals does as much good as that in natural rivers.[38] Let the peoples of Latin America take immigration policy into their own hands and not let it be misguided by their governments, for "if in a certain sense to govern is to populate, it is even truer that to populate may mean to render brutish, to corrupt, impoverish, and contaminate." [39]

In a long life in which there was time for much writing, Alberdi touched upon an infinity of topics. Many of them may be ignored here, including the essay on a new method of learning to play the piano, but a few major works do, as the Spanish say, impose themselves.

Among these is the early fragment on the "Study of Law" (1837). The impossibly lengthy subtitle proclaims that it is "accompanied by a numerous series of considerations forming as it were a program of the future tasks of the Argentine intelligentsia." The young philosopher did not see independence as anything simple: "It is a complex of all the liberties, which are infinite, and like the virtues, related and interdependent: or rather, there is but one liberty, that of reason, with as many phases as there are elements in the spirit of man. It follows that when not all these liberties or phases of rational liberty exist at once, it may be said that no true liberty exists. . . . What our fathers gave us was only

[35] *Id.* at 268.
[36] *Id.* at 269.
[37] *Id.* at 270.
[38] *Id.* at 274.
[39] *Id.* at 276–277.

material liberty: it is for us to achieve a form of civilization that is our own, achieved by our own genius. Two chains bound us to Europe: a material one that was broken, one of the mind that is still there. . . . Thought is called upon to work for order in all things. . . . The reign of action is over; we are entering upon the reign of thought. We shall have heroes, but they will arise from philosophy." [40] Where our fathers were timorous in thought, he continued, we must be bold, for we have many intellectual worlds to conquer, and South America must yet have its Bolívars and its San Martíns of the mind.

In other words, South America has proved its will to freedom, but it still needs eyes, for complete freedom is a matter of intelligence, morality, religion, as well as formal political arrangements. An ignorant people cannot be truly free. Alberdi was as anxious to work for the spread of that ill-defined ideal, civilization, as any of the North Americans whose story the Beards have eloquently told in *The American Spirit*. His whole argument might be taken as his attempt to pour meaning into the word "civilization." When it captivated his imagination he went on to speak of "hastening the coming of democracy, learning to think, to acquire, to produce, making ourselves safe for democracy. . . . If we wish to be free, let us first be worthy of so being. Liberty does not come all of a sudden. It is the slow part of civilization. It is not the conquest of a day: it is one of humanity's ends, an end which we shall never achieve wholly. . . . But liberty is not impatient; she is patient, because she is immortal. . . . The people that would be free must be industrious, artistic, philosophical, believing, moral. Let one of these elements be lacking, and we return to barbarism." Here Alberdi employed the same contrast between civilization and barbarism

[40] Alberdi, "Fragmento preliminar al estudio del Derecho" (1837), in *Obras completas*, I, 112–113.

that played so large a part in Sarmiento's thinking. "Without religion, man is not a whole man," he continued; "so the larger part of our independence remains to be achieved, the slow, enormous, costly part; the inner, spiritual part that comes with intellectual development. Let us not fool ourselves: it will not come in our day. We shall sow the seed for our grand-children. . . . The Golden Age of the Argentine Republic is not passed; it is ahead of us: it lies in the perfecting of the social order. Our fathers did not see it: our sons will one day reach it: it is for us to break the trail." [41]

If we look at ourselves in the mirror, we must confess the anarchy in our minds, the absence of a philosophy, the dividing lines that prevent unity. Some of these qualities, he said, we share with humanity in general in the nineteenth century; our hope for the future, too, we share with humanity, or at least with Europe, for we are every day more closely bound together; the Atlantic has become an agent of civilization, and every step that Europe takes toward true freedom is a step forward for us.[42] If we can boldly lead the way into the new era, Europe will receive democracy from the hands of the new world. Education is the motto of the century, education of the common man, and improvement of his material and moral condition. "Know thyself" was the old command of philosophy to the individual; political science now bids whole peoples to know themselves, and upon the resulting knowledge hopes to build the new free world.[43]

Another essay, on what Spanish writers call *sociabilidad* (with doubtful propriety, since the meaning is not derived from *sociable*, but is closer to "the nature of society"), returned to the unworkable nature of constitutions if they do not grow out of the mores. A constitution works in the United States, where it is congruent with custom, ideas, and

[41] *Id.* at 114–116.
[42] *Id.* at 119–123.
[43] *Id.* at 127–131.

beliefs; the same one does not work in Mexico, where it lacks that backing. Liberty does not come into existence by decree; it grows as part of a culture. If you would change a people, work on their customs; judge their customs in the light of your supreme goal — democracy or any other — and strive to modify them in the direction of that goal. "Among us," Alberdi argued, "a custom is good if it is in accord with the principle of equality. . . . No style or fashion or belief or idea or doctrine should be admitted if it is not in conformity to this great principle." It is a principle that led him logically to attack the status of women in Latin countries, where they were, he maintained, still treated as mere children, as aspects of their families, of their husbands. The change that will bring woman's status into line with the principle of equality will come slowly, through education.[44]

A prize offered by a peace society in 1870 for the best essay on war encouraged Alberdi to put his thoughts in order and gave us "The Crime of War." It was a subject that came home to him, a citizen of a continent that had suffered much from war; and a subject that belonged to the field of his professional specialization, for war considered as a crime is just the penal chapter in international law. Finally, his Christianity made war a crime, although not always, for it may be required by justice when it is the punishment of a criminal war. Justification had commonly been lacking in South America, he maintained, where war was a means to the seizure of power; the wars of independence, general spontaneous movements of the population in line with the law of progress, are the chief exception. To speak of civilized war is to Alberdi as ridiculous as to speak of civilized barbarism.[45] If we handled the problem in a civilized way, applying to the crime of war the same principles of law that we apply to the

[44] "Sociabilidad" (1839), *Obras completas*, I, 392–397.
[45] *Id.* at 31. "The Crime of War."

responsibility, complicity, criminal intent, and punishment of individual crime, we would find our procedure equally efficacious, and wars would become progressively less and less frequent.[46] He is not even sure that an international tribunal would be necessary. Public opinion the world over would pronounce sentence, and this sentence in itself would be the most terrible of punishments.[47]

The discussion soon takes a turn characteristic of Alberdi. The military power of any nation rests entirely on its financial structure. This in turn is not just a government question, but depends upon the wealth of the nation, and that wealth comes from work. Work makes wealth, and war destroys wealth, and ends in ruin.[48] The conservation of wealth if nothing else makes it imperative to minimize war. He suggests "hanging the Kaiser," or bringing home the charge of guilt to the highest and most responsible parties, not those who merely obeyed orders.

Although neither this nor any other procedure can entirely eliminate war, he predicts that it will become less frequent, less general, less cruel and disastrous.[49] Arbitration, taking the decision out of the hands of the vitally interested parties, will do something. Government of the people, by the people, will do more, for such governments do not need large armies.[50] Such governments will one day learn to associate themselves in a larger society, just as they themselves were once constituted by union. World government may not be exactly like that of the United States, but it will possess both unity and authority.[51] Regional unions, such as a Pan-American one, are natural steps in the direction of the more inclusive one.[52]

Returning to South America, he opined that it had wanted

[46] *Id.* at 52.
[47] *Id.* at 53.
[48] *Id.* at 61.
[49] *Id.* at 98.
[50] *Id.* at 116.
[51] *Id.* at 183–184.
[52] *Id.* at 203.

two incompatible things, glory and liberty; one can be had
only at the price of the other. Now that we have a measure
of liberty, he said, war and revolution can only mean reaction, the crime of *lèse* America, *lèse* civilization, criminal
because it prevents the steady flow of immigration, depopu-
lates, delivers the continent to imperialism, kills agriculture and commerce, results in general impoverishment and
misery.[53] Until war ceases, the world will be "civilized in
detail, savage as a whole." [54]

Among the posthumously published writings of Alberdi,
the "Economic Studies" deserves most attention. This book
is the distilled essence of a lifetime of thought about the
problems of South America and what can be done about
them. Provocatively, Alberdi begins with the assertion that
"South America is inhabited by poor people who live on rich
soil, and Europe for the most part, by rich people who live on
poor soil." The study of the reasons for this anomaly is what
interests him in economics.[55]

It cannot be said, he avers, that Latin America's poverty is
a crisis; it is a secular condition, inherited and deep-rooted.
There is no escape from it until we first of all recognize it and
face the facts. The facts are that "the wealth which might
be produced is not produced, and that the soil and the
climate, which we take for riches, are only instruments in
the hands of man to produce riches, for he is the immediate
producer, through the two methods of work and savings." [56]
The "capital of the country is nothing other than its civilization." [57]

If the government is interested in increasing the greatness
and power of the nation, it ought to get down to business and

[53] *Id.* at 225–227.
[54] *Id.* at 239.
[55] Alberdi, *Escritos póstumos* (1895–1901), vol. I, *Estudios económicos*, p. 1.
[56] *Id.* at 2–3.
[57] *Id.* at 12.

study the causes of the general poverty, and the causes that elsewhere produce wealth, increase in commerce, a high standard of living, immigration, an increase in population, high credit rating — in a word, prosperity, progress, and civilization.[58] It will be found that the deepest causes of poverty are moral, and that a campaign must be organized against them just as we have done with endemic diseases.[59] To live on other people's money, as South America does by borrowing, is to spend an income which one has not known how to produce.[60]

Every war, even a just and glorious war, destroys both men and material means of production, unproductively, and is a cause of impoverishment. Talk all you like about glory and honor, but do not forget their cost in loss of wealth, decrease in work, the fall of wages, flight of workers and capital, paralysis of industrial enterprise, decrease in tax receipts, disappearance of precious metals, contraction of credit — in a word, general poverty.[61]

Latin America has known chronic poverty for three hundred years; it has now reached the stage where it can also know depressions.[62] Since poverty and wealth depend upon social conditions, every society has the poverty it deserves. From its labor and its abstinence, or from its idleness and dissipation, come the economic characteristics of every country. If one would arrest poverty, it must be by working on these things, not on the soil. The example of the industrious immigrant is again invoked as the best of all solutions.[63] If soil has an effect, it is indirect; the equatorial regions of Brazil will never attract the right kinds of immigrants; the richest soil is that which attracts and holds French, English, Swiss, German, Italian, and north Spanish immigrants.[64]

[58] *Id.* at 14.
[59] *Id.* at 18.
[60] *Id.* at 48.
[61] *Id.* at 50–51.

[62] *Id.* at 61–62.
[63] *Id.* at 65–68.
[64] *Id.* at 73.

South America deludes itself with the fact that it is able to borrow, or with complacent optimism about what its soil will be able to produce, and avoids all mention of the productive qualities of its people.[65] It lives bemused in the "idolization of an ephemeral self," as Toynbee calls it, absorbed in the memory of its own heroic infancy, the military period that it should have outgrown, as England, France, and the United States have done.[66]

"Hispanic America was warlike, not industrial, commercial, or agricultural, from the very beginning. Unfortunate in its population . . . it received as its inheritance ignorance and disdain for work; hatred of dissenters; love for gold acquired without work; the false belief that to possess mines was to be rich, provided you had slaves to work them for you; the delusion that to extend one's dominion meant increase in power and greatness; hatred of foreigners, especially if they were Protestants; commerce and trade looked upon as crimes dangerous to the security of the land; isolation as the very principle upon which existence was based and the safeguard against foreigners; government prohibition of all trade with the rest of the world and between the colonies themselves; lack of roads, bridges, ports — this, too, a government policy consciously adopted; savage Indians left unconquered in nomadic hordes, disturbing the communication of the colonies, and fighting among themselves; the geometric growth of convents, the burden of the tithe and of the dead hand of charity and mendicity preventing the prosperity of agriculture; the love of feast days and holidays; the vice and luxury that accompanied them; the policy of dividing to dominate; the favoritism displayed toward the mountainous countries of Mexico, New Granada, Quito, Peru, as being rich in mines and in Indians who would work for the lazy owner, and as being isolated from foreign influences; the abandonment of

[65] *Id.* at 81–85.   [66] *Id.* at 93.

the land on the eastern side of South America . . . to pasturage . . . the fear of work which might have led to wealth, and through wealth to independence; the cultivation of a life of pleasant leisure, which was a cause of poverty, and therefore of weakness and dependence." [67]

According to his theory, Alberdi can find only one source of wealth which the Spaniards exploited, namely, the unwarlike, docile Indians who inhabited the land. It was their work that built the cities, the only permanent addition to wealth that was made here. But the conditions under which this work was done made even it in the long run unproductive, since it enslaved the Indian, and demoralized his slothful owner as well. Saving was discredited, and work considered an attribute of the slave; to sum it up, an antieconomic society was created. [68]

When South Americans read about the United States, he holds, they do not learn what a really economic society is, for they read De Tocqueville, who was no economist, and skip the latter part of his book, in which he most nearly approached being one. [69]

The ideal of civilization cherished by South Americans, he continues, is to spend money living as they imagine Englishmen, Frenchmen, and Germans live, that is, to spend freely, buy much, and forget that the men of other nations work and produce. South American cities want to be little Parises, and forget that Paris, which accounts for a third of all French production, works hard. [70]

Argentine history shows us that the system bossed by Rosas was just the colonial system, with more blood and terrorism. [71] "The worst of its poverty has consisted in its absolute lack of statesmen; that is, men who through their

[67] *Id.* at 100.
[68] *Id.* at 112.   [70] *Id.* at 158.
[69] *Id.* at 119.   [71] *Id.* at 217.

knowledge and common sense have realized the nature of the
problem, and through their upright, disinterested character
have been capable of making their views prevail." [72] As long
as the power is concentrated in Buenos Aires, this state of
affairs will continue, whoever rules, for "things govern by
means of men, not men by means of things." [73]

Alberdi was one of those who believe Latins have a great
propensity to solve all problems by "reason"; they were left
with nothing else after the revolution, he said, for certainly
they could not be guided by the regulations of the very
colonial régime they had found it necessary to overthrow.[74]
What policy would he advocate? The reader already knows
it by heart, and is heartily tired of its key-word, immigration. The only new element here is more discussion of the
safeguards that must be thrown around imported labor and
industry to make it contented. Capital, too, says Alberdi,
must be assured the enjoyment of complete liberty in choos-
ing its field, and its profits must be respected.[75] Besides importing labor and capital, South Americans must train themselves to be labor and to employ capital. Doubtless science
and literature are the fine flowers of civilization, but its
foundation is something else, namely, industry and commerce. One of the causes of the situation which he laments
is precisely a too-literary education. Even the intellectual
minority must have a reoriented education. The country
might be inundated with professors and books, but barbarism would still triumph without the increased population,
the rapidly growing commerce and industry, that he con-
tinually urges. "Science is the light, it is reason, cold thinking, deliberate conduct. Literature is all illusion, mystery,
fiction and passion, eloquence, harmony, intoxication of the
soul, enthusiasm. . . . Literature has fulfilled its mission, its

[72] *Id.* at 251.   [74] *Id.* at 463.
[73] *Id.* at 325.   [75] *Id.* at 484.

time is past in South America. Only science can furnish what this new age requires: light, reason, the calm and peace necessary to the foundation of its institutions and the development of its wealth. . . . In educational matters it is the Argentine Republic that is most backward. . . . In the River Plate region science has been strangled by literature."

In economic even more than in political matters, America is its own best model. The great model for South America to copy is North America.[76] In the best models, he insists, we will find that men do not merely work. Work must be intelligent, moral, enlightened, civilized, and it must go hand in hand with saving for the formation of capital. Alberdi seems to believe that life is nowhere so difficult that it puts insuperable obstacles in the way of working and saving; the lack of land and money is not the cause of poverty; the cause lies within men themselves.[77]

The ideas of Alberdi are clear enough, and we turn, perhaps with relief, from the man of ideas to the complete man, who was, take him all in all, the greatest man Argentina has produced, and the most Argentinian. This is Sarmiento.

Domingo Faustino Sarmiento (1811–1888)

The completeness and representativeness of Sarmiento lie in his manysidedness. He was less the cultivated European than he wished to be, and more the *gaucho* than he knew. From his own efforts to educate himself came that vast passion to educate others which more than any system of thought defines the man. Not always are the great fighters for civilization themselves the most exquisitely civilized. The flowers of civilization are not its transforming forces. There is little of the evangelist left in a Henry Adams.

Ricardo Rojas, who thinks of himself as continuer and cor-

[76] *Id.* at 506–520.   [77] *Id.* at 626–630.

rector as well as admirer of the work of Sarmiento, has a
paragraph which sums up the reasons for regarding him as
the leader-symbol of South America. "We shall be Argentines when we feel in ourselves the attachment to the soil
that the Indian had, making it the source of his art and
myths; when we feel the urge to create civilization which the
Spanish founders of cities possessed; when we feel the plasticity of the gaucho on the limitless pampas and his inspiration to rise above his environment and to tell of it in song;
when we have the capacity for disciplined work, like the
gringo; when we are neither Indians, nor gauchos, nor Spaniards, nor gringos, but Argentines, as Sarmiento was." [78]

If this analysis seems to make of Sarmiento a highly complicated figure, the reverse is really true. He was, as Echagüe
says, the "man without a mask," the man who found strength
within himself to pursue single-mindedly a single ideal, that
of creating a civilization, educating a people, leaving the in-
delible imprint of his personality and work on the institutions
of his country. Echeverría and Alberdi believed in their
ideals; Sarmiento brought his to life. They called for more
education, especially scientific education; he created it. His
limitless ambition for his country would have done away
with the uncivilized pampas, the giant obstacle of the Andes,
with war and with social classes, with everything that im-
peded the development of a civilized and classless society.
The struggle was never ended, and he was a fighter to the
last. Where he was most the thinker is in explaining the
fight, finding explanations for the warring elements in Argentine life, and throwing the light of his genius upon the way
they have retarded the movement of civilization. Aside from
this, the confused mass of his fifty-two volumes is the raw
material of a history of his crusade for more knowledge, a
crusade which he himself defined in the cry: "We must not

[78] *Sarmiento: cincuentenario de su muerte* (1939), I, 140.

give up being independent: but we must give up our barbarism."

The child of poverty, born in far inland San Juan, Sarmiento took full advantage of such meager opportunities as he had for education and supplemented them by reading the Bible and the *Autobiography* of Franklin that he wished to see in every school. Making oneself is a serious business, and Sarmiento took it seriously, never learning to play games until as an old man he did it under doctor's orders.[79] Storekeeping and a business trip to Chile did not for a moment stop his campaign of self-improvement. With the definitive triumph of the gaucho chieftain Facundo Quiroga in 1831, Sarmiento, because of his political opinions, found Chile a more congenial residence than Argentina. The penniless youth secured a job as elementary school teacher, with a salary of thirteen pesos a month. In 1833 he worked in a store in Valparaiso; here he spent half his salary on English lessons, but got up in the middle of the night to study, and was so sure of himself that he dropped the lessons, satisfied with his knowledge, after about a month. This stay in Chile lasted five years. The third and most fruitful sojourn began in 1840.

It was still necessary for him to eke out a living by many means, but Sarmiento was beginning to find himself, and to use writing as he always did to prick sleepers and to attack tyrants. For a time he wrote three or four editorials a week for *El Mercurio,* and he thought he had arrived when Andrés Bello spoke well of one of them. At the same time, his attitude toward literature was both more social and more romantic than that of Bello, and when the master scolded Chile for her careless speech and ignorance of the classics, Sarmiento was not slow to suggest that such high standards were out of place in Chile, and that Bello may be the type of

[79] Leopoldo Lugones, *Historia de Sarmiento* (2d. ed., 1921), p. 51.

humanist who would feel more at home in Europe. This shows a sense of the reality of the American scene which did not desert Sarmiento; he found inspiration with Echeverría and Alberdi in European political and social ideas, chiefly French, but he adapted them to local conditions. Freedom of worship, civil marriage, pacifism were among the social ideals which he preached, together with an insistence that never relaxed on the necessity of education.

The despot Rosas deigned to notice the journalist and sputtered threats. Sarmiento's friends urged a reply, and the pamphlet masterpiece *Facundo* (1845) was the result. Ostensibly a life of the less important *caudillo*, it attacks all tyranny by implication. and asks why it arises in Argentina, what is the way out? All of this makes, as the author admitted, "a strange book, without head or feet." Strangest of all is the fact that his villain, like Milton's Satan, gained his grudging admiration; after all, he is Argentine and a kind of hero.

Travels through Europe, Africa, and America, beginning in 1845, left an impress not only on Sarmiento's literary production ("Travels," 1850) but on his whole subsequent life and thought. Seeing the world between the ages of thirty-four and thirty-seven, he was mature enough to profit, young enough to be affected. Starting with Montevideo, he went on to France, where he talked to General San Martín; to Spain, North Africa, Italy, Austria, Germany; and finally to the United States in 1847. He began to feel that enthusiasm for things North American which continued unabated during the rest of his life, and which gives so much trouble to later Argentines who want to admire him but cannot share this view. Almost everything that he saw in the United States seemed superior to its counterpart in Europe, and he adopted a tone familiar enough in North America: Europe is the effete, decadent continent; America is the land of hope; America is realizing its hopes through education. Sarmiento knew personally the most notable leader of educational reform, Horace Mann, and began with Mann and his wife a long and noble inter-American friendship. Mrs. Mann translated his *Facundo*, remarking that she felt that she was translating a nation, not a man.

The year 1850 saw the publication of his "Memories of Provincial Life," which expressed in a style he never equaled in other writings a nostalgia for the tranquility of the old colonial régime, and a love of home. At the same time, it is, like everything he wrote, an apology and a proclamation. Even his tenderness grows out of the formula: "I am accused? Well, here is my answer."

Sarmiento, the man of passion, "the crazy man," reached a point where he could not refrain from telling General Mitre, "You, Mitre, will be the first president of the united republic, but remember, I reserve the second term for myself." The prophecy was fulfilled in 1868. In the meantime, however, there were more ideas to be sown in Chile, three years of directing *El Nacional* (succeeding Mitre), laborious and effective work in the Argentine Senate, with a succession of carefully prepared speeches, governorship of the province of San Juan (1862), polemics and more polemics, his designation as Minister to the United States, where he arrived in May, 1865, with letters for President Lincoln, who had been assassinated the month before. Sarmiento was an outstanding member of the diplomatic circle in Washington, tireless in traveling and informing himself, collecting endless statistics for the edification of Argentina. From New York State or wherever he might be, he continued to agitate Argentine questions, writing repeatedly to recommend books for public libraries in that country — Humboldt, Motley, and the

Macaulay he had himself just purchased at seven dollars a
volume.[80] Questioned about his own country, he admitted
frankly that the situation there was much like that in the
southern States.

When he returned to Argentina to be president, in 1868,
he exclaimed: "I come from a country where education is
everything, where education has succeeded in establishing
true democracy, making races and classes equal!" [81] His
term as president was dedicated to the ends he had served all
his life, but he perhaps found reason to agree with the Chinese sage who said, "Those who are not in charge speak
lightly." He continued to serve as senator, as minister of the
interior, as director general of schools of the province of
Buenos Aires, after leaving the presidency. Toward the end
of his life he returned to the explanation of Argentina's basic
problem, confessing that in *Facundo* he had studied only
certain aspects of it, and that its persistence led him to suspect that it had deeper roots than the surface of the land.
This time, in the formless and incomplete "Conflict and
Harmony of Races in America," he deserted his old master
Buckle for Herbert Spencer, writing also as the heir of
Bolívar, and like him embracing a whole continent. If this
volume is *Facundo* grown old, and exhibits a writer who had
also grown old and had been busy with a thousand other
matters, it still proves the depth and permanence of his
interest in political and social theory. There may be some
falling off in the quality of this last work, but still Carlos
Pellegrini spoke for all when he said after Sarmiento's death,
"This was the most powerful brain America has produced." [82]

A career so varied refused to be tagged with one label. "In
him journalism does not kill the writer, the writer does not
kill the teacher, nor the teacher the statesman, nor the states-

[80] *Sarmiento: cincuentenario de su muerte*, IV, 90.
[81] *Ibid.*, III, 332.   [82] Palcos, *Sarmiento*, p. 236.

man the sociologist and political philosopher. He was all these at once." [83] He had something of the scientist's love for truth, plus a large dose of the humanitarian's compassion for ignorance.

The attitude that he wished to inculcate can be described summarily as liberal (he was a Mason, and at the end claimed the right to die outside the Church), as progressive and scientific (thirty thousand miles of railroads constitute a proper source of pride). He was utopian in his great dreams ("put it down in the record, Mr. Secretary, that they laughed at my proposal"), but the dreams were of practical and utilitarian things. Esthetic sensibility was not entirely lacking in Sarmiento, but there were gaps in it; everything was seized by the social angle, and if he was tolerant of novels it was not only because they are human life and society but also for the curious reason that while reading even a bad novel one will be temporarily out of mischief. The goal is civilization, which is defined in terms of European customs, institutions, and population; or rather, it is the North American variant of European culture that attracts him; he recognizes the United States as the greatest Europeanizing agent of modern times. It is the United States that has been most successful in avoiding the segmentation of society into fixed and changeless classes arrayed against each other, Europe which displays the lamentable results of such social schism. Sarmiento cannot be claimed by socialism, however, for he was always the advocate of private ownership, of individual initiative, to such an extent that public welfare and social security impressed him as dangerous. Yet in his own career he paid little practical attention to the needs of Domingo Sarmiento; "I think," "I propose," "I did thus and so," are words that were always on his lips, but the thinking, planning, and acting were for the common good.

[83] *Id.* at 241.

The first book of Sarmiento that marks a notable advance over Echeverría and the others from whom he had learned European thought is his *Facundo, or Civilization and Barbarism*. In it he expounded the ideas that were to guide his own policy when it was most statesmanlike; he did not merely bemoan or attack the civil wars that had ravaged his country: he explained them. Avellaneda found in this book the clue to Argentine history which he could not discover elsewhere, and was one of the first to call it sociology, although it might better be called philosophy of history. The nature of Argentine history is, for Sarmiento, to be explained by the physical and social environment and the way they mold the rural inhabitant; from geography he goes on to collective psychology and studies the prevailing sentiments and beliefs, probes the very spirit of his country, resultant as it is of the influences of nature and of tradition.

Facundo is more a collection of articles than an organic book, and it fits no convenient pigeon-hole of the literary historian. It was struck off red hot in a struggle that Sarmiento believed to be one to the death. It took sides in that struggle most vehemently, and yet without awareness of the fact that the author had ties that bound him to more than one party. For "he was an Indian in his feeling for the land, a gaucho in his free individualism, a Spaniard in blood, passion and language, and also a European, like the immigrant stock, in his capacity for work and his eagerness for progress." [84] It is because he was all these things that he has reached the height of being hero and symbol of his country, its conscience while alive, its incarnation in history.

The subtitle of *Facundo* strikes the keynote, for the question is, shall we be savage or not? Men like Facundo and Rosas are not isolated facts in history, but manifestations of a social condition, of an underlying barbarism. It is of the

[84] *Sarmiento: cincuentenario de su muerte*, I, 138.

nature of Argentine life that it is ruled by "brute force, the preponderance of the strongest, the authority without limits or responsibility of those in command, justice administered without forms or debate." [85]

Two societies exist side by side here; they are hardly the city of God and the earthly city, but the contrast is striking. "The man of the city wears European clothes, lives the same civilized life that we know in all parts of the world; in the city are laws, ideas of progress, means of instruction, more or less municipal organization, regular government, etc. Leave the bounds of the city, and everything changes in appearance; the man of the country wears other clothes, which I shall call American, since they are common to all American nations; his habits are different, his needs peculiar and limited; they seem two distinct societies, two peoples quite alien to each other." [86]

The vast plains of Argentina have created a life that is appropriate to them, a pastoral life with little association. Families are scattered and isolated, and in their isolation feel no need to live with dignity or luxury. "The necessary privations of their life are used as justification for their natural indolence, and frugality in enjoyments brings with it all the manifestations of barbarism. Society has disappeared completely; there is left only the isolated feudal family, withdrawn into itself; since there is no organized society, all government becomes impossible." [87] Religion is reduced to bare natural religion; Christianity exists, but only as the Spanish language does, corrupted, superstitious, without ritual observances or firm faith. Education is equally neglected, for schools and other means of civilization cannot exist on the frontier, but only when supported by a numerous population.[88] The life of the frontier has developed the gaucho's

[85] Sarmiento, *Facundo* (ed. Sopena, 1940), p. 23.
[86] *Id.* at 25.   [87] *Id.* at 27.   [88] *Id.* at 28.

physical powers, but not those of his intelligence. His moral character is such as results from his habit of triumphing over obstacles and over the power of nature; he is strong, sure of himself, energetic. He is happy in the midst of his poverty and his privations, which are not such to him who has never known anything better, who has never had any higher ambitions. If the roots of barbarism are found in this dissolution of society, because of the impossibility and uselessness of any moral and intellectual education, it still is a life not without its attractions. The gaucho does not work; food and clothing he finds prepared at home; both are furnished him by his herds, if he owns cattle, by the boss or a relative if he does not. The care demanded by the cattle he makes into sport and pleasure.[89]

The sub-varieties of the gaucho are described with a vivid pen, although Sarmiento had not personally lived the life of the pampas. He distinguishes the round-up man, the scout, the "bad gaucho" or outlaw, the gaucho with guitar, voice, and the bard's impulse. The bad man is defended, for essentially he is no worse than the men of the city. The singer is customarily idealized; socially he is the marginal man between a society that is disappearing and new forms of life that approach inexorably; he is the troubadour of the struggle between city and country. The gaucho admires above all physical strength and skill, ability to handle his mount and bravery, and exhibits these qualities whenever he can get together with his fellows. He carries a knife because it is indispensable to him in a thousand ways, he cannot live without it; occasionally its use ends in tragedy. It is apparent that a society of such men has no use for cultivation of the spirit.

The history of recent decades falls into place neatly according to Sarmiento's formula. First, revolution of the cities against the Spaniards; second, revolution of the coun-

[89] *Id.* at 30.

try against the city. One city after another has fallen to the gaucho leaders, but in the end Buenos Aires, so strong in the things that go to make civilization, must educate even a Rosas, and domesticate even his bloody and barbarous instincts.[90] Even though the Dictator has closed the schools and the university and expelled the Jesuits, young Argentines will educate themselves abroad and return to fight in their own country for the free institutions they have seen functioning in foreign lands, and will not rest until the tyrant is overthrown.[91] We can even be grateful to Rosas for having completed our political education; we have had to learn many hard lessons, and we shall not forget the lessons learned with so much shedding of blood. "Precisely because 'he' has persecuted the very name European, and has fought the immigration of foreigners, the 'new government' will establish great associations to bring more inhabitants to the country . . . and in twenty years' time the same thing will happen here as in the United States, and cities, provinces, and States will spring up in the desert as if by enchantment." [92] The immigration which up to 1840 moved toward the United States will be diverted to Argentina, and will become the principal agent of order and moralization.[93]

The exact nature of the conquests Sarmiento looked forward to is summed up in his definition of civilization, with its strong emphasis upon technique, or rather its failure to distinguish between mere technique and culture. Civilization is command over nature by man in order to achieve perfection, which will have both physical and moral aspects, and will be achieved through religion, philosophy, science, technique, industry, art, and politics. He sought the reasons that lie in geography for failure to achieve these goals; as an old man, he returned to look for them in racial considerations.

[90] *Id.* at 49.
[91] *Id.* at 176.
[92] *Id.* at 179.
[93] *Id.* at 182.

He never quite became aware of the difficulties that lay in his own thought; how could he reject Spanish civilization and yet glorify the cities which were Spanish if they were anything? Wherever the cause for failure lay, its cure, he was confident, was education. He thought in order to act, and all his concern with the past was directed to the elimination of evil. His perennial message in the field of social action was that of "educating the sovereign people." He pursued education furiously for himself and mapped the road to culture for his nation. Did he, like other mapmakers, jump too thoughtlessly to the conclusion that the shortest road thither was the best?

He was not all optimism. There are two terrible warnings to the United States in Sarmiento. European immigration, he says — who would believe it? — can easily be a contribution to barbarism, rather than to civilization. It must be carefully selected. The other warning carries no solution with it; within a century there will be in the United States either a race war, a war to extermination, or else an abject and retarded Negro people living side by side with the most powerful and most cultivated white people of the world.[94]

Most sociologists have found themselves at different times calling a variety of things the most serious problem that confronts us. Sarmiento is no exception. At other times it was international or industrial rivalry that appalled him. We find him telling the Chileans in 1849, "Against the violence and injustice of the Yankees there is no appeal on this earth"; and in 1855 he was looking into the crystal ball and reporting: "We seem to see something graver than the struggle between races, the very traces of which will have disappeared from the earth. May it not be the struggle of indus-

[94] Ricardo Rojas, *El pensamiento vivo de Sarmiento* (1941), pp. 73–77.

tries, of powers, of development, of forces of expansion which is beginning?" [95]

His sociology is of that moralizing and evaluative kind which is not content with narrative history. "History is the science which deduces from facts the march of the human spirit in all parts of the world, in accordance with the grade of liberty and civilization which the various human aggregations have reached, and the best historian of the world is he who can rank the nations according to their moral, intellectual, political and economic progress." [96] Most history has seen the world upside down and glorified the natural in all things, the noble savage; we who have seen with our own eyes what these savages are like can furnish a corrective, and put the golden age in the future as a conquest of science and civilization.[97] This conquest has already been aided greatly by America, which has taken the torch of Renaissance ideals from the hand of Europe just in time, and which will solve the great problems of humanity, unencumbered with the débris of a Gothic tradition.[98] In peroration, he alludes to equality, equitable distribution, common education — characteristic American institutions since the Revolution, initiated by North America and imitated in South America. The gloomy side does not belong in perorations, so we must turn to another lecture to find his admission that all the flaws due to the Spanish colonial tradition are not worse than the results produced by slavery in the South of the United States.[99]

An interesting corollary of his philosophy of history is the observation of the "archaism" (see Toynbee, *A Study of*

[95] Sarmiento, "Espíritu y condiciones de la historia en América" (1858), *Cuatro conferencias* (1928), pp. 11–12.
[96] *Id.* at 31.
[97] *Id.* at 33.
[98] *Id.* at 36–42.
[99] "La doctrina Monroe," an address before the Rhode Island Historical Society (1865), *Cuatros conferencias*, p. 111.

History) of societies that looked toward the past; take languages, for instance: the Greeks studied Egyptian, the Romans studied Greek, the barbarians Latin. In an age that looks toward the future, the two languages that must be studied are Spanish and English.[100] For the sake of the many who do not know English but depend upon the scanty supply of good books in Spanish, he recommends a plan for securing the translation of selected books, an ideal which only today is being realized.

One despairs of abstracting a book like Sarmiento's "Conflict and Harmony of Races," but some idea of its aim can be given by his opening question, "What are we Argentines?" and by his professed ambition not to write history but to explain it, and to continue the analysis that was begun in his *Facundo*, a book that was a historical event and made history.

"To set before the eyes of the American reader the elements that make up our society; to explain the partial failure of republican institutions over so great a territory and on so many separate occasions due to the resistance of inertia . . . to point out deficiencies . . . without stepping over the boundaries of the future that its destiny has in store for America, such is the object of 'The Conflict of Races in America' which I present to the public and demand to have read."

He goes on to give the conclusion of the whole matter. "Without more ado, what is it that distinguishes the colonization of North America? The fact that the Anglo-Saxons did not admit the indigenous races as associates or even as serfs in their society. What is it that distinguishes Spanish colonization? The fact that it made a monopoly of its own race, that when it migrated to America it did not leave the Middle Ages, and that it absorbed into its own blood a prehistoric and servile race." [101]

[100] *Id.* at 122.
[101] Sarmiento, *Conflicto y armonías de las razas en América* (Buenos Aires, 1883), II, 415.

"What can this part of America do to follow in the foot-steps that have taken the other part to prosperity and freedom? Raise itself to a higher level; it is already doing so with other European races, correcting the aboriginal blood, with modern ideas, putting an end to the Middle Ages. Bring up the intellectual level, and in the meantime refuse to admit to the electoral body any who are not capable of fulfilling its functions." [102]

This book, like his last speech, remained faithful to the enthusiasm of almost half a century, and pointed to the United States: "South America is falling behind and will lose its God-given mission as part of modern civilization. Let us not hold up the United States in its forward march; that is what some are proposing to do. Let us overtake the United States. Let us be America, as the sea is the ocean. Let us be the United States." [103]

[102] *Id.* at 416.
[103] *Id.* at 421.

CHAPTER III

The Generation of '42 and After

Andrés Bello (1781–1865)

B ELLO, who knew so much, did not know the date of his own birth; he missed it by a year less a day. As to the place, there never was any doubt. He was a Venezuelan unless you allow more years spent in Chile to make him a Chilean, which is an old South American custom. In Venezuela he began that education that was to produce "the greatest Spanish humanist since the Renaissance"; Quesada found him the perfect pupil, and he won prizes; Humboldt, visiting the country at the age of thirty, found the youth worthy of his friendship. In 1804 he won applause with an ode on the introduction of vaccination, but he failed to keep a copy of it, and in later years is said to have forgotten that he ever wrote it.

The fact that he graduated from being the docile pupil into being a government secretary so docile that he found it comfortable to work first for the Spaniards and then for the revolutionary régime has been held against him. It was the latter régime that sent him, with one companion, to London and Bolívar in 1810, to secure the good will and protection of England. He stayed some eighteen years, years which left a severe Britannic stamp upon his life. Here he knew and admired Francisco Miranda and, of the English, above all James Mill and Jeremy Bentham. The revolution failing, he resorted to translating and language teaching, for the record says that in those days even women wanted to learn Spanish. He married (in succession, for he was no Miranda) two Englishwomen. Perhaps the second, Isabel Dunn, was not one of those who wanted to learn Spanish; at any rate the great grammarian never succeeded in teaching her.

For a time Bello was secretary to the Colombian Legation in London, but the Colombians, too, paid very irregularly, and he resorted to the language work again for supplemental income. He also played a principal part in the journal, *El Repertorio americano*, but this doubtless failed to do any supplementing of the meager income. He contracted a friendship with Olmedo, another of the great classic poets of Latin America, and wrote his own best poetry, the "Silvas," including the one "On Agriculture in the Torrid Zone" (1826).

There was talk of his representing Colombia in the United States, but he found the Colombians cold and inconsiderate, and Egaña had been writing home to Chile that here was a chance to make an important acquisition in the person of an excellent employee. Bello, he said, was disposed to move to Chile, and he would be a splendid choice for under secretary of foreign affairs. Ask the people who know him, he concluded, and you will find that you could not get a better man; we must have people who have experience in the way things are done in the great nations.[1] The upshot was that Bello landed in Valparaiso in June, 1829, and had the chance for the rest of his life to do what Bentham always wanted to do: to civilize a people and legislate for them.

He began modestly enough. He had no powerful friends, and was poor; by temperament he was no fighter, no active politician, but the wise man, the balanced man, whose life was all of a piece, and harmonious. But one thing got under his sensitive, civilized skin; these people didn't *read*, and their Spanish was terrible. It was immediately clear to Bello what was the social problem of Chile and what was its solution.

[1] M. L. Amunátegui, *Vida de don Andrés Bello* (Santiago, 1882), pp. 298–299.

The people needed education and then more education — always education. At this task he worked for thirty-five years, and before the end of that time he could look upon a transformed country; in the change he had played a principal part. Amunátegui's quaint old biography describes his method in teaching, which was his first and always his principal activity: "Instead of getting lost in long dissertations, he began by expounding precisely and concisely the point they were studying. This done, he conversed about it with his young hearers. Every question was debated at length, going into details and applications. Bello hated anything that was vague or nebulous." [2]

His approach to the larger public was through the pages of *El Araucano* and through textbooks which grew out of his classes. He tackled anything: the sciences, the Scotch school of philosophy, grammar, the study of *El Cid*, international law. Whenever he was dissatisfied with the textbooks, he seems to have written one. He agitated the question of primary education, and opposed the censorship of books which was still being carried out by ecclesiastical authorities. For Bello, who read "whenever he could, even just after eating," anything that prevented his getting books was wrong. He pointed out the fact that *The Spirit of Laws* was still on the Index, along with the *Essai sur les Mœurs* and Llorente's *History of the Inquisition*, and clamored for suppression of the censorship, which he did not obtain. He lectured the Chileans on their spelling, grammar, and pronunciation. He labored for the development of a theater, considering "theatrical representations an excellent means of civilization, and even of improving moral character." [3]

These were the questions that he attacked most boldly. In politics, while he had never stood for monarchy, he was a

2 *Id.* at 344–345.   3 *Id.* at 437.

most temperate liberal, certainly not approving the abuses
of authority, but quite incapable of rushing furiously into
public declamation against them.

It was in 1841 that Manuel Montt asked Bello to draw up
a plan for the improvement of the teaching of the arts and
sciences. The resulting proposal, with certain modifications,
became law on November 19, 1842, and created the University of Chile, of which Bello was the first rector. His
statue stands outside the door of the main building, and
when in recent months the hundredth anniversary of the
institution was celebrated, Bello's was the most eulogized
name.

It was in connection with the university that Bello did one
of the strangest things of his career. The statutes called for
the periodic reading of a paper in solemn session of the faculties. At the end of the first year, it seemed time to meet this
requirement, and Bello turned to José Victorino Lastarria
and, as legend has it, said, "You seem to be the most revolutionary of the young fellows; why don't you pick a topic
and develop it your own way?" The result, as we shall see,
was such that Bello felt it necessary to break the glacial
silence with which Lastarria's blast had been received by an
article in *El Araucano*. He commented on its vigorous style
and abundance of ideas, the correctness with which "in general" it was written, and predicted a future for Lastarria.
But he refused absolutely to accept the latter's gloomy picture of the condition of the colonies as lacking in all social
virtue, for the revolution itself, he said, gave the lie to such
statements; and he refused to blame Spain for everything,
since it was precisely the Spanish element that throughout
America had risen in revolt and expelled the Spanish government.[4]

[4] Bello, *Obras*, VII, 84 (on Lastarria's *Investicaciones*).

It is natural that much of Bello's thought should have been given to education. He has one essay on the subject which furnishes the following gems:

 The distinctive character of man is his susceptibility of improvement. Education, which enriches his mind with ideas, adorns his heart with virtues, is an efficient means to promote his progress. . . . But not all men are to have equal education, for each has his own way of contributing to the common felicity. Whatever be the equality which political institutions establish, there is nevertheless in all peoples an inequality — we shall not say a hierarchy (which cannot exist among republicans, especially in their share in public rights) — but an inequality of condition, of needs, of mode of life. To these differences, education must adjust itself. . . . In a matter of such vital importance, governments cannot be too careful. To develop public establishments meant for a limited portion of the people is not to develop education, for it is not enough to turn out men skilled in the learned professions; it is necessary to form useful citizens, it is necessary to improve society; and this cannot be done without opening the path to advancement to the most numerous part of the public.[5]

A warning note against expecting too much from legislation is sounded in the essay on "Government and Society":

Liberty does not stand alone as some people think; it is allied with all the national traits, and it improves them without changing their nature; with natural intelligence, to which it gives vigor and audacity; it gives wings to the spirit of enterprise, wherever it meets it; it breathes breath into it where it does not exist. But it cannot work without the two great factors of all human work: nature and time. Administrative measures now retard the movement, now hasten it, without doubt. But it is necessary that we should not exaggerate its power. There are moral obstacles that it cannot banish. There are natural accidents that it is impossible to change.[6]

There is so much temptation to think of Bello solely as the codifier of laws and as the educator that brief mention of his

[5] "Educación" (1836), *Obras*, VIII, 213–220.
[6] "El gobierno i la sociedad" (1843), *Obras*, VIII, 288.

article on roads is needed as a corrective. There never has
been a time, he says, that has not needed means of communication; we certainly need them in Chile, and opinions can
differ only as to which way the need is to be met. Roads —
or channels of communication — are the most necessary and
efficacious instruments of civilization; to forget or postpone
action in this matter is not possible unless the government is
completely to fail its people.[7]

Is it the Englishman in Bello or the moralist that speaks,
when as early as 1836 we find him deploring the harm done
by holidays?

Among the evils which have most struck us are those which result from public diversions in which we with pain have seen time
and money, honor and health lost by those who take part in them.
We know that it is impossible to deprive the people of all entertainment or to reduce at once their irregular pastimes to some
sober compass, or prevent for the future certain disorders from
occurring in connection with them; but we are sure that others can
be developed which will furnish rest and innocent distraction at
appropriate intervals, and be reconciled with decency, and help
to inculcate those forms of behavior which man needs in social
life. . . . There still remains much to be done, for in most of the
towns there are still authorized diversions from which serious
harm results . . . scenes in which, on the pretext of celebrating
the highest and purest part of religion, instead the worst forms of
vice are publicly displayed, and a week or two given over to idleness and the most unrestrained dissoluteness.[8]

Bello was not a popular hero.

José Victorino Lastarria (1817–1888)

Chile has perhaps not been sufficiently grateful to Lastarria. The boldness of his opinions was not designed to
conciliate, and the inflexible dogmatism with which he im-

[7] *Discurso de instalación de la Universidad* (1846), *Obras*, VIII, 303, at 322–327.
[8] *Obras*, XV, 324 ("Fiestas perjudiciales," 1836).

posed himself and his opinions did not please. Today if it
were not for two brilliant critics, Domingo Melfi and Ricardo
A. Latcham, and one biographer, Sady Zañartú, this creator
of Chilean progress and independence in thought during the
half-century after 1842 would be almost totally forgotten.
He was, however, not only the doctrinaire exponent of rationalism and positivism, but a thinker who cared deeply for
the welfare of his country and sought to trace back the
causes of its problems to their roots.

Once freedom had given the right to choose, every South
American country faced an option between Europe and
America. The struggle with Spain was too recent and the
temptation to place upon Spain and the colonial régime the
blame for all the troubles that plagued them was too great
for thinking men to choose her as mentor. So, if they were
Europeanizers, it was in revolutionary France that they
sought inspiration; if they were wholeheartedly men of the
New World, it was to the United States that they looked.
It was also quite possible to harmonize the two views, empha-
sizing in the case of France its science, literature, and ideas,
and in the case of the United States its free political institutions and economic progress. It is of this tendency that
Lastarria is a magnificent example.

A poor provincial boy from the down-at-heel town of
Rancagua, a few miles south of Santiago, Victorino Lastarria
came to the capital to study during the restless times of
Portales' conservative dictatorship. The lack of liberty in
the atmosphere seems to have made the word ring in his
mind ceaselessly. He read, as we who take freedom for
granted do not, the classics that told the story of liberty
and how to continue it; Comte, Rousseau, Montesquieu,
Bentham. In Andrés Bello's house, with a select group of
students, he listened to the great teacher's disquisitions on
Roman law, grammar, and literature. The restraint of the

older man must have irked him, for we read that only
Domingo Tagle could make Bello relax and be human, even
laugh. Bello on the other hand must have heard enough of
Lastarria's opinions to know he was a Hotspur and to recognize his great gifts.

When he began to teach, Lastarria felt that he was himself
still learning, was a part of this historic movement toward
freedom and progress which was the burden of his teaching
to others. Picking up in a second-hand book store a history
of the United States, he acquired from it the habit of com-
paring the two Americas, and it strengthened his conviction
that the political régime of 1836 stood squarely in the way of
progress. In 1840 we find him translating a French romantic
play, *The Exile*, and later adapting it, giving it a Chilean
setting. Literary liberty was closely related to political freedom. Romanticism, which means so many different things
in different places, did not mean nostalgic longing for the
past in South America; the past was Spain and the enemy of
romantic ideals.

When Lastarria's son was born he called him Washington,
and "the name was a hymn of liberty." [9]

He sought out the Argentine exiles, Sarmiento and Vicente
Fidel López, and admired their bold stand against tyranny,
even though he hardly considered them well grounded in the
faith of freedom.

The year 1843 was an important year in his life. In June
the first number of his fighting journal *El crepúsculo* ("The
Twilight") appeared; the following month he entered Congress; and the new University counted him among its professors in the Faculty of Humanities. The Rector's address
did not please him too much, in spite of its "liberty in all
things." There was not enough demolition of the errors of
the past in it. He wanted to find the ideas that had made

[9] Zañartu, *Lastarria* (1938), p. 29.

history what it was; Bello was afraid of anything but facts and distrusted the element of subjective interpretation to which Lastarria would open the door. But it was Bello himself who dryly gave him his chance, asking him to prepare the address on the occasion of the first anniversary of the University. This address was the bomb-shell, "Investigations on the Social Influence of the Conquest and the Colonial System of the Spaniards in Chile" (1844).

It was not only his own freedom of utterance that got him into trouble. The even more outspoken essay on "Chilean Society" by Bilbao was published in his journal, and there was a terrific outcry accusing it of being blasphemous and seditious. Moreover, the presidential election of 1846 gave further occasion for passion on behalf of the liberal cause. When political persecutions broke out, Lastarria was one of the first victims, and a boat called the *Chile* carried him to exile in Peru. When he returned, however, it was with unchastened spirit, preaching still that there were great obstacles to be overcome if his country was to achieve democracy: "the difference of classes, the indolence and ignorance of the masses, the monarchial habits and sentiments which the colonial system instilled in us, and the demoralization produced by the immoral government of the viceroys and the civil war." [10]

Without following him in detail through the years of his struggle against these obstacles as teacher and writer, we may note his term in Congress from 1855 to 1858, and his mission to the emperor of Brazil, which was a measure of recognition for the first native Chilean to win the name of "master," with all that that means to Latin-Americans.

"The Investigations" is a short book but it must have been a very long speech. It proposes to use history as a precious deposit of experience from which men can extract

[10] *Id.* at 90–91.

lessons that will save them from disaster and light that will guide them in the darkness of the future.[11]   Concretely, Lastarria asks, "What is the history of our republic? What profit can be drawn from its study for the direction of our affairs in their present condition?" and he answers, "The history of Chile is still that of a new people who can look back upon three centuries of a gloomy existence without movement." But the philosopher who examines this history, he continues, can find in it heroic acts which are the foundation of our political liberty and the beginning of a happiness which is the brighter because we remember the sufferings caused by that despotism from which we have just been delivered.[12]

The original part of the book is Lastarria's attempt to tell the story of the influence of facts upon the nature of Chilean society. His interpretation is one of the classic documents which have built up what is called the Black Legend of Spain. The Spanish conquerors were torrents of adventurers who came not to colonize the new world but to exploit the precious metals which it produced in abundance. The system of government that the Spaniards set up in the new world prohibited with heavy penalties the selling and printing in America of books of any kind, even of books of devotion. The schools and universities which they established were monuments of imbecility designed to keep men from true science.[13] The government employees that Spain sent to America became veritable despots who used the most arbitrary authority for the sake of their own private profit.[14] The law did not protect the native inhabitants of the country, but authorized tyranny over them.[15] The Spaniards in Chile were the same as those in Peru, and if the abuses in Chile were not so great it was only because the natural pov-

[11] Lastarria, *Investigaciones sobre la influencia social de la conquista i del sistema colonial de los Españoles en Chile.*
[12] *Id.* at 13–15.
[13] *Id.* at 42.
[14] *Id.* at 45.
[15] *Id.* at 50.

erty of the country did not awaken the same greed as did the mines of Peru. The administration contained the same destructive and anti-social element as the government of the other colonies, but it perhaps did less harm.[16]

✓ The laws of the colonial regime, like the laws of every period, were an expression of the habits and sentiments of the society. They had no other name than the king and his interests, God and the glory of arms.[17] The king's officers were arbitrary and despotic because they were representatives of an absolute ruler, and under their administration the people of Chile were profoundly depressed, reduced to a complete state of helplessness and without a single social virtue, at least so far as one could see, for their political institutions were designed to make slaves of them. "Their customs were simple and modest it is true, but anti-social . . . their simplicity was that of slavery." [18]

✓ The mixture of races that took place in the new world was a complete misfortune. "The mestizo bore on his forehead the mark of degradation and infamy, his birth condemned him to be the pariah of society. His condition was a thousand times worse than that of the native Indian: he at least was ordinarily treated as a conquered enemy." [19]

The class situation was perhaps equally unfortunate in the results it produced at the other end of the social scale. The Spaniard had so high a conceit of himself that he easily became an oppressor and made much greater claims upon society than could be justified by his contribution to it; if he knew some mechanic art or useful profession, he abandoned it on removing to America, and for this reason industry stagnated in its primitive condition. Only Indians and mestizos were employed at it.[20] "You see here," exclaimed Lastarria,

[16] *Id.* at 52–53.
[17] *Id.* at 60–61.
[18] *Id.* at 71.

[19] *Id.* at 80.
[20] *Id.* at 89–90.

"the cause which has perpetuated down to our days the immoral and pernicious custom of looking down upon all who devote themselves to industrial pursuits! Never did our fathers recognize any merit in industry or commerce, and if they gave some slight attention to agriculture, it was because that was the chief source of wealth which Chile offered." [21]

All, he maintained, that can be said by the apologists of the colonial order to prove the virtue that flourished under that régime can be summed up in the statement that Chileans were docile followers of the religion they had been taught. Religion among them had been made the instrument of despotism instead of the basis of civilization and freedom, the highest guarantee of the rights of man.[22]

It seemed evident to Lastarria that no society can fulfill its object so long as it is subject to a foreign power "which does not know it and which treats it capriciously, with the sole object of exploiting to the limit." The war of independence was, therefore, absolutely necessary and justifiable. We must recognize in addition, he continued, that the Spanish régime left a heritage of conditions and even of character which constituted a great handicap to a people who would be free and progressive. The struggle between the past and the present goes on. "It is for us to study our own peoples, to come to know their errors and their problems, and thus appreciate the obstacles which stand in the way of their greater perfection and happiness . . . and destroy completely the resistance offered by the old Spanish system embodied in our society." [23]

As early as 1844, then, Lastarria made his attitude perfectly clear. One could almost anticipate what he would write when in a calmer moment he turned to prepare a treatise on Constitutional Law for university students to ponder and memorize. He began by studying the relation

[21] *Id.* at 90–91.
[22] *Id.* at 111–113.   [23] *Id.* at 138.

between society and the state, a problem that still has the
world divided into opposing camps. Like most North Americans, he believed that the state is only an instrument for
achieving general happiness and that we involve ourselves in
endless error when we confuse the end of society with the end
of the state. "Society as an aggregation of men can have no
other goal than that which is given in the nature of human
nature. Good for man consists in the development of his
faculties and of his relations with the general order of the
universe." [24]

The state would have no business with religion at all if it
were a purely internal matter; but man embodies his religious beliefs in external forms and institutions which necessarily enter into relation with the state. The principles which
govern their relations are the requirement that the church
should neither mix in politics nor practice its forms of worship outside the places meant for such use. On the other
hand, Lastarria would provide for the complete independence
of all religious communities, prohibiting the state from imposing or modifying any religion or religious dogma and from
appointing any of the functionaries of the church. If it happens that the society has a single homogeneous belief, he
would permit the state to pay its officers a salary.[25]

Lastarria the positivist speaks in the "Lessons of Positive
Politics." Like Comte he seeks a law of progress in order
that, knowing the law, men may actually progress; that is,
move forward simultaneously in all the principal spheres of
their activity.[26]

The forward movement that history reveals is not regular
and steady. Society comes to stopping places and rests; it
may rest for centuries, but finally new ideas and beliefs arise

[24] Lastarria, *Elementos de derecho público constitucional: Teórico ó filosófico* (1846),
Obras, I, 1–196, at p. 29.
[25] *Id.* at 181–183.
[26] *Lecciones de política positiva* (Santiago, 1874), *Obras*, II, 33.

and a struggle ensues between the old and the new; society
passes through a transition period of conflicts and restlessness. The details with which this scheme is filled in are borrowed directly from Comte. Most of the Christian people of
Europe and America, he holds, who are at the forefront of
the march of progress, are now in one of these transitional
periods, attempting to establish human relations upon the
basis of freedom.[27] If the hoped-for progress is to be achieved
there must be a plan, a system, a faith with regard to human
progress. It is just this need which he then attempts to meet.
Human evolution, he argues, is nothing but the last stage in
a general progression found throughout the realm of the living, and it consists in assuring the predominance of faculties
that are characteristically human over those that are shared
with the animal creation. His examination of the social institutions of his own time reveals the fact that the Catholic
Church has not been bound by those principles which he
considers essential. It has, on the contrary, erected into
religious dogmas all its aversions to the moral conquest of
modern philosophy, and finds itself opposing the social and
political right which modern civilization demands for its
members. The result is an irresistible movement toward the
separation of church and state.[28] As a part of this movement,
he maintains, education will be taken away from the church
and will become a positivistic and scientific education without ceasing to inculcate the knowledge, love, and practice of
what is just and true, making the good and useful citizen.[29]

One of the things that he is very sure the state will not do
is to set up the national workshops of which Louis Blanc
dreamed, to provide work for all the unemployed; nor will it
fix a minimum wage, nor take the side of organized labor
against industry and capital. All of these proposals are re-

[27] *Id.* at 47–48.
[28] *Id.* at 110.   [29] *Id.* at 157.

jected on the ground that they destroy freedom.[30] The social
hierarchy which results from the natural operation of liberty
and is based on the natural inequality of human beings is not
objectionable to him. It is inevitable that some should
direct social activity and others be subordinate, as for example in the relation of management and labor.[31]

The state is severely limited by science, he says, to the role
of ensuring justice, which means furnishing every sphere of
social activity the conditions necessary to its existence and
progress.[32] He presents a scientific theory of reform, not too
well integrated with the theory of the state's reduced functions. Its object is to cause the disappearance of that disturbing factor in modern society, the persistent vices of the
old régime, and to bring about social reform through a
gradual evolutionary process as the natural result of the
relation between the political régime and the ceaseless forward movement of civilization.[33]

Lastarria was also one of the first to attempt a survey of all
Latin America, a *genre* in which he was followed by Alfredo
Colmo and Francisco García Calderón. This volume is called
simply *América*. His point of departure is the belief that
Europe and America have a common origin and a common
task in the world. It angers him, however, that "America
knows Europe, studies her incessantly, follows her step by
step and imitates her as a model; but Europe does not know
America, and in fact looks down upon her, or refuses to look
at her at all, as if she were a child gone to the bad, for whom
there is no longer any hope." [34] He ridicules the theory that
the Latin race is so different from the Germanic race that it
cannot hope to evolve a parliamentary régime, but must per-
force live under absolute government.[35] The truth, he says,

[30] *Id.* at 165.
[31] *Id.* at 197.
[32] *Id.* at 206.
[33] *Id.* at 218.
[34] Lastarria, *La América* (Buenos Aires, 1865), p. 5.
[35] *Id.* at 7.

is that Europe is profoundly ignorant of South America, at least on its human side. A hundred naturalists have been sent specimens of its flora and fauna, but who has come to make a careful study of its society? [36] The attitude of complacent superiority which Europeans assume toward Latin America would be the worst of all preparations for arriving at a fair and accurate judgment.

Lastarria pleads for more recognition of the contribution that America can make. We Americans understand, he says, that liberty is nothing other than the practice of law. Really the light of the future is to be found in America, and Europe can be saved only if it imitates America and heeds the redeeming voice of democracy.[37] He argues for the teaching of history, philosophy, ethics, law, political science, in line with the new teaching of democracy, which is the faith of the future and has been the American credo ever since "the Revolution of 1810, which was the greatest event of the ages since the coming of Christianity." [38] That revolution had as its ultimate aim the emancipation of the spirit of man, and was a revolt against Spanish civilization, which rested upon the contrary principle of the enslavement of the human mind.[39]

The fact that Europe clung to monarchy and had not learned the lesson of democracy was for Lastarria sufficient reason why America should not enter into a federation with the European nations. As for the idea of a league of Latin or Hispanic nations to combat the power and influence of the Anglo-Saxon race, it was "as false and absurd as it is behind the times and pernicious."[40]

The line that divides the world is that between exploited colonies and their exploiters, between Spanish and American

[36] *Id.* at 11.
[37] *Id.* at 133.
[38] *Id.* at 136.
[39] *Id.* at 191.
[40] *Id.* at 223.

civilization. "The principal cause of our political and social
disaster lies in our Spanish task, and we cannot remedy these
disasters except by reacting frankly, openly, and energetically against that civilization, in order to free our minds and
adapt our society to the new form, democracy." [41]

✓ The special circumstances of Chile attract his attention
again. Of all the Latin-American countries, it is the most
law-abiding and orderly. Democracy is surer to come there
than in any other country. However, the excellent work-
habits of the Chileans, their morality, sobriety, and energy
also imply a certain passiveness and clinging to the *status quo.*
Their conservative spirit must be reckoned with. [42]

✓ All of Latin America will continue to need immigrants.
"European immigration is undeniably a powerful stimulus
to the development of American population; provided with
the immigrant there come civilization, capital, and industry
and not ignorance and immorality . . . and provided that
the immigrant comes with the intention of being a part of
our society, as happens in North America, and not to form a
European colony with nationality and interests antagonistic
to the nationality and interests of America." [43]   In the
American population, ignorance and indolence are the
enemy, and he pleads for the establishment of industrial
enterprises and an education which will fit men to take part
in such enterprises. Already great material progress has
been made, and he presents the statistics that prove it. Side
by side with this progress has come an intellectual progress
of which America can be very proud. If science is international, the literature should be, and increasingly is, an expression of the spirit of American democracy, completely
emancipated from "the traditions of the outworn and anti-
social Spanish civilization." [44]

[41] *Id.* at 228.
[42] *Id.* at 380–381.
[43] *Id.* at 449.
[44] *Id.* at 466–467.

Francisco Bilbao (1823–1865)

Lastarria was a valiant fighter for freedom, but he seems almost stodgy compared with the fiery Bilbao. You may say all you like about the fragmentary nature of his work, his failure as a practical organizer, and the fact that he was always under the influence of someone or other, but you still will wake up with a start when on the dusty yellow pages of old books you read the clarion call of his manifestoes. Perhaps your opinion will be a reflection of your own personality and attitude. If you are conservative and find his writings clamorous but empty, you will have Armando Donoso on your side; if you think the world has need of more revolutionaries, and that Bilbao was a great one, Luis Alberto Sánchez is your spokesman.

Lastarria's rejection of Spanish civilization was vigorous enough, but he retained Christianity. It was Bilbao's contribution — and it soon got him into hot water — that he could not separate Spanish civilization from Catholicism. The famous essay on "The Nature of Chilean Society" (*sociabilidad* has nothing to do with being sociable, and some purists have tried, unsuccessfully, to coin a more logical word) was published in June of 1844. It reminds one of the *Communist Manifesto* of the year before.

"Our past is Spain," he wrote. "Spain is the Middle Ages. The soul and body of the Middle Ages were Catholicism and feudalism." [45] The faith was an instrument that the church used in its relations with the barbarians. It tried to subject everyone to its sway. While there is no doubt that the coming of Christianity marked the greatest step forward in religious history, Catholicism was a reaction which deformed the primitive purity of the doctrine of Jesus. Its effects on women, children, citizens, and intelligentsia are

[45] Bilbao, "Sociabilidad Chilena" (1845), *Obras*, I, 5.

analyzed by Bilbao: "The wife is subjected to the husband. Slavery of the wife. . . . The child irremediably subjected to the father. Slavery of the child. . . . The individual subjected to authority. Slavery of the citizen. . . . Thought chained to the text, intelligence bound to dogma. Slavery of thought." [46]

It was Catholicism that carried out to its logical conclusion the medievalism of Spain; it was Catholicism that put the same stamp on the colonial régime in America. It was a true society, for it had a single system of belief; but it was a slavery. All that a society needs to know of whence it comes and whither it is going were given by the faith. Once that faith is destroyed these questions must be answered scientifically, that is, rationally. We must determine what we are, he says; what is our tradition and our destiny, whether we will go the whole way in completing the revolution. To complete the revolution means to make another revolution by doing away with the beliefs that come to us from the past and that still clutter up the minds of the people. [47]

The present spectacle is lamentable. We see around us intellectual anarchy, but that anarchy is transitory. The triumph of the past survives in the forms of the old civilization. There are still monarchies, there are still aristocracies, there is still papal and ecclesiastical authority. . . . Our task in the political and religious sphere is to accept the facts. . . . The liberty of the individual as a body and a thinking thing. This is a fact.

The equality of my fellow man because he is another temple in which God has installed liberty. This is another fact.

Liberty is social equality, that is to say it belongs to all; sovereignty of the people. This is another fact.

Liberty of worship, that is to say, religious democracy. This is another fact.

Liberty is political equality, that is to say, democracy properly so called. This is another fact. . . .

[46] *Id.* at 10–11.
[47] *Id.* at 21.

On these facts is based the future system of belief. They are few but they are irrefutable. They are indisputable. They must serve as the basis of the future religion.[48]

Future religions were not a popular subject in the Chile of 1844, and Bilbao's accusation and condemnation for blasphemy, sedition, and immorality followed as a matter of course.

Thereafter, however, from whatever part of the world he happened to be living in, and he was a wanderer from this time on, Bilbao continued to play his part in history, which he conceived to be the manifestation of the efforts of human beings to arrive at the realization of an ideal. "The problem of the philosophy of history reduces itself to learning what man's duty is and the nature of the being who is to fulfill that duty, and then moving toward the God-given end. . . . The problem is simple. The ideal is the perfection of the human being. The perfection of the human being is the absolute dominance of the universal spirit to cause to live in every one of us universal freedom." [49]

When we examine America in the light of this distant goal, he continues, we see that it falls into two divisions: the English United States, and the Spanish Disunited States: "In the United States we see all the elements of their history united in a movement toward greater and greater liberty. In the Disunited States we see the impotent efforts of Liberty, falling and rising again, always threatened, never secure, living through all the vicissitudes of a terrible alternation between despotism and attempts at freedom." For this striking contrast, Bilbao can find no other valid explanation than the difference of religion between the two continents.[50]

What has been the role of Catholicism in this continent of

[48] *Id.* at 37–38.
[49] "La Ley de la historia" (1858), *Obras*, I, 156.
[50] *Id.* at 159–160.

South America? he asks. To exterminate, to brand as heretics those who thought freely. To strive to keep in slavery
a world that had won its political independence; to impose
itself as a state religion, banish liberty of conscience, hinder
immigration, lay an economic burden on the people, oppose
all reform and progress, arouse the baser instincts of the
multitude, fight reason, personality, sovereignty, and the
principle of nationality.[51]

Bilbao's more positive statements are vague but violent:
"The Good is Liberty. The law of the good is Equality. The
Bad is usurpation or slavery. The law of the Bad is Inequality or Privilege. Liberty is in ourselves. Equality is in our
relation with others. . . .[52] There is no country without men;
there are no true men without liberty. Liberty is our
country." [53]

To this cry that the people is all and must have liberty, he
maintains, the constitutions answer that the people are a
myth, that inequality is necessary, that there is no escape
from classes and the war of classes, nor from the misery and
ignorance that are their consequence. They decree therefore
that the people have no voice, may not meet freely nor learn,
nor legislate, and that a happier future is impossible for
them.[54]

Bilbao does not find a way out in anarchism, but in newer
and better constitutions, this time international ones. In his
"Plan for a Federal Congress of the Republics" he proposes
a "Union Now" which would provide citizenship in the international federation, a system of international law, common weights and measures, abolition of customs duties,
creation of an international tribunal, a system of coloniza-

[51] "Movimiento social de los pueblos de la América Meridional," *Obras*, I,
174–175.
[52] "El gobierno de la libertad," *Obras*, I, 174–175.
[53] *Id*. at 245.
[54] *Id*. at 277.

tion, universal education, a plan for intellectual coöperation, the settling of boundary disputes, creation of an American University, joint planning for reform, granting of power to the Federal Congress to represent the member nations before the world, determination of policy by majority of the individual (not national) votes.[55]

Since there was no such federation in existence, events like the French invasion of Mexico and the naming of Maximilian as Emperor were still possible. They moved Bilbao to write his "America's Danger," published in Buenos Aires in 1862. Bilbao always had a French master; in his writings on religion he followed Lamennais; this political and historical work was dedicated to Quinet and Michelet, with whom his mind lived, although his body was far away.

The message of this book is that the hour is fateful for America; it must take thought about its destiny. That destiny is to preserve independence in order to bring about the federation of humanity, under the aegis of reason and with a régime of civil and political liberty.[56] But Bilbao cannot resist telling us once more that reason and Catholicism are incompatible; we must choose between them.[57] And he prints an embarrassing list of Latin-American revolutions and dictatorships to prove that the continent has known few years of true liberty.[58]

"The American Gospel," published in 1864, is the same gospel he had been preaching since his twenties. It is still needed, he maintains, for America has no American Bible or Koran. He aspires to write it. Readers of his other books, he continues, hardly need to be told that Spain conquered America, the English the northern continent, and that the

---

[55] Id. at 301–302. Iniciativa de la América: idea de un congreso federal de las repúblicas (Paris, 1856), Obras, I, 301–302.

[56] La América en Peligro, in Obras, II, 177.

[57] Id. at 199.

[58] Id. at 240–241.

result of their divergent policies has been that the United States takes first place among nations old and new, while for the Disunited States progress consists in the task of "un-Spanishing" themselves.[59] For Spain and Spanish history can be epitomized in a word, and that word is Catholicism. The liberty to think for oneself, which Spain proscribed, is a thread that runs through the origins and subsequent history of the United States. He even dares to use the word Protestant, and admits the close relation between the liberty of North America and the form its Christianity took. There have been few South Americans who would go this far; nearly all have been Catholic enough to be very sure they were not Protestants. He admits again, as few Latin Americans have done, that the United States is more than a rich or progressive nation; "it is the creative nation"; and he lists the glories of its thought and literature.[60]

To be sure, he says, rationalism is even better than Protestantism; the smell of theology and of biblical learning clings to Protestantism, and leads to a perfect fury of interpretation and discussion which cannot be settled by the immediate appeal to reason that he would use. There is still revelation in the Protestant view of the universe; it is the best attitude that has been adopted by any historic society, but it is not the best possible attitude.[61]

Valentin Letelier (1852–1919)

A half a century later in Chile the fight for intellectual expansion was still going on, as it always must. Valentin Letelier was carrying the banner and writing a volume called "The Struggle for Culture." This collection of political articles and pedagogical studies, issued in 1895, sums up a dis-

[59] *El evangelio Americano* (Buenos Aires, 1864), *Obras*, II, 338.
[60] *Id.* at 400–401.
[61] *Id.* at 406.

tinguished career devoted to the defense of education and of
the liberal (i.e. not ultramontane) cause in Chile. Its author
was professor of administrative law and later Rector of the
University of Chile.

Letelier felt that he lived in the epoch predicted by Bilbao.
"In every period the social order is based on the dominant
philosophy; their [the authoritarians'] philosophy is theo-
logical, their organic principle, authority; our philosophy is
a scientific philosophy, and its organic principle, liberty." [62]
But the fact that he is writing shows that liberty still needs
defenders.

Mere party allegiance did not mean so much to Letelier as
a man's attitude toward culture and education; those whose
policies are favorable to the development of culture and
human faculties are for him liberals, and those who take the
other side are conservatives.[63] The touchstone is thought,
not public works, docks, bridges, and railroads. "We deem
to be anti-scientific that school which in our times teaches
that personal liberty, liberty of thought, the right to work
and to equality are natural rights, inalienable and inherent
in human nature." For science reaches no such conclusion;
however enthusiastic one may be about freedom, one must
recognize in the cold light of reason that liberties are granted
or withheld by society, used or abandoned as means to ends,
depending upon circumstances.[64] The feudalism which today
we decry had its good reasons for being and served a social
purpose, that of defense, in its day. Even today, authority,
for all the bad name it has acquired, may be necessary and
useful, and he refuses to be frightened by being called an
authoritarian:

When we judge it to be necessary, let us make education com-
pulsory, or vaccination, savings, or insurance; let us forbid the

[62] Letelier, *La lucha por la cultura* (Santiago, 1895), p. 11.
[63] *Id.* at 13–14.   [64] *Id.* at 24.

employment of children who have not finished their schooling; let us fix the hours of labor, with no other considerations in mind than those of science and hygiene; let us regulate prostitution, intoxication, examination, degrees, professions . . . let us make the authority of the State prevail over that of the Church; and let us not worry if they call us authoritarians, provided we are by these means giving man more power, making him more master of himself, and endowing him with greater vigor, originality, and independence of mind.

Above all, let the label of authoritarians not bother us so long as the freedom to think, to speak, to write, to read, the freedom of worship, of public meetings, of printing, of teaching, of movement, in short all the liberties that man needs to develop his capacities and society to develop its culture find in us the surest guarantee of their existence.

Let us be men of science, and as such remember that the aim of government is not liberty, nor yet authority, nor any abstract principle whatsoever, but to satisfy social needs in order to arrive at the perfection of man and the development of society.[65]

In another article he returns to his pet theme, playing on Alberdi's motto and insisting that to govern is to educate — every good system of government being a true system of education and every general system of education a true political system. The two are so intertwined that a state can never surrender the control of public instruction to any other power in society.[66]

His impatience of anything that is not instructive is indicated by his grumbling that what we call literature, that is, intellectual productions without moral aim, philosophic concepts, or scientific content, is an invention of decadent societies.[67]

If a people lacks desirable qualities — and he admits many defects in the Chilean character, many absurd errors in the Chilean mind — the blame lies at the door of public educa-

[65] *Id.* at 30–31.
[66] *Id.* at 44.
[67] *Id.* at 49.

tion, which has failed to cultivate the potentialities of youth, or has positively stifled its curiosity by a routine and uninteresting education.[68]

By this time a policy had been adopted of importing German professors to raise the level of the Teachers' College and install the best European methods. Some objection was raised to paying public funds to foreigners, and the whole system came under attack. Letelier rose to its defense as the advocate of high standards in education, and pointed out the noble contribution of these professors to the culture of the nation, their notable research, and the ridiculously small salaries they received. Not one of them was a clock-watcher; not one displayed the slightest tendency to proselytize for the German Empire.[69] There is, he concludes, not one single fact to substantiate the groundless fears of the detractors of the German pedagogues.[70]

Especially in the second and enlarged edition of his "Evolution of History" Letelier embarked upon broader and more abstract themes, including the still prickly one of the difference between history and sociology, so often confused by historians who do not know what sociology is, and by sociologists who challenge history's right to an independent existence.[71] Letelier entered the lists equipped with an acquaintance not only with Comte, but also with Gumplowicz, Lacombe, and Durkheim. He is, he says, quite aware of the superficiality of individual explanations in history and of the need for studying the whole state of society if one is to understand why the individual action of men like Luther or Hampden bore such fruit as it did.[72] He is positivist enough to advocate studying social phenomena directly and giving up

[68] *Id.* at 370.
[69] *Id.* at 415.
[70] *Id.* at 440–441.
[71] Letelier, *La evolución de la historia* (2a ed., Santiago, 1900), I, xiii.
[72] *Id.* at 471–472.

the pretense of explaining them by abstract speculation.[73] He is not misled by the organicist school, the history of which he traces, into seeing in the analogies between society and an organism anything more than analogies, and he points out a number of very real differences in structure, nature, and activities. There is even a bit of semantics in his observation that the error lies in supposing that organism means the same thing when used of the individual and of society. With sociology surveyed and defined, he is able to conclude that a line can be drawn between history, the science of the past, and sociology, which studies the permanent laws of the social order. History records what man did, the steps in the development of industry and science and institutions; sociology studies industry, science, and institutions without names or dates, embracing all societies rather than narrating the facts about one society in chronological order.[74]

*   *   *   *

We are tempted to follow Chilean thought into its contemporary forms and say "four words" about friends like the gentle philosopher Enrique Molina; Chile's great woman, Amanda Labarca; that amazing mixture of anthropologist, politician, and literary critic, Ricardo A. Latcham; and the sincere and intelligent analyst and meliorist of medico-social conditions, Salvador Allende. But both chronology and logic forbid, and we turn instead to Uruguay, where a reaction to the Americano-phile tendencies of Sarmiento and the generation of '42 was to appear in the person of José Enrique Rodó.

[73] *Id.* at 516–518.
[74] *Id.*, II, 510–512.

CHAPTER IV

A Reaction—Rodó

José Enriqué Rodó (1872–1917)

E VEN A PATRIOTIC North American becomes a little un-
easy at the continued panegyrics of his country in the
pages of Sarmiento, Lastarria, and Bilbao. It would not take
a prophet with any very extraordinary knowledge of human
nature to predict that Latin Americans would eventually
react, have to find some reason for cultural affirmation. This
reaction and affirmation is at least part of the significance of
Rodó in the history of Latin-American thought. At least
part of his success in writing the pillow-book of a generation
of Latin-American youth is due to his having spoken the
eagerly awaited word.

Another part is due to the way he spoke it. "He speaks to
our souls . . . with more than earthly music . . . a message
deep and grave, luminous and revivifying, that seems a
psalm to life, a song of hope, a bugle call of victory." [1] This
is "the magician of Spanish prose, the publicist who of all
men on this round globe writes the best Spanish, who best of
all knew how to handle in all its majesty the instrument that
is our language." [2] When he speaks, "he gives the impression
that everything he says is mature wisdom, that he has tried
to make of his works a cathedra and to put into his voice an
accent at once doctrinal and elevated. Whatsoever things are
evil and despicable in the mind of man are excluded from the

[1] Victor Pérez Petit, *Rodó: su vida, su obra* (Montevideo, 1918).
[2] Andrés González Blanco, *Escritores representativos de América* (Madrid, 1917),
p. 3.

writing of Rodó; not a perverse paradox, not a cruel irony, not a cry disturb the calm of his style." [3]

This man who in life haunted libraries, played not a very glorious part in politics, wore thick glasses, and was diffident and cold in manner, sought to be the intellectual leader of America — to scale the most remote heights of idealism and speak from above the saving word, and speak it in a way that permitted no debate.

It is a surgical operation to separate his thought from the manner of its expression. He himself would not have submitted to the operation. Once in conversation he remarked, "But these men are not writers! They are men of thought, and nothing more. Above all, the writer must know how to say things beautifully." [4]

In the exquisite refinement of his culture, in his love for truth and for beauty, in his balance between the humanistic tradition of European culture and the needs of American life, Rodó seemed to multitudes to be the writer Latin America had been waiting for. He had extracted from all books not dull learning but living wisdom that could be the guide of noble and aspiring souls.

The biography of Rodó is so unimportant that even his disciples neglect it, and Pérez Petit, who purports to give it, turns to rhapsodies instead. He was born in Montevideo of good family, he studied, read and wrote, was briefly professor of literature and twice member of Parliament. Most European of Latin-American thinkers, he went to Europe only during the World War, poorly supported by a journal at home, and after eight months' wandering and illness, died there.

The important thing about Rodó is his writing, and it is only by letting his ideas speak for themselves that one can

[3] Arturo Marasso Rocca, *Estudios literarios* (Buenos Aires, 1920), p. 93.
[4] Max Henríquez Ureña, *Rodó y Rubén Darío* (Habana, 1918), p. 9.

decide whether he deserves the encomiums he has received
both as thinker and as writer — whether he actually achieved
that harmony between Hellenic paganism and Judaic Christianity that he (and Matthew Arnold) sought: between the
positivism on which he never quite turned his back and the
idealism that he certainly preached, between the rational
liberalism that made him less than orthodoxly religious and
the sentiment that made him reject all attack on religion,
between the aristocracy that a fastidious culture glorifies and
the democracy that he dared hardly criticize.

The most successful attempt Rodó made to deal with these
problems was his classic little book, *Ariel.*[5] The setting is a
farewell of the revered master, called lovingly Prospero, after
the Duke in Shakespeare's *Tempest.* The farewell to the master, an obvious surrogate for Rodó, himself not impressive in
such gatherings and morbidly timid, takes place in the old
man's study, dominated by a bronze statue of Ariel. He in-
vokes Ariel as his inspiration, for he has derived from his
favorite Renan the idea that Ariel represents the noblest,
most wingèd part of the spirit of man, all that rises above
irrationality and sensualism into disinterested action, the
play of intelligence, culture and spirituality. The rest of the
book is Olympic discourse, a kind of sacred oratory; it deals
with the most serious matters, and is addressed to youth, and
may change the course of lives.

Youth must in each generation conquer anew, by its own
efforts, a faith in the ideal and come to an awareness of its
own mission with relation to the ideal. To watch it do so is
the most inspiring spectacle in the world. Only the vision of
the future and hopeful movement toward it gives the soul its
"sweet and ineffable beauty."

Rodó bids his hearers possess in serene confidence the
strength that is in each of them and calls them to consider the

---

[5] *La vida nueva*, vol. I: *Ariel* (Montevideo, 1900).

life that lies ahead of them. "Some of you will be men of science; others, artists; others, men of action." All, however, will be men, and this is what concerns Rodó. For each must somehow be above all a representative of an unmutilated ideal of Humanity, in which none of the finest qualities are lost or covered over. "The necessity that each of us is under to devote himself especially to a particular calling, a part of culture, certainly does not prevent his trying to achieve, by the harmony of the spirit within him, the common destiny of all rational beings." [6] Specialization must not be allowed to lead to an indifference to the general interests of Humanity; that could only be disastrous.

Can our complex civilization find again the harmony that simplicity made easy and natural for the Greeks? It can if behind and beyond the inevitable differentiation that comes with progress it maintains its unflagging interest in the things of the soul, of man as rational being. Keep your inner freedom; never give all of yourselves to utility or passion, that is the way to slavery.

Inner freedom is necessary to morality and to beauty, which in the last analysis are one, for duty is not an imposition from without felt as restriction or coercion; it is most virtuous when felt from within as harmony. The supreme harmony would be represented by the union of the spirit of charity with Greek elegance and good taste. In those rare instances where this union has occurred it has not been superficial form or mere compromise between opposing ideals, but an inner, spiritual, and esthetic harmony.

This ideal of the free and harmonious development of our nature is countered by the utilitarian conception of life, in which all is directed at interest and its immediate satisfaction. People miss the point that utilitarianism is only justifiable as a prelude to idealism. Many explain it as indis-

6 Rodó, *Ariel* (3a ed., 1926), 27, 28–29.

solubly connected with democracy. Renan has dealt with this problem and suggested that democracy inevitably renders men mediocre, making them bow the knee to Utility. This, however, is a view that centers our attention only on the negative function of equality in the past, when it was doing away with *unjust* superiority; its positive function is to clear the way for the recognition of *true* human superiorities. To govern is to populate only if we add, and then educate and select. Democracy and science are not rejected as incompatible with humanism and intellectual aristocracy, but are accepted as the necessary supports upon which our civilization rests. Mankind must be taught what subordinations to the superior are necessary and how the superior may be recognized. Democracy means equal possibility, not equal reality of influence and power within society. All may aspire to be morally and intellectually superior, not to be treated as if they were when they are not. A rational democracy includes the idea of aristocracy; it recognizes its own best elements and establishes them in a position resting on the free consent of their fellows. In this formula we have already achieved the fusion of Christian and Greek ideals, for it is "from the spirit of Christianity, in reality, that is born the sentiment of equality, vitiated by a certain ascetic underestimate of spiritual selection and of culture. From the heritage of the classic civilizations come the sense of order and hierarchy, an almost religious respect for the genius, vitiated by a certain aristocratic disdain for the humble and weak. The future will bring together the two suggestions of the past." [7]

In the part of *Ariel* that has always been best known, but that is in reality only an illustration of his thesis, Rodó examines Americanism as the very spirit of utilitarianism. He does not know the United States, but this fact never pre-

[7] *Id.* at 70–71.

vented either him or his disciples, in spite of their vaunted love of the truth, from being very dogmatic about the subject. Admiration for the greatness and progress of the United States has been growing by leaps and bounds in the minds of those who lead and govern South American countries, and perhaps even more in the minds of the masses. It is fatally easy to pass from admiration to imitation. To give up Latinity of their own free will has become the dream of many sincere men, truly interested in the future of their countries. In opposition to this tendency some later thinkers have gone further than Rodó himself, for he is not absolute in his opposition; the example of the strong, he says, has much to teach us, and we must not close our eyes to foreign experience. But to go so far as to give up our own essential nature — that is another matter, and he calls a halt.

He salutes the enemy, and generously states that "to neglect her defects is less foolish than to deny her good qualities." [8] "Without sacrificing the sovereignty of the individual, she has at the same time made out of the spirit of association the most admirable instrument of her greatness." [9] He has only praise for the curiosity and love of learning of North Americans, the marvelous results of investigation, philanthropy, and industry. Their culture is not refined or spiritual, and they have not added to science a single great principle, but in application they have been wonderful. In the general shipwreck of idealisms, they have preserved the highest, keeping alive a religious feeling that puts a firm basis under morality even if it does not rise to the heights of a delicate spirituality. They are strong and have a kind of primitive robustness. But the worst is that Americans live for the present, and have neither the deep traditions of the past to guide them nor a noble and disinterested con-

[8] *Id.* at 77.
[9] *Id.* at 78.

ception of the future. The ideal of the beautiful makes no appeal to the descendant of the stern Puritans, and he is not concerned with thought or the true in any absolute sense, but only as a solution of the present and practical problem. All research, he remarked at the moment when Willard Gibbs was working in New Haven, is directly related to utilitarian application. Even if he had known of Gibbs, and a hundred like him, he would have said they were not representative, refusing to judge North America by the few, and insisting on judging Latin America by its élite. All her war on ignorance, he says, has only made the United States a half-educated nation, in which the highest forms of culture languish. It is a civilization which may have a glorious future before it, but that "may" does not constitute any valid reason why South America should slavishly imitate it and abandon its own heritage.

We in Latin America, proclaims Rodó's spokesman, must stand for the things of the spirit — art, science, morals, sincerity in religion, a politics based on principles; we must educate our wills "in the persistent cult of the future." The past belonged to the fighter; the present belongs almost entirely to the arm that levels and builds; the future will offer unlimited possibilities for the development "of the superior faculties of the soul." He bids youth consecrate a part of its soul "to the unknown future." Savages live in the present; as we advance our horizon widens, and we live increasingly in a universe not bounded by our grandfather and by the next meal. The civilized man thinks of posterity, and governs his actions by the thought of conditions ever farther removed from him in time and space. "The future is in the life of societies the thought that kindles ideals par excellence. From pious veneration of the past, the cult of tradition, on the one hand, and on the other from the bold drive toward the future, comes that noble force which, lifting the collective

spirit above the limitations of the present, imparts to the
social agitations and sentiments an ideal goal." [10]

No other writing of Rodó need detain us so long as *Ariel*.
"The Motives of Proteus" (1909) is a much longer book, and
one on which Rodó lavished loving care, but it has neither
beginning nor end, and even his admirer Zaldumbide admits
that "its uniformity appears monotony, and is perhaps a
bit excessive; 450 closely-packed pages to prove to us, when
all is said and done, that each of us ought to follow his vocation is perhaps too many pages for one book." [11] The form at
least was deliberate on Rodó's part; it was never to have an
end or an architecture, but always to be "becoming." For
the ideal of life is also a perpetual becoming and self-renova-
tion. The chiseled marmoreal beauty of the aphorisms and
parables in this volume has its own appeal. The thought is
essentially unsystematic, but it contains insights that no one
has expressed better.

He recalls the experience we all have as part of the crowd,
and our return afterwards to our own personalities, amazed
at what we have said and done. But the crowd spirit is more
ubiquitous than we think; "all human society is, in a sense,
a crowd. Every society to which you remain bound robs you
of a part of your essence, and replaces it with a speck of the
gigantic personality which is its own." [12] Primitive man's
vocations are simple and limited in number; as societies advance, their specialization requires each individual to choose
from an ever greater number of callings an ever more re-
stricted and precise one that he will follow. [13]

Although Rodó gives other examples, he must also have
been thinking of Latin Americans when he remarks that the
journey of a superior man has often been determinative, has

[10] *Id.* at 108–109.
[11] Gonzalo Zaldumbide, *Montalvo y Rodó* (New York, 1938), p. 204.
[12] Rodó, *Motivos de Proteo* (2a ed., 1941), p. 44.
[13] *Id.* at 93.

marked an epoch for the society of which he is a part, whether its result be enthusiasm for what he has seen and would copy, or disillusion with the real and renewed determination to achieve something better.[14] Tolerance he would understand to be not a mere matter of intellect, possible of attainment for the indifferent or the skeptic; no, it involves warmth of feeling, the strength of love; it is not lack of enthusiasm or conviction, but is affirmative, creative.[15]

The fatality that steals from ideas something of their essence, their aroma, when schools or sects are organized around them is noted; even if the institution exists to further the idea, it deforms it. For ideas are most alive and fluid when they are in the minds of their discoverers, evolving, transforming themselves freely into other ideas. Even before action and organization crystallize them into death, the very need of using words and categories to describe them is an injury to their delicate nature.[16] History and public opinion, which are so hard on those who change their habits or tenets without good reason, fail to observe that other falsity, no less frequent, no less harmful, which lies in preserving the outward appearance of loyalty to an idea which has no longer any living roots in one's heart. Is this not also apostasy? [17] But *mere* ideas in our minds are part of our intellectual history, not of our personality. We do not change nor are we reformed by ideas; it is passions that reform us, or ideas that arouse our passions.[18]

The unity that persists through varying experiences in the individual personality finds its match in the spirit of a people or race, and there is no reason for denying societies the attribute of personality. These larger personalities are of many varieties, change easily or resist stubbornly, find harmony or

[14] *Id.* at 225–227.
[15] *Id.* at 293.
[16] *Id.* at 315–316.
[17] *Id.* at 320.
[18] *Id.* at 328–329.

bend and break under strain, just as the personalities of individuals do. "The ideal epic of nations is to maintain this personality." [19] This can be done only by accepting change; the tree that does not change by growth is eliminated. But we must not think that the way the twig is bent is the only way it could grow. Hidden potentialities lie within us, individuals and societies.[20]

The Mirror of Prospero, which first appeared in 1913, is a collection of criticisms, articles and speeches which can hardly be compared to his other books, although Rodó was a supreme critic. It is his most American book, and contains one statement of American ideals worth quoting. At the celebration of the hundredth anniversary of Chile's independence, Rodó represented Uruguay, and said: "I have always believed that in our America it was not possible to speak of many fatherlands, but rather of one great, single country; I have always believed that in America, more than anywhere else, it behooves us, without destroying this idea of a fatherland, to make it greater and wider and purify it of all that is narrow and negative . . . and raise above the idea of the nation, the idea of America." [21]

The reader will draw his own conclusions as to the greatness of Rodó's thought, but inasmuch as the twentieth century has seen a division of opinion into the Arielists and anti-Arielists, and Rodó has become a symbol — the incarnation of an attitude to be accepted or rejected — it is in place to indicate the reasons which lead men like Luis Alberto Sánchez or even the Uruguayan critic Alberto Zum Felde to conclude that Rodó has been overestimated in the past, or has distracted attention from the real problem. The counts on which Sánchez would criticize are these:

[19] *Id.* at 366–367.
[20] *Id.* at 368–369.
[21] Rodó, *El mirador de Próspero* (Montevideo, 1913), p. 161.

The preoccupation with style in Rodó is narcissistic, static, abulic. His love of form prevents his living up to his own ideal of renovation. It amounts to literary decadence, and prevents serious thinking. On the ideological side there is complete lack of originality, and utter subservience to French masters. Not admitting Rodó's application of European culture to American conditions, Sánchez considers him a *déraciné*. The only time he ever took an interest in Indians (in his essay on Montalvo) it was for esthetic reasons. His anti-United States attitude fails to appreciate certain elements of idealism in the United States and on the other hand neglects the danger both of economic imperialism and of the active penetration of North American ideals in South America. The theme of the vocation which runs through so much of his work is vitiated by estheticism, which in reality leads to instability. His obstinate optimism is groundless and logically leads to skepticism. Like most esthetes, he is anti-democratic, and like most individualists, fails to see social problems, although in this respect he did a little better toward the end of his life. His philosophy is a poor thing and his ideals vague and literary. The practical outcome of his school has been unproductive; the idealism which became a myth to his followers was only a myth and led to no social action.[22]

Zum Felde's criticisms are the same, but less violent. He adds a natural explanation of the triumph of *Ariel* both in Latin America and in Spain; it was "the justification of their racial characteristics, the compensation for their practical backwardness, the claim to spiritual superiority over the Titan of the North." [23] The essential subject matter of Ariel is values, and it begins to seem insufficient as a discussion of

[22] Luis Alberto Sánchez, *Balance y liquidación del novecientos* (Santiago, 1940), pp. 71–88.
[23] Alberto Zum Felde, *Proceso intelectual del Uruguay* (Montevideo, 1941), p. 236

values for it lacks any metaphysical foundation. It was never anything but pretty words. The man that Rodó talks about is an abstract, non-existent creature, and the author was neither a psychologist nor a sociologist.[24]

Carlos Vaz Ferreira (1873–　　)

There have been few genuine philosophers, as distinguished from professors of philosophy, in all Latin America. Vaz Ferreira, besides being a distinguished educator, is one of them, and deserves to be better known. Besides the fact that he is Uruguayan, he has a number of qualities in common with Rodó: the extreme sensitivity which brought both to periods of crisis and suffering; the emphasis on the fluid, living, and never-completed character of thought; the fragmentary form in which both deliberately present their work.

To those who can tell by inspection that they will not be satisfied by these characteristics may be added those who label as bourgeois any writer whose analysis does not lead him to Marxian conclusions. Ceruti, for instance, finds Vaz completely conservative and all his talk about taking all possible ideas into account mere camouflage. On the other hand, Gil Salguero, in an eloquent study, "Limits of the Human," prefixed to Vaz's "On Feminism," combats the view that we are dealing with eclecticism or doubt, while admitting that the philosopher is very hesitant about generalizing or drawing conclusions. In this case we have an instability that comes from depth, not from superficiality. The courage of Vaz is seen in his frank reservations as to certain "truths" very generally accepted or tendencies decidedly fashionable in his period. The novelty of his method is presented as a type of thinking as plastic as life itself; he thinks reality directly, without the tool of a system, and

[24] *Id.* at 242–243.

when he thinks enters into an endless process that is without beginning or end.

The words "living" and "fermenting" occur in the work of Vaz with a frequency which suggests that they are explicative of the core of his thought. He has sought to infuse into the rather stereotyped program of studies of the universe something of the ideological ferment that goes on in the mind of a sensitive and thoughtful person who lives his philosophy. He has tried not to imprison or deform ideas, but to catch them on the wing; not to tie himself to any system, which would result in his seeing things from one angle only, but to hold all relevant ideas in his mind at once. In this way only can ideas exercise on the thinking process a suggestive and renovating action which he calls *fermental*.

If this sounds like intuitionism it is not misleading; yet that is only a part of his thought, for he has his allegiance to positivism, too. In the course of his life he has moved from an attitude resembling that of John Stuart Mill to something much more fluid and intuitional. His teaching has been to some extent a rebellion against the current rote methods of the University and secondary school, for he has sought to provoke thought rather than to impose conclusions, and has summed up his own courses as being "some facts, some empirical laws, some more or less probable theories, and as to the rest, a classification of questions." [25] He collects ideas, but it is life that he has confidence in. The curious result of this attitude is that, believing in life, he is less ready to act in it than the system builders whose rigidity he deplores. The ideas and solutions that history has proved appeal to him more than those that a rigorous logic recommends, for if they have survived the historic process they have the plasticity that life demands.

Many of these trends in the thinking of Vaz are expressed

[25] *Id.* at 379.

as early as the "Living Logic" of 1909, which in its second edition is provided with an appendix giving questions and examples and illustrating what he calls the *penetrable* method in education, or immersing the students in as many ideas as possible rather than pre-digesting their education for them.

You must think, he teaches, with all the ideas you can, taking them all into account, balancing them, adapting them. When you try this you will feel lost, for the human mind finds difficulty in avoiding the impression of abandon when it is left free. Our minds desire exactitude in our knowledge; we come to rest in it. Now that exactitude is a good thing — the ideal, in fact, when it is legitimate; but when it is not, when it is false or illegitimate, the effects are very bad. Interpretations are falsified, even facts are hidden or disfigured, investigation is held up, and we reach no depth in our thinking. Look for such unwarranted precision in thinking and you will find it in entire systems, such as Herbart's. System building is acceptable where you know everything — facts and principles — and when everything can be combined or integrated, but it is bad when these conditions are not present, as in the more complex fields of morals, psychology, literature, philosophy, all the social and practical.[26]

Like Pareto, who would be good reading for many Latin Americans but is never mentioned by them, Vaz believes that to base living on a dogma strengthens belief in it, just as if it had been proved experimentally; this he calls the illusion of experience.[27] Classifications, like systems, have their dangers, but he warns against throwing them out just because they do not cover all the possibilities or because cases do not exactly correspond to their categories. They are schemes for thinking — instruments, and useful as such if you do not take them for pictures of reality in all its complexity. Max

26 Vaz Ferreira, *Lógica viva* (2a ed., 1920), pp. 166–167.
27 *Id.* at 214.

Weber might be speaking of his Ideal-Typus, except for the crystal clarity of Vaz Ferreira's style, but there is no indication that the Uruguayan reads Weber. Our very language is full of implicit and often fallacious classifications, he says, which we use without realizing that names commit us to a view of reality. This is so important a point that it is one of the two criticisms he has to offer of classic logic. The older logic forgot the fluctuating, vague character of terms and the penumbra of connotations they bring with them, and the inadequacy of language to express reality.[28]

His own method in philosophizing cannot be better savored than in the 1940 edition of his *Fermentario*, or the "Mind Vat." Here the reader is introduced into the stream of consciousness of a philosopher, in which fragmentary essays, glimpses of truths, or would-be glimpses that turn out to be nothing but the framework without the substance of thought (two pages of "On the one hand . . . but on the other . . . it is inconceivable that . . . some have maintained") are presented and defended. This is truer, more sincere than to write a book, according to Vaz; this is the way thinking is actually done; systems are artificial, not living.

Every reader will have his favorite sayings from this volume. Ours are the following:

Folks talk about men of thought and men of action as if they were opposed to each other. . . . Men of thought are also men of action, but of much more action. This is not understood because this action works a different way.[29]

Moral books, which set out to be more or less pedagogical or pragmatic, are often ingenuous. Everyone feels this and understands it. But books, and in general art, which has to do with evil, with vice, with sin; in life itself, too, what has to do with evil and vice, is usually just as naïve, at times even more so. But this no one feels.[30]

[28] *Id.* at 228–235.
[29] Vaz Ferreira, *Fermentario* (1940), p. 21.   [30] *Id.* at 31.

The best of our acts do not live on in history; moreover, only acts are recorded, not sentiments. . . . And above all, history tends to eliminate men who feel all the feelings, all the ideals, men whose action is therefore less symmetrical and less easy to describe, although it is more intense and good.[31]

The people . . . do for their progress, for their success and conservation, much more than is conscious and deliberate; what good results — what *comes out* — in democracies is usually more and better, and above all more efficacious, than what is consciously planned and discussed.[32]

Nostalgics are almost always men of more feeling and sincerity, deeper men, more real than futurists. For a feeling for the past is present in almost everyone . . . but true feeling for the future is very uncommon; what is mistaken for it is nearly always theories, words.[33]

We are told in our thinking to avoid extremes, to aim for the golden mean, but "in reality, in things, there are no extremes or means. These expressions make sense when they refer to theories, doctrines, formulation. As to reality, it is as it is, and the future will be as it will be." [34]

About Vaz Ferreira, and about him only, one wishes there were more.

[31] *Id.* at 48.
[32] *Id.* at 56.
[33] *Id.* at 59.
[34] *Id.* at 78.

CHAPTER V

Positivism and Idealism in Argentina

Agustín Enrique Alvarez Suárez (1857–1914)

IT WAS NOT only the teaching of Agustín Alvarez, master of a secular idealism like that of Emerson or Guyau, suspicious of Utopianism, that made him an exemplary figure to the youth of Argentina, but his career as a self-made man. His own efforts led him from military life and politics to the honor of being the founding vice-president of the University of La Plata, and one of its most influential professors. His thought reconciles a noble and optimistic message with a frank facing of reality, a positivist's confidence in scientific method and impatience with all metaphysics and theology. No other Argentine thinker so reminds us of Anglo-Saxon mentality, and the names of Carlyle, Horace Mann, Emerson are as often on his lips as that of Guyau. No other fought more strenuously to set the feet of the people of Argentina on the path to progress and well-being, and away from supine acceptance of life's ills or actual worship of ignorance and pain. No wonder that to Evar Méndez this profoundly human thinker, whose life was one long struggle for social betterment and personal growth, represents what is most worth while in the inspiration of the youth of his country.[1]

It is characteristic of Alvarez that when he reviews the "History of Free Institutions" he concludes that the lesson of history is the failure to prevent evil by punishment and

---

[1] Méndez, in Alvarez, *Manual de patología política* (2a ed., 1916), p. 23.

the fear of punishment, with a vengeful and castigating deity in the background; the church, it seems to him, has served to set bounds to human capacity, and we must substitute for it schools, which find their objective in positively increasing the powers of the individual. The only useful vestige of Christianity — its emphasis on fraternity and love — will enter into the secular ideal of the future, a society without oppressed or oppressors, in which the motive of conserving and serving the life of the community shall become ever stronger and more sufficient.[2]

It is in his *South America* (so entitled in the original, with the connotation of the prevailing opinion about the continent in Europe and the United States) that he makes his greatest contribution to the explanation of the history of his country. The history of America, and particularly that of Argentina, reveals to the reflective mind as its principal trait the dominance of pure reason over practical reason, or of natural reason over experimental reason.[3] Claiming no more than to make an application of Taine to local conditions,[4] Alvarez points out that the eighteen nations of Hispanic America enjoy political constitutions which are the quintessence of the scientific reasoning of other lands; under them live and evolve half-civilized peoples who in politics can scarcely be said to have advanced beyond natural reason.[5] This attempt at pulling oneself up by the bootstraps is foredoomed to failure; one might have known, he insists, that public opinion cannot be more advanced than the public.[6] In such countries, all tends to excess; pure reason, in default of experimental education, sees all in black or white, everyone is a savior or a

---

[2] Alvarez, *Historia de las instituciones libres* (Barcelona-Madrid, 1909), pp. 301–308.

[3] Alvarez, *South America, Historia natural de la razón* (Buenos Aires, 1894), pp. 50–51.

[4] *Id.* at 79.

[5] *Id.* at 90.   [6] *Id.* at 102.

traitor, and moderation and abstention from politics is only another form of treason.[7] Pure reason loves endless futile argument over forms of free, constitutional government so perfect that by adopting them any people can behave as if it were in reality advanced. It is as if a man set out to buy a suit of clothes in which he would be sure to act with more common sense than he has.[8] The intransigeant, all-or-none attitude carries its enthusiasm for progress to the point of destroying moderate governments, and the South American pendulum swings endlessly from one extreme to another, each in the name of salvation or of the good, burdening society with its very real misfortunes.[9] We live — perhaps a little less than our ancestors, but still too much — in a world of appearances, cheating ourselves with a religion of words, applying opinions as medicines to be used externally.[10] South America must learn the lesson that words do not imply the existence of the things they name,[11] and that no amount of verbal guaranty of civil rights will assure them as effectively as a system of checks and balances among the three branches of the government.[12] Do not imagine that by playing with words, he says, you can change social conditions; our institutions will not improve that way, but naturally and spontaneously; when we are mature and have attained a high cultural level, our institutions will be the workable expression of that culture.[13]

Alvarez's inclination to look for the reality and not the form of things leads him to criticize the "hidalgo" spirit and its precious "honor," so readily insulted, so impatient of gradual improvement, so eager for the miracle that in a moment will pay all life's arrears. South American vanity is cousin to its intransigeance.[14] One's own party has the mis-

[7] *Id.* at 106.
[8] *Id.* at 110.
[9] *Id.* at 122–123.
[10] *Id.* at 132.
[11] *Id.* at 135.
[12] *Id.* at 138.
[13] *Id.* at 140–142.
[14] *Id.* at 143–147.

sion of saving the country, the other party deserves the
worst names in the dictionary; such is the fruit of "honor"
and "glory." In reality, the Anglo-Saxon dependence upon
the self-seeking of the individual is more conducive to social
well-being than the South American's vanity, his principle —
honor, and his object — glory.[15] But just as Christianity has
been modified in the course of history, so the "political religion" of South America may change little by little, and its
practitioners come to view themselves in a less messianic
light, with less of a liberating, purifying, or restoring function.[16] Social progress in general will come of itself if we do
not in our impatience destroy the bud, and when it does, we
shall find our impracticable laws (e.g., those against dueling)
no longer needed; the lack of social approval will of itself
have eliminated dueling.[17]

These are hard sayings for Latin America to accept, he
continues. They are so salutary that we should all go out of
our way to learn what our enemies think of us; they can
hardly help seeing us from a point of view which reveals
things that we, with the best will in the world, cannot see,
and that will is generally lacking; we are by nature a hundred
times more competent to recognize others' defects than our
own.[18]

Alvarez does not hesitate to return to the attack on such
essential defects as he sees, especially the deplorable tendency of the Latin-American politician to manufacture manifestoes, programs, and theories — to live in a world of words,
of pure fantasy, cut off from reality by the impenetrable
cloud of his own ideas.[19] This unfortunate state of affairs
has an historical rather than a racial explanation: independence destroyed the traditional basis of the colonial

[15] *Id.* at 150–154.
[16] *Id.* at 190.
[17] *Id.* at 304–305.

[18] *Id.* at 310.
[19] *Id.* at 328.

regime, and the new one had to grope to found itself on pure reason.[20] Wherever it comes from, it brings with it the paralysis of endless pros and cons, the folly of depending on pure reason instead of experience, the continual amending of the opponent's impossible program by one's own equally foolish and impossible program.[21] Society needs to base as large a portion of its activity on automaticity as does the individual, who would find life a heavy burden if it were not for habit. Both habit and custom spare us much taking thought, and much error.[22] In the early days of the North American nation, it did have at least the routine of self-government by the town meeting to fall back on.[23] South America did not find its course thus simplified and its practice habitual; there everything had to be discussed, and a complete new legislation drawn up.[24] It is possible, of course, to suffer from an excess of tradition and routine; Europe does. It is possible to fall even more into the dolorous extreme of pure reason, seeking a futurist's mortal leap into a scheme of things for which life has not yet made us ready as in Central America.[25]

This volume ends with a warning that a perfect future is not to be attained by complete emancipation from the past; the most stable nations of Latin America — Brazil and Chile — are those that have followed in the footsteps of despotism, or preserved the forms, at least, of the past.[26] How Alvarez would have enjoyed Ortega y Gasset's epigram asserting that revolutions are attempted rebellions of the abstract against the concrete!

In the *Manual de patología política*, Alvarez permits himself an enormous number of quotations from his favorite American and European authors, including Elbert Hubbard. With their support he points the finger of scorn at those who

[20] *Id.* at 335.
[21] *Id.* at 342.
[22] *Id.* at 345.
[23] *Id.* at 346.
[24] *Id.* at 347.
[25] *Id.* at 251.
[26] *Id.* at 362.

cannot or will not face reality, who are drunk with ideas and partisans of the impossible.[27] Too often, lifting a people's ideals means only making them conscious of new needs and decreasing the means of satisfying them.[28] The first step in achieving ideals is to see defects; those who have lost the ability to see their own defects have lost the power to correct them.[29] South Americans love to decry the utilitarianism of England and America, but fail to see that that utilitarianism has been more productive of social good than all the empty idealism of their own countries; these nations of "abject materialism" have a record of philanthropies that far surpasses the pious foundations for the good of the founder's soul that one finds in Latin America. Doing good for its own sake has found few cultivators or admirers in these "glorious peoples with a future that is always magnificent and a present that is always detestable." [30] Alvarez is now willing to label the program-making tendency an embryonic form of the grandiose delusion, and to call for better men and fewer programs.[31] For a little good actually achieved is always that much accomplished, he argues, and many such little goods make a great good; but a great good that is only proposed and not achieved is an evil, often a great evil.[32] The Latin proposes and often accomplishes the heroic, but too often lacks the common sense to preserve the freedoms he has won. To be sure, Spain has never educated her colonials for liberty or self-government, but only to be governed by and for the King of Spain.[33] Perhaps, he hints in a parting shot, Spain was right: those who cannot govern themselves individually do need a lot of governing.[34] Anglo-Saxons, seeking health and energy, and through them independence, seem to him

[27] Alvarez, *Manual de patología política* (Buenos Aires, 1899; ed. cited that of 1916), p. 37.
[28] *Id.* at 56.
[29] *Id.* at 127.
[30] *Id.* at 204–205.
[31] *Id.* at 259.
[32] *Id.* at 260.
[33] *Id.* at 294.
[34] *Id.* at 296–297.

better behaved and less in need of external coercion than the
turbulent Latin, living for ostentation, political or social
position — in short, glory, with its Siamese twin, rivalry.[35]

The volume entitled *La creación del mundo moral* traces an
unflattering picture of the character his people inherited
from the mother country, unable as they were to oppose a
steady and principled resistance to despotism, and steadfast
in nothing but their religious bigotry.[36] They could and did
learn to be ashamed of their former passivity. They can
learn, he maintains, that rationalism provides a higher morality than Christianity, because it is more altruistic.[37] They
can learn to reject or to improve upon the religious and patriotic fanaticism which eight centuries of warfare against the
Moors and three of Inquisition directed against the heretics
had inbred in the Spaniard; they can scrap a social system
based on privilege and social status, which considered the
ideals of liberty, equality, and fraternity detestable and a
nuisance.[38] Just as life on this globe became possible as it
cooled off, so the cooling off of men's belief in hell will make
possible a right appreciation of work and the use of our intelligence, of rationalism and science, of joy and good humor,
of letters and the arts, of cleanliness and comfort, irony,
laughter, skepticism and tolerance, all of which had been
sacrificed to the religious fanaticism which played so central
a role in the history of the mother country.[39] His own ideal
has a place for all of these, but the root of the matter is the
idea, the hope of improvement *de la condition humaine*, and
the struggle to make it a reality.[40]

In spite of an easily observable tendency in Latin-American thought, as in our own, to move on from the facile ex-

[35] *Id.* at 369–372.
[36] Alvarez, *La creación del mundo moral* (Madrid, 1913), p. 183.
[37] *Id.* at 192.
[38] *Id.* at 197, 210–211.
[39] *Id.* at 219–220.   [40] *Id.* at 225.

planations of the influence of the geographic environment
and essential ethnic qualities to the more complex truth
which lies in the cultural approach, few thinkers have been
able to avoid paying their respects to physical environment
and race. Alvarez does so in his "Transformation of Races
in America," if only to prove to his own satisfaction, and to
ours, for his heterodoxy has been the accepted view today,
that Latin America is not doomed to retardation by its racial
composition. Beginning with a somber picture of conditions
under church domination and feudalism,[41] our moralist-
historian damns those social institutions for their responsibility for social, economic, and moral conditions which made
impossible the prosperity of the people and the progress of
the nation. Civilization is for him the supreme good, un-
questioned and undefined, except for the reiteration of these
words "progress" and "prosperity." The retardation which
in reality is due to institutions we have a tendency to assume
is a necessary concomitant of race; "what is really a question
of mentality seems to us a question of racial structure," and
we assume that a race and its customs are inseparable.[42]
The truth would more nearly be found in the statement that
race is a result; a race is a grouping of human beings who
have long been subjected to the influence of the same culture. Thus Spain has half-a-dozen physically defined races
that "have been reduced by the adoration of the dead and
the cult of relics to a common mental denominator in the
special psychology of the superstitious, ritualistic, madly
fanatical Spaniard, obedient follower of the Inquisition and
the Jesuits." [43] It is not race, he maintains, that accounts
for our notorious incapacity for modern progress, but the
mass of old superstitions which make us inept for modern

[41] Alvarez, *La transformación de las razas en América* (Barcelona, 1906), p. 60.
[42] *Id.* at 148.
[43] *Id.* at 150.

ideas and ways of feeling.[44] The result of our mentality is
that Latin-American civilization after four hundred years is
less advanced than that of Australia, a penal colony founded
in the second half of the last century. To cure this situation
it will not be enough to borrow the political and external institutions of liberal peoples; we must, he repeats, manage to
acquire their mentality.[45]

It is no wonder, then, that education plays a central role in
Alvarez's thinking. If we may with perhaps undue simplification think of Sarmiento as finding the answer to his country's political and social problems in education, and Alberdi
in economics, and Gálvez in something more spiritual and
more a matter of feeling, in which religion, tradition, and
patriotism are fused, for Alvarez the answer is character education. This is the burden of his eloquent "Moral Education."[46] The secret, he maintains, of English greatness and
progress is not her coal mines; the true wealth of England is
English character. But character can be made, and Argentine character can be transformed by an education of muscles,
of the will, and finally of moral character.

Carlos Octavio Bunge (1875–1918)

The voluminous writings of Bunge, "the sociologist," include one volume of criticisms of representative writers of
Latin America and much more than sociology. He was a
novelist as well as a professor, and wrote on law, psychology,
education, philosophy. Nevertheless, it was a book to which
he gave the subtitle "An Essay in Social Psychology" that
attracted most attention and takes a natural place in our
study of the books that have made Latin-American ideologies
what they are.

[44] *Id.* at 153.
[45] *Id.* at 165, 171.
[46] *Educación moral; tres repiques* (Re-edición Buenos Aires, 1917).

He begins this book, "Our America," by saying that he recognizes, of course, the element of exaggeration in his description; and after this curious opening he prefaces his unflattering description of the Spanish character by the statement that it is silly and futile to look down on the men and things of Spain. One wonders what Bunge thought he was doing.

The Spaniards receive this cavalier treatment in the first book of the five that constitute the work. The other four deal successively with Indians, Negroes and mestizos; with the Hispanic-Americans; with Hispanic-American politics; and with three eminent or notorious figures of that political life.

Bunge proposes to develop a scientific theory which will explain the psychology of the Spanish people in terms of the geographic configuration of the Iberic peninsula.[47] Every people has a typical psychology which changes only slowly and gradually. Its qualities are shared with other peoples, but the ensemble is peculiar and characteristic.

The essential quality of the Spaniard is his arrogance, based on the fact that any peninsula has to struggle against invaders. Analyzed, it can be reduced to a sort of introspective individualism, as if the Spaniard were always saying to himself, "Be a man!" Being a man is a warlike ideal, rather than one of good workmanship, for work he despises. He insists upon being treated with an etiquette that can only be called Spanish, for there is nothing like it. The form that avarice takes among this proud people is the desire to get much with little work, and it does not preclude the tendency to spend prodigally. That conspicuous consumption which Veblen found in North Americans and anthropologists among the Northwest Coast Indians is called ostentation by

[47] Bunge, *Nuestra América* (Barcelona, 1903). The second edition (1905) adds the subtitle "Ensayo de psicología social." The edition used is that of 1926, with a prologue by Ingenieros. See p. 52.

Bunge, and listed as a typically Spanish trait. Despotism is a consequence of arrogance in religious and political organization, and in practical economic life it leads straight to misery and famine, which are due to the combination of no industry and spendthrift habits. The Spaniard is too arrogant and stiff to be addicted to sports and pastimes, and only unbends to collect artistic antiques. His cruelty has been, but his dislike for methodical, continuous work can scarcely be, exaggerated. In speaking ill of his fellow men he is, however, really ferocious. These qualities do not make for co-operation, and the true description of Spanish society would be anarchic democracy. Spanish laziness has been in turn philosophic, contemplative, spendthrift, and indigent. Because of their arrogance Spaniards (except Becquer; he was not of Spanish origin) have no idea of delicacy. Their very language is arrogant rather than delicate.

The South American Indian reveals as his most essential trait a fatalism or resignation that recalls the Orient, together with a passion for vengeance. The Negro is characterized by servility and infatuation of the Emperor Jones or Henri Christophe variety. The mestizo inherits something from all, and the mixture itself contributes psychological lack of moral sense. The mulatto is impulsive, false, and petulant, a cheat and a chiseler, incapable of successful open competition with the white; irritable, neurotic in his addiction to innovation, lacking in personal bravery.

The Hispanic American, heir of various bloods, has three fundamental qualities, laziness, sadness, and arrogance.

His laziness is an absolute lack of activity, physical or mental, unlimited and universal, including the failure to have ideals, for they imply mental effort. It leads him to take the easiest way out of every situation by lying. He writes many books, but where is one that has been deeply thought and is a grand, finished work?

His sadness or resignation is that of a slave people, without liberty, individualism, and discipline. Fortunate is Argentina that she has attracted immigrants who do not have these qualities! They have brought the capacity for sustained work which means progress, just as laziness means decadence. Their presence means that it is impossible to generalize about the Argentine character, which is still nebulous and unformed, and varies from class to class and as between the coastal population and that of the interior. Bunge has great hopes for the emergence of something "beautiful and powerful," especially in the east, where the immigrants have congregated.

There is one remedy for all the ills of the country, a remedy in which he succeeds in fusing the ideals of Sarmiento and Alberdi, for it is culture — the high level of culture that Europe has — to be reached by work.[48]

Alcides Arguedas (1879-   )

Bunge's self-assurance and acerbity find an admirer and follower in Alcides Arguedas, who, although he is a Bolivian, may be appended to this discussion of Argentine thinkers. Historian, novelist, and essayist, Arguedas first attracted attention with a contribution to the understanding of South American social psychology entitled "A Sick People." While he writes of Bolivia, much that he says can be applied to other countries, and his clinical examination of social ills has been so appreciated that this book has gone through three editions, and he has continued to revise it and add new material.

Like many other authors who have attempted to give an explanation of the puzzle of Latin America, Arguedas appeals to geographic, racial, and cultural factors. For him, the geography is determining, for it lies back of the racial factors. "The physical conformation of this solemn and

[48] *Id.* at 53-231.

desolate reason has stamped . . . the character and constitution of the Indian with their harsh traits. . . . Down in
the valleys the same race takes on a more attractive aspect;
there you see in the women smiling and even pretty faces."[49]
The race that has been shaped in the highlands of Bolivia by
its relentless struggle with an ungrateful soil, depressing in
the extreme in its psychic effects, is destined by its moral and
physical deformity and its inferiority to final extinction,
unless it can be saved and raised by the process of miscege-
nation.

The tradition of telling the whole truth with absolute
frankness (if not with love, which some critics find lacking in
Arguedas) finds in him its leading exponent. Those who
found their hopes for the future on a facing of all the ills of
the present have called this book, on account of its blunt
sincerity, the most patriotic that has come out of Latin
America.[50]

Arguedas not only attacks the innate characteristics of his
countrymen, but also carries his implacable denunciation
into the area of their customs and says severe things about
their alcoholism, their lack of interest in art, and their intellectual sterility. In contrast, he praises the United States,
which, he says, is not merely the technological giant of
popular mythology but has done more for the book than any
other nation, and has an amazing interest and productivity
in art and music.

When he surveys the history of his country, he finds more
tragedies. His long and unfinished history of Bolivia sets out
to be a treatise in the style of the new history, with much
attention to the price of potatoes. For "man is not only a
political or military being, but a social and economic one,

[49] Arguedas, *Un pueblo enfermo* (Barcelona, 1910; 3rd ed., Santiago, 1937),
p. 36.
[50] Benjamín Carrión: *Los creadores de la nueva América* (Buenos Aires, 1925),
p. 173.

or in other words, man always and everywhere has had ambitions, produced, created and consumed. But the historians
never paid much attention to this man." [51] Arguedas hardly
lives up to his own program, for his history is in large part
military and political, and comes to the conclusion, in "The
Barbarous Leaders" that the predominance of people like
Melgarejo and Morales, who ruled Bolivia between 1864 and
1872, is responsible for the backwardness of many nations in
Spanish America.[52]

Joaquín V. González (1863–1923)

There emerges from the pages of history from time to time
a figure so noble and complete that he seems to embody in
one personality the ideals of a whole people. Such a figure is
Joaquín González, a man of noble character, sensitive feelings and abilities that carried him to the highest positions in
pedagogy, politics, jurisprudence, and literature. He is one
of the great builders of the Argentine spirit. In the field of
education he continued the splendid work of Sarmiento. The
University of La Plata was virtually his creation, and he was
its first president (1909–1918). Always receptive to new
ideas, he left behind him in this university a monument
which is one of the most living in Argentina.

If we were to assign first place to any of the manifold
aspects of his busy life and his fifty-one works, it would be
to González the educator, the apostle of culture. Yet to
emphasize any one thing is to forget another quality almost
as important. If González believed in freedom of access to
ideas and in culture in the highest sense of the word, it was
because he was first of all a "mystic poet, with a human and
social mysticism that was no less fervent than that of the
religious mystics." [53] And if he accomplished magnificent

---

[51] Arguedas, *La fundación de la República* (La Paz and Madrid, 1920), p. xii.

[52] Arguedas, *Los caudillos bárbaros* (Barcelona, 1929), p. 8.

[53] González, *Obras*, (Buenos Aires, 1936–1937), I, 24.

things in his lifetime in the field of culture and education, it was because he was also a practical statesman and administrator. Himself the highest type of intellectual aristocrat, he was at the same time a proponent of democratic ideals. He succeeded, as few people can, in cultivating his own inner spiritual life, turning out research of the highest quality in the field of his specialization, and playing a constructive part as legislator, minister, and administrator in giving concrete form to his highest ideals. There is no gulf between González the humanist, González the sociologist — who continues the work of Alberdi, with a masterly understanding of the political and juridical institutions of his society — and González, the citizen, the man of action, the reformer. These aspects are fused in one highly impressive personality by the conviction of this Argentine sociologist that social reality is not to be explained in economic terms but rather psychic or ideological ones, and that by ideas it can be changed. Of all the human and social ideals to which González gave his adherence none comes before that of international peace. Although he did not hesitate to criticize Alberdi severely, he has nothing but praise for the latter's "The Crime of War," and he feels that if it had been written in another country, in a language more widely used, it would have attained universal acclaim.

No extreme radical, González began his career with a thesis on revolution, which attempted to demonstrate the right of the people to defend their sovereignty by arms and gave a definition of revolution which lifted it above the sometimes petty skirmishes of Latin-American politics into the realm of the transcendental and universal: "Revolution is any radical transformation of the existing order in all or some spheres of life, in the direction of progress." [54]

In his political thinking, González is the best Latin-

[54] *Id.* at 106.

American exponent of a fervid patriotism harmonized with the broadest and most tolerant humanity, for the content which he pours into the idea of patriotism is one of justice, sacrifice, sense of honor, and love of one's neighbor, and is far from the ideals of territorial aggrandizement and mere material progress. Love of country, democracy, humanity — it is because these are his ideals that González is such a fighter for education. Democracy cannot succeed and patriotism will be ignoble unless education can make the competent and loyal citizen. González is brave and frank in his observation of how far Argentina falls short. In his frankness there is a conscious harking back to Echeverría. Like Echeverría, González attached a high value to the religious factor in social life and hoped that morality and religion, in harmony with science, would make possible social peace and progress without violence.

It is in the charming university town of La Plata that the spirit of González most visibly lives on. Here he created a university which in its statutes proclaims its three-fold aim: to teach its students, to raise the level of public culture through extension work, and to further progress in science through its research fund. In this modern university city one finds not only a handsome bronze statue of González in front of the University, but monuments that he would have preferred — the museum of natural science, the astronomical observatory, and the entirely admirable library which the University shares with the city and which preserves in a separate collection the private library of González.

The originality of González is sufficiently emphasized in what has been said. It does not detract from his merits to point out that in education he was profoundly influenced by his good friend, Dr. Leo S. Rowe, then professor at the University of Pennsylvania and for many years since Director General of the Pan American Union, and that in his international politics he was an ardent admirer of Woodrow Wilson. Nor does it lower in our eyes this intellectual of contemplative habits to recall that he did not love a fight or have the pushing qualities which might have brought him to a presidency he would have adorned. The versatility of Latin-American thinkers is likely to do them harm in a nation which believes as heartily in specialization as North America does. In this connection it is worth while to recall the statement of Rojas: "It has always moved my admiration, when I read the vast works of González, to see how this diversity which might so easily turn into dilettantism, charlatanism, or mere pretense, is, on the other hand, in all its branches a monument of real solidity. The author possesses the technique of the poet in his literary work; the technique of the statesman in his political works; the technique of the lawyer in his juridical works; the technique of the educator in his pedagogical works; and besides all that there is fantasy, sensitivity, virtue, intelligence, meditation and an astonishing and polyglot erudition." [55]

Some inkling of the nature of González' thought must be given by surveying a few of the works in his twenty-five handsome and bulky volumes. We may mention first one that deals with "The United States and Latin America." All states that become first-rate powers, he holds, and the United States is certainly one of them, have in addition to shaping their own destiny the mission of being virtual representatives of the integrity of the smaller powers in their part of the world and to some extent in all the world. It is their role to protect the weak and to defend justice against possible abuses by the strong. The United States, with its Monroe Doctrine, must be particularly circumspect in its relations with the nations of the western hemisphere. González accepts the ideals of Pan Americanism and finds that the sov-

[55] Rojas: *Elogio de González* (Buenos Aires, 1925), p. 124.

ereignty of the American republics is not at all infringed by
it but that on the contrary it increases the respect in which
they are held in the rest of the world and offers many advantages for wealth, peace, and education. The United States,
which has in the past made many contributions to international law, is now, under Wilson, assuming the high function of being a guardian of the right and insuring the future
peace and safety of a whole continent. It is evident that
González does not exaggerate when he says he loves the
foreigner as a brother and dreams of a common fatherland in
which justice, liberty, and coöperation will reign. He does,
however, insist that immigration is a domestic question.[56]

When he turns to "Spain and the Argentine Republic," he
expresses the feeling that he is only being a good patriot in
trying to spread throughout the mass of the Argentine people
the same affection for Spain that he himself has. Why should
the old artificial hatred be kept up? Why not behave like
reasonable people, as England and the United States have
done? There is no subject which has stirred up more bitter
passion and on which more diverse judgments have been expressed than this matter of America and Spain. For his part,
he rejects absolutely the "Black Legend" and the easy way
out of difficulties by blaming them all on the Spanish inheritance. It cannot be denied that Argentina has a particularly
intimate relation to Spain, and it is futile to adopt any cultural policy which will not give a prominent place to Spain
and the Spaniards in that eventual harmony which will constitute the new nation of Argentina. He has studied the old
Spanish codes which governed the life of the colony and gives
them credit for establishing a stable order and even for being
progressive; that active political life which might be called
democracy did not exist in the colonies, but it would have
been utopian to expect it. In addition to her institutions,

[56] González, *Obras*, X, 52–61. Written in 1917.

Spain gave Latin America something that was more precious, her race. For the moment in which Spain expanded into the new world was the moment in which the Spanish people won immortality by their energy, their capacity for suffering and resistance, and the way they defied the unknown. Is it nothing that Spain gave her blood to discover and conquer, to people and civilize, this land — and to give it a racial composition than which nothing better could be asked? He is frankly glad that Argentina is a nation of pure South European blood, with some additions from other immigrant stocks but scarcely any native element, and that Spain, besides her blood, gave Argentina, in her traditions and habits and in her language, a soul that is Spanish. The United States, if it comes closer to Latin America, will not impose its culture but will be conquered by that Spanish soul. True enough, the Spanish soul needs support from more Spanish bodies; and he pleads for a population policy which will strengthen and renew the racial capital by securing more immigrants from Spain.[57] In spite of his criticism that the Spanish government has shown little disposition to coöperate in recent times, it is no wonder that it has coöperated with him. Spain has to pick her Latin-American thinkers with care; not every day can she find a tolerant and friendly Bello to glorify, as she did on the centenary of independence.

The unity and harmony which have been mentioned as leading ideals in the thought of González are not easily achieved:

Neither passing laws nor possessing a common blood is enough to create real fraternity and suppress the infinite causes of discord and separation and fruitless rivalry among the children of the same family or the same nation. Holding common ideals and working together on a common task, these are the things which unite our hearts and create the indestructible nuclei which in their expansion come to constitute first the nation and then all humanity.

[57] *Id.* at 86–118.

In the creation of such a sense of national mission the University finds its highest function.[58]

González had always been concerned with things that would create a strong feeling of nationalism. An early and brilliant work entitled "The National Tradition" (1888) raises the question, what raw material do we have for the making of a great national tradition? We began, he answers, with a revolution, and revolutions do not happen unless the process of forming a nation has been long at work. National feeling is the very soul of revolution. Now the historic fact of the revolution has entered into our tradition and is part of a tremendous force which will shape future history. The traditions that bind our history into one and play so vital a role in the present life of the nation go back not only to Spanish municipal institutions but to the native peoples and their traditions of freedom. The Creole who fought for freedom was unconsciously inspired by the ideals and memories of the Indian he had conquered. In rebelling against Spanish misrule, America is carrying on the tradition of Spain's most glorious days, and saving the honor of that tired and unfortunate country. To have an heroic tradition is a social and spiritual necessity, and far from criticizing this absorption in the past, González would make of it a cult as sacred as religion. He hopes for the coming of artists and poets who will help to idealize the events and happenings of the revolution, which are still a little too close to us to be revered. Note the word *revered*, for González is talking of settlements and of the soul rather than of the brain; of virtue, not intelligence. The literature that might be written — finding its inspiration in the mountains, deserts and rivers of Argentina and the ocean that bathes its shores, the adventures and accomplishments of its people — is eloquently described: "The literature of a people is a copy of their nature and their his-

[58] *Obras*, XV, 512.

tory; in its creations we find all the influences which nature
and history exercise on the spirit of man." [59] González disclaims any intention beyond pointing out the materials
which may be made into the national legend. Five years
later he was to publish a book of the kind of loving and eloquent description which he here pleads for: "My Mountains" (*Mis Montañas*). One can see how natural it is for
him to praise Sarmiento's *Facundo* and "Provincial Memories" and why critics have thought that González himself is
the best sequel to these unmistakably Argentinian books.

The "National Tradition" is in part a sociological analysis, long needed — perhaps still needed — of the function of
tradition in the social process; it is in part a passionate ode
to Argentina. Something of the same sort might be said of a
book published in 1900 under the title "The Fatherland."
This is again an earnest plea for the higher patriotism and an
argument that it cannot be won unless the people are educated for it. Children educated to be merely citizens of the
world do not automatically become good members of the
smaller communities to which they belong. It is possible,
however, to work out a curriculum which will give due attention to the mother tongue and to the history of the nation
and at the same time permit the teaching of foreign languages and world history. What is intolerable is that foreigners should be allowed to set up schools which neglect the
language, literature, and history of a country in which they
are located. Nothing binds us better to the tradition of our
ancestors than the language we share with them. Since the
language is Spanish, González embarks again on the praise of
Spain and the liberty, the culture, and the Christianity she
brought to the new world in spite of "the classic errors of her
colonial system" which have just been shown in her final
complete loss of her new world possessions. [60]

[59] *Obras*, XVII, 261.   [60] *Id.* at 131.

José Ingenieros (1877–1925)

In so cosmopolitan a country as Argentina it is not surprising to find distinguished intellectuals who are the sons of
non-Spanish immigrants. This is true of Ingenieros, who
was of an Italian family, and of Korn, who comes of German
stock. The two men happen to have in common a most unusual background for philosophers, for both worked with the
police, Ingenieros as an alienist and clinic director, Korn as a
police surgeon and later superintendent of a hospital for the
mentally diseased. It is difficult to see what contribution
this service made to Korn's thinking except to make him a
mature man when he turned to philosophy, but in the case of
Ingenieros the position and the interests it indicates are by
no means negligible.

The story of Ingenieros is that of a brilliant, intellectual,
and forceful personality rising unaided from poverty and
obscurity to a position of spiritual and scientific leadership
that extended far beyond the boundaries of his country. He
is said to have been for a time the most widely read author
of Spanish speech. He did not allow himself to be cooped up
in a mere twenty countries, but became the first Latin-
American scientist with a European reputation. He shares
with Rodó the honor of being the favorite author of Latin-
American youth, and if he is a less polished writer, compen-
sates for it by the prestige of his scientific accomplishments
and the mere bulk of the 535 items in his bibliography. Less
elegant than Francisco García Calderón, less dramatically
intense than Vasconcelos, less profound in his thought than
Korn, or Vaz Ferreira, or Caso, he is perhaps altogether a
greater figure, with a newer message. The attempt to be a
man of science — psychologist, psychopathologist, criminol-
ogist — and at the same time a philosopher-moralist cost him
admiration in certain quarters, and, in fact, he was not able

to reconcile the two careers completely, but turned more and more away from scientific work after 1914.

It is typical of Ingenieros that, after graduating from the Colegio Nacional, he started at the same time to take the courses in law and medicine. At the end of the year he took examinations in medicine only, but the two interests continued, and took him into forensic medicine. As if his studies did not keep him busy enough, he became secretary of a socialist group of students, drew up their manifesto, "What is Socialism?" and took to the soap box. This kind of thing drew fire, and it is said that he walked into the church of a priest who had been attacking him, waited until the service was over, and then marched up to the pulpit to deliver an impassioned defense of his own ideas and activities. Propaganda continued side by side with medicine. Ingenieros discovered his own amazing facility for writing, to which he later added method and the self-protection that came from doing all his writing at night. Even so, he would not have been able to accomplish so much if he had not used the same writing repeatedly, publishing it first as an article, then incorporating it in a book. To trace the history of a given chapter might require a good deal of detective work.

With that baffling writer Leopoldo Lugones, who later turned to nationalism and apology for dictators, he founded in 1897 a magazine called, no one knows why, "The Mountain." After three numbers it was in trouble, after the seventh it did not exist. An article entitled "Bourgeois Reptiles" seems to have been the thing the censor could not swallow. The magazine suffered from lack of advertisers but was highly regarded by intellectuals. Its three parts — sociological studies, art, philosophy, etc., and current events — are an indication of the broad interests of its directors. Ingenieros was not blind to the values of literature, but he accused the literary lights of being blind to the need for re-

search, and education and intellectual life of being absorbed
by the literary obsession. His own favorite authors in this
period were those with social and moral leanings, Ibsen and
Tolstoy and Nietzsche. In social science, he read Loria,
Tarde, Spencer, Durkheim, some of Marx and Engels.

These interests were in addition to the combination of
biology, criminology, and abnormal psychology which was
coming to be his specialty. In this specialty he had the
benevolent guidance of Ramos Mejía, a psychiatrist with
interests in sociology and the author of "Argentine Masses."
Ramos Mejía made Ingenieros head of his clinic, and was
looked up to as a father. By 1904 Ingenieros had become
director of psychiatric observation for the police department;
this post he held until 1911. Between 1902 and 1913 his review, the "Archives of Criminology, Legal Medicine and
Psychiatry," gathered in the writing of all the most distinguished men who wrote in Spanish on those subjects. With
these beginnings and a first book to his credit, Ingenieros was
sent to Rome in 1905, to attend the International Congress
of Psychology. The part he played in this congress was most
remarkable for a young man of twenty-eight, and Morselli
urged him to stay in Europe as his assistant. The unbeliev-
able product of this year and a half in Europe includes five
books, forty travel articles, thirty scientific articles published
in Buenos Aires, and over sixty articles in European journals.
No wonder a somewhat bewildered admiration was expressed
and Morini hailed him as the most productive and original
alienist writing in Spanish.

On his return he took up the question of an Institute of
Criminology, impressed González with its necessity, and was
named director by the latter. As if he had exhausted the
subject, Ingenieros shortly turned to new interests, and the
cycle of his activity that began in 1908 was mainly focused
on psychology and sociology. His opportunity to enter the

medical faculty seemed to have come in 1911, when de Veyga resigned, but his application for the chair of Legal Medicine, supported by a bibliography of hundreds of items in five or six languages, did not win him the merited appointment, and Ingenieros betook himself to Europe, this time for a longer stay.

The stay became so long that the Dean of the Faculty of Philosophy and Letters pursued him with a letter, asking how long this leave of absence from his chair of Experimental Psychology was to continue. Ingenieros replied politely but firmly from Heidelberg, saying that his experience in the matter of the medical school had taught him that the government made appointments without consulting the faculty, and that consequently he had sent in his resignation as psychology professor directly to that same government; he supposed that the authorities had been a little negligent about passing on the news. And Ingenieros continued to stay in Lausanne and Catalonia, sending back the inevitable articles and chapters of books.

Shortly after returning from this stay in Europe, Ingenieros founded his *Revista de Filosofía*, from the pages of which he pontificated as the acknowledged leader of the positive or scientific school of thought in Latin America.

Always a lover of youth as well as a frequenter of labor circles, Ingenieros put his shoulder to the wheel for the University Reform movement in 1918, and soon thereafter gave his enthusiastic approbation to the Clarté group of Anatole France and Henri Barbusse, which had many followers in Latin America. He endeavored to provide program and organization for the amorphous anti-imperialist movement, as well as to "renovate" the country from within. In the midst of all these activities death came, and found him working, leaving on his desk the finished "Treatise on Love."

A few directive ideas provide the key to all the works of

Ingenieros. He is a Darwinian and sees everything as part of the survival process; he is interested in the pathology of the individual and social life, that is, in insanity and in criminology; he is a moralist who believes that ideals are necessary for progress, and a philosopher who believes that science can give us both truth and ideals. These elements are combined in various proportions in an amazingly prolific output.

Ingenieros made two studies of simulation or pretense, and at first published them together. The study of madness simulated by criminals as a means of escaping punishment is sufficiently technical to be ruled out of the present study by the rather arbitrary procedure we have adopted. The other, "Simulation in the Struggle for Existence," is of general interest, indeed so general that it more nearly belongs in the field of literature, in the tradition of La Rochefoucauld and La Bruyère, than in that combination of biology, psychology, and sociology which it carves out for itself.

The essential ideas of the theory of struggle for existence are too familiar to be repeated here. Ingenieros, observing with the trained eye of the psychopathologist, adds to the familiar his own version of the psychopathology of everyday life: the pattern of survival is compounded of two elements, strength and fraud; we get on in the world, defend ourselves, and survive, by using the instruments of power or of guile. When he looks about him to find examples of the latter, so essentially human and therefore so neglected by the biologists, he finds them everywhere. If he had looked for conflict, or coercion, or intimidation, or pressure groups, or social distance it would have been equally easy to persuade himself that he had hit upon *the* explanation of social life in each case. But there is no use whittling away the merit of an extraordinary book by such criticism.

The world is full of so-called race conflicts, and perhaps,

he says, there will be more of them in those future days when the United States and Japan are the two great world powers. But these are not really racial conflicts, since no pure races exist. The cry of race is raised to cover up the real interests involved or to incite the apathetic to greater enthusiasm in the struggle; the questions at issue are cultural or national questions parading as racial, and the racial aspect is feigned. National rivalries are being attenuated like the racial ones in the history of mankind, and the propaganda that is used to rouse patriotic ardor and conceal the real nature of war and the nature of the groups that profit by it is the old pretense of nationalism. The "lies that schoolmasters tell little boys" about the history and power of their country are fraud, but fraud justified as useful in the struggle for existence. The white man's burden, the necessity of civilizing backward peoples or preserving order — so much more pretense. The laws by which one class keeps in the saddle and renders others powerless are justified by other fictions as to their usefulness to the whole nation. The struggle between the sexes involves constant use of pretense, chiefly by women; women's modesty and morality are chiefly pretenses designed to interest men in their bodies, and their intellectual interests are usually assumed for the purpose of attracting men. They pretend affection, which has no other object than to lure a man into matrimony. The "sweet deceit" is not all on one side, but men, even Don Juans, are generally less adept at it.

Every profession has its own favorite means of imposing upon the ignorant public, from the doctor's inscrutability and bedside manner to the tenor's excuse of his laryngitis. Every job and activity known to man has its own hocus-pocus by which it renders itself impressive or mulcts the public of more money. Of them all, politicians and the clergy win the prize for being more skillful at deception and employing it most.

But the point is made that wherever there is struggle for existence there is simulation as a means for success in it, and further examples are not needed.

Bureaucracy offers a tempting field for pretending to work while all that one really does is read the paper and draw one's check. Human parasites are less frank than those in the lower part of the animal and vegetable kingdoms, and are actors as well as leeches. Skeptics simulate belief in order to avoid trouble or to set a good example to the children or the working class. The simulation of disease is often a means by which a petty tyranny over the lives of others is exercised. There is no end to the strategies that human nature has evolved out of the necessity to injure others and defend oneself. "A world of pretenders and hypocrites induces the individual to deceive his fellow men. Everything says to him: Lie and pretend! and he does. The fault is that of mores which have bases in the lie; education is poisoned by it: the general tolerance of it adds to everyone's already too great willingness to deceive in order to live." [61]

The historic evolution of such means of survival is a part of sociology. The Darwinian key to evolution is excellent as far as it goes; but an economico-sociological conception is more scientific, and Ingenieros accepts such a modification of the purely biological view. For the biological, while it enters into all things social, is only a part of the whole picture. The biological theory has been used to justify a struggle à l'outrance which is neither morally acceptable nor scientifically accurate, for the principle of mutual aid has developed alongside that of conflict and coöperation is as natural as "nature red in tooth and claw." The progressively greater and greater use of methods of fraud, hateful though it is, should be viewed as a diminution in the intensity of the struggle for existence. In the long view, it has constituted

[61] Ingenieros, "La simulación en la lucha por la vida," *Obras*, I, 186.

an advance. It is the method of society, and at least indicates mental awareness of "the other" and is a confession of the necessity of our living together instead of eliminating the rival. The moralist and idealist in Ingenieros speaks in the conclusion that those men are happiest who can forget the necessity of appearing and concentrate on being, can depend upon the sincerity of others and not live in constant apprehension of being fooled by hypocrisy; those who can love and be loyal. Perhaps in a future day we shall all have learned the folly of spending our time cheating each other.

Even when Ingenieros is writing a travel book, like the "Travel Chronicles," he is very much on the margin of science, surveying the state of culture and the progress of science in the countries he visits, reporting the Congress of Psychology, and somewhat shamefacedly including stray articles that have at least an autobiographical value. One of these articles records his opinions, in 1905, on the subject of inferior races. That there are differences in the capacity for becoming civilized he admits; the Japanese, who might seem an exception, are racially different from the Chinese. The Malaysian base has been mixed, especially in the upper strata of Japanese society, with white blood, and this fact accounts for the success in adapting themselves that deserves our good opinion; if the others tend to disappear, it is only because of the slow operation of the law of natural selection, which in the long run is a beneficent one.[62]

The operation of nature is indifferent to our opinion, anyway. Even when it produces imperialism, it is petty of us merely to like or dislike the phenomenon; it is to be studied as an historic process and with complete objectivity. When we engage in such study, we may come out with a quasi-defense of imperialism, for its ideal is peace rather than war. It, too, is part of the great process of natural selection, and

[62] Ingenieros, "Crónicas de viaje," *Obras*, V, 196–197.

our sentimental interest in the "rights" of the weak cannot prevent the strong from exercising their strength. There is no right without strength to enforce it; if a nation is weak and feels that its rights are being trampled upon, its only course is to become strong. As a traveler in Germany, Ingenieros observes that the individual who is part of an imperialistic nation is hardworking, coöperative, proud of what his country is doing. When European nations have dropped out of the race, these same qualities of individual initiative will make the United States and Japan the great imperialistic nations, and after them, who knows? Perhaps the turn of Argentina and Australia will come.[63] They are young nations, which do not need such morphine as the bullfights of Spain, and he has great hopes for them. On his return to Argentina his first address is a plea for the development of science, the development of a national art, a strong feeling of nationalism, and the adoption of a real national policy. Argentina may rightfully aspire to be someone in the family of nations.[64]

What Argentina may become is conditioned by its past, and in a constantly growing and changing volume, "The Sociological Evolution of Argentina," he attempts to trace the outstanding trends of that past, laying stress on its economic aspects as well as its biological foundations. He never forgets to situate his sociology or history within the larger framework of biology, which teaches that association is a favorable variation in that struggle for existence which is universal, and that there are other societies than human ones. Association began a long while ago. The economic interpretation is added to this; it is really an application of biological sociology, and economic laws are a special type of biological laws.[65]

[63] Id. at 224, 235.
[64] Id. at 305.   [65] Ingenieros, "Sociología argentina," Obras, VIII, 14-26.

The Spain which conquered the New World was worn out and was beginning to go down in the struggle for existence. Unlike González, Ingenieros has little good to say of the Spaniards of the age of conquest, but he accepts the view that they came to exploit and sack. He approaches Toynbee's theory that such expansive activities are in reality a symptom of internal decay; only those who are uncertain of themselves strive so desperately for a support in things. If he had faced this theory frankly, he would have rejected it in all probability, for it is difficult to harmonize with his previously expressed views about imperialism. Spain did not spread culture nor pass overseas the new techniques which other European nations were using in production; she only organized her exploitation, and that not too well. Because she was in a different stage of her evolution, what Spain did in the New World was different from the colonization of the northern continent by Anglo-Saxon peoples, and the evolution of North and South moved in divergent directions. South America, without a true economic organization and the balance of differentiated interests, fell a prey to her landowners and *caudillos*. In later days, the feudal regime was transformed into an economy of farming and cattle raising for the world trade; European immigration determined once and for all the racial composition of Argentina and added enormously to her productive capacity. *Caudillismo* gave place to capitalism. Europe and the United States poured their millions into South America and made of her nations mere economic colonies, contributory to the economy of the investing country. Further economic changes are in store, he continues, for a middle class is forming, and there is a growing rural and industrial proletariat which will ultimately refuse to be a mere instrument in the hands of the conservatives and will develop a politics related to its class interests.[66]

[66] *Id.* at 71–75.

The future evolution of Argentina, if it can avoid or throw off Yankee domination, offers splendid possibilities. No other South American nation can compete with it. Chile is neither large nor fertile enough. The climate and the racial composition of Brazil are against her. Argentina alone has the white race, temperate climate, fertile soil, and vast territory which are the ingredients of progress. A few decades more of peace is all the country needs.[67]

Ingenieros' "Principles of Psychology" is better explained by one of its original titles, "Principles of Biological Psychology," or by the suggestion that critics have made that it is really a philosophy of psychology. It repeats, almost word for word, the discussion of the struggle for existence that we have met before. This struggle takes three forms: between social groups, between the group and the individual, between isolated individuals. Groups of men who live in adaptation to similar conditions of life show similar psychic traits which constitute their social psychology. This collective psychology is subject to modification in the course of history. The individual within each society acquires his beliefs and attitudes from collective representations which are handed down by tradition out of a very remote past. Collective mentality is one of the traits in which societies differ, and those that have the favorable variations will progress and surpass the others in the struggle for existence.

In spite of the unity of each society, the division of labor and social selection have resulted in the formation of social classes. There is room in social psychology for a study of their behavior as well as for that atypical manifestation, the psychology of the crowd. Social progress is seen as consisting largely of invention and imitation, two subjects which have been thoroughly studied by Tarde and others.

Customs, morality and institutions are essentially mental

[67] *Id.* at 85–93.

in their nature, but are acquired by the individual in social life and have a biological function, since they serve to protect the group in the struggle for existence. While every human society believes, and derives strength from the belief, that its morality is the only true morality, the scientist regards moral systems as products of evolution and necessarily relative. Morality, as John Dewey once said, "for all practical purposes means customs." As for that most definite part of custom which we call law, "in every period and place, the laws in force are those that are most useful to the group which imposes them in the name of the social class or party; they prevail only by reason of the force that is behind them."[68]

It is not until he has laid the foundations of scientific method, biology, and sociology in a full half of his book that Ingenieros feels justified in turning to individual experience, for every man is conditioned by the society in which he lives and moves and has his being. His individual experience is a function of social experience. There is no human individual living outside of society. Every man represents on the one hand his species and on the other his culture, and his psychic life is absolutely inexplicable without a knowledge of his social environment.[69]

It is undeniable that some men never do anything more than adapt themselves to the society around them; but there are others, of more capacity and more character, who impose certain variations on the culture and introduce modifications. Even these men, for good biological reasons, lose their vision as they grow older, and end as apathetic and prudent conservatives, even if not as senile misanthropes.

Ingenieros finds, then, that he does not need any such slippery terms as instinct, conscience, or intelligence in order to write the natural history of psychic functions through the

[68] Ingenieros, "Principios de psicología," *Obras*, IX, 222.
[69] *Id.* at 225–226.

evolution of the species, of society, and of individuals. In every case he goes back to experience. Thus, personality is not an entity which mysteriously exists or appears in individuals; it is a natural result of biological conditions and is built up in the course of experience, beginning with the recognition of the difference between the ego and the non-ego. The unity of conscious personality depends on the unity which is given by biology, and its other essential trait, continuity, is the result of the continuity which it experiences. Pure intelligence no more exists than the immaterial entity called consciousness. Man thinks when he has to in the struggle for existence. There has been too much attention given to logical operations and not enough to the real processes by which man thinks, which are quite different. Thinking is a functional activity. This function results in the formation of beliefs never based on perfect knowledge but, if our education is good, moving in that direction. Our primitive or spontaneous beliefs and those that we absorb from social environment are tested and corrected. The mere classification of correct forms of reasoning is a far less realistic study than that psychology of how men think which Ingenieros, like Pareto, wants to see developed. What passes for thinking is usually the acceptance of a belief which fits in with our previous beliefs or which serves a practical purpose at the moment. Beliefs are often formed by vague, incomplete, and incorrect processes of reasoning, as well as those that satisfy the logician. It is not too much to say that those neglected processes, implicit reasoning, unconscious reasoning, and the other types that he calls affective, volitional, imaginative, by analogy, sophistic, pathological, social and contradictory, play so important a part in life that practically all of our mental operations fall outside logic. This section of Ingenieros' psychology is as close a parallel as we know to the second and third volumes of Pareto's *The Mind and Society*.

The way in which Ingenieros can weave together different themes and make them part of a unitary structure is almost as remarkable as the musical phenomenon in Bach or Wagner. What has gone before seems disillusioned in the extreme, but now the idealist is ready to prove to us that ideals, too, are founded on experience and have a natural history. Our thinking reaches a point at which imagination can anticipate experience and form beliefs about the possible perfection of the future. Anything regarded as perfection will do; the name idealism has been unfairly preëmpted by fanatical religious and moral cults. An ideal may be anything, provided its realization lies in the future and someone regards it as better. Experience decides whether the ideal was a good and possible one. Evolution selects the best of ideals, as it selects the best of everything. There is a strain toward consistency between the ideals, and they ultimately converge. Ingenieros, who is attacked as a positivist, is no less in love with the ideals of truth, good, and beauty than Korn. In fact, in a last analysis, what interests him most in history is the great men who feel or symbolize man's longing for perfection, and what worries him most is the complete incapacity for idealism on the part of the mediocre masses at every moment of the human adventure.

This "Principles of Psychology" is an unusual book, remarkable for its synthesis of philosophy, biology, and sociology, as well as for the small amount of what is usually called psychology that it contains. It ends with a plea for supplementing the genetic method in psychology with three methods of observation. Experimental observation can be applied to only a small number of very elementary psychic processes in individuals, and is even more limited in animal and social psychology. Introspective observation has at its disposal only a small part of psychic functioning. We must rely more and more upon extrospective observation. Unorthodox to the end, Ingenieros proposes that this type of

observation has much to learn from the profound psychology
of writers like Cervantes, Goethe, Bourget, and Dostoievski.
Professors of psychology can be made in the library and the
laboratory, but psychologists, who are very different, can be
made only by imitation of these writers — or perhaps cannot
be made at all.

There is a direct connection between the volume we have
just examined and "The Mediocre Man," which won Ingenieros his largest audience, including, doubtless, thousands
who would be deterred by more scientific work. In this book
he continues the discussion from the point at which we
learned that ideals are beliefs or hypotheses about the future
and that they play an important part in human evolution.
"There are as many idealisms as ideals; and as many idealists as there are men capable of conceiving perfections and
shaping their lives with a view to their realization." [70]

In this sense, idealism cannot be monopolized by the oppo-
nents of so-called materialism. The materialists of Argentina
have had just as many ideals as the so-called idealists. They
have been different ideals, or the means proposed for bringing
them to realization have been different.

The morality of primitive peoples excludes idealism. It is
characteristic of modern man to oppose to the imperfect
reality of the present an ideal, which, if he is wise, he realizes
is always relative. Progress would be inconceivable without
ideals, and the practical man who has none is the worst enemy
of real progress. Its friends are to be found in youth. Ingenieros admits that not all the young in years have the
youthful, idealistic spirit, and that it may be possible, here
and there, to find an old man who has not lost it. The exaggeration, sentimentality, and romanticism which are the ear-
marks of the idealist are, however, characteristic qualities of
youth. It is obvious that it is this type of excitable idealist

[70] Ingenieros, "El hombre mediocre," *Obras*, X, 17.

that arouses the enthusiasm of Ingenieros, although he admits that there is a more stoical type which is characterized by open resistance to the organized mediocrity around him and a disdainful refusal to make any compromise with that which he cannot change. He will not have anything to do with evil; he awaits the hour when it will be possible to eradicate it and in the meanwhile lives his ideal.

But the book is about the enemy of the ideal, the man without ideals, and that is the meaning of the phrase, "the mediocre man." He is so common that he might almost be called the normal man. Neither his mediocrity nor his normality can be defined except in relation to the society in which he lives, and the part he plays in it. That part is certainly not to be a model; he is a man without personality, a shadow, but for all that he is a force. He has been drilled into a docile imitation, patient and passive, rather than imaginative and creative. He seeks to be like those around him, not to stand out; he is afraid of being different, of having a character of his own. He is only a shadow thrown by society. Below him is the sub-human or sub-social inferior man, the criminal who has not been adjusted even to the low requirements of our present-day civilization. Above him is the superior man, who has a personality of his own, who in his life and thought is ahead of the society in which he lives. This discussion of the role of a creative individual in a custom-bound society can be profitably compared with a similar discussion in Toynbee's *A Study of History*. It is only because such men are inventive that the masses have anything to imitate. The routines that they defend are vulgarized versions of ideals that were once original. To be quite fair, we must recognize that the masses of mediocre men do provide continuity in history and do perform the function of resisting ideas that would be destructive. The trouble is that they make no distinction between constructive ideals and the dissolution of society. Feeble individually, as a herd they have a dangerous power.

Latin-American youth found in this provocative book a ringing denunciation of things that they could hate and ridicule and a call to action and to thought, to a campaign for a better world. Ingenieros taught them to rebel against the official education which implanted prejudices instead of developing originality, and against the contagion of mediocrity which was all about them in society. He taught them to recognize intellectual mediocrity by its commonest signs. Ingenieros, who was a friendly and tolerant soul, not prone to use invective in personal attack, would seem to have expressed the spleen of a common disease from which many of us suffer and which might be called "disrespect of persons" by generalizing it. His thumbnail sketches of mediocre men who are not identified even by initials have a liveliness which leads us to think that they had originals. Intellectual mediocrity makes a man solemn, modest, undecided, and obtuse. Such men pass their life in a dreamless sleep; they are cogs in the machinery of routine; they never lift their eyes to the heights; they vegetate. As a writer, the mediocre man is worse in his style than in his morality; when he speaks, his morality is worse than his style, for he gives free rein to backbiting and gossip, which nearly always please his mediocre hearers, anxious to debunk and bring the great men down to their level. Having no glimmering of an idea of what glory can be, the mediocre man has no higher object in life than success.

Here Ingenieros returns to simulation, the theme with which he began his writing career. For the mediocre man is likely to try to get on in the world by hypocrisy, by selecting and professing, without inner conviction, the faith that seems most profitable at the moment, thus making his whole life a methodical and organized lie. Hypocrites cannot have true friends, for they are disloyal and ungrateful. Their hypocrisy is their homage to a virtue for which they are impotent and the result of the fact that they are too cowardly for vice. Their morality is mediocre like everything about them and consists in not attracting attention. True virtue is not afraid of public opinion, nor does it calculate the profit that lies in action. The mediocre man is essentially fearful and calculating.

Ethical progress is slow, but it does take place. Men learn to imitate the new models set by saints who are virtuous in a new way. We have used the word saint, but it is characteristic of Ingenieros that for him the highest virtue is inseparable from intellectual superiority. His highest ideal is that wisdom which includes the integration of personality, the superior intellect, and sheer goodness. Socrates was right: a genius is a man who teaches a new virtue or practices an old one with a new intensity. He does not limit himself to a mere vision of the ideal but lives it. There are times when it is the element of goodness or sacrifice in the morally superior man which is most needed. There are other times, and Ingenieros thinks our own is one of them, when the intellectual aspect is the most important, and dying for one's country is less important than resisting the prejudices which would strangle honest intellectual life. The superior man who is serving an ideal needs a certain self-love. What would be vanity in the mediocre man is dignity in him. Sarmiento would have been incomplete without his megalomania. Such dignity is difficult to attain without freedom, and for all the teaching of the Stoics as to the possibility of an inner and spiritual freedom, the material aspect cannot be neglected. To starve with dignity is extremely difficult.

The relation of the superior to the mediocre man is the occasion for some very enlightening pages on envy and admiration, two attitudes which have the same root. Admiration arises in the strong who can hope to achieve the qualities they look up to, envy in the weak who give up and are bitter. There are some deeply felt remarks on literary criticism in this connection, and the comforting assurance is offered the superior man who has suffered at the hands of critics that he must expect to be envied; if he were not, he could be sure of his own mediocrity.

Unfortunately, if we live long enough, fate has in store for us a sad end. The old, with rare exceptions, are mediocre. The decay of intellect and the loss of idealism are simple biological necessities. We lose first the mentality characteristic of each of us as individuals, then that which we share with society, and finally we may cease to be human. The greatest, like Kant and Spencer, have suffered this fate; the rest of us cannot hope to escape. We cannot be born mature, and we cannot die naturally and of old age in the prime of life. Much more remains to be said about the psychology of old age than Ingenieros has said, but his beginning is stimulating and should arrest the attention of a civilization which faces in the near future a great increase in the proportion of its population which will be old.

What has all this to do with democracy? Can a superior man live his ideals and impart them to others in democratic societies? Ingenieros is a believer in democracy, but he would put even higher the ideal of civilization, and he believes that to make all men equal would destroy the very possibility of civilization. Society must have the man of talent and of genius for its progress. Unfortunately, true democracy, which is not to be confused with the rule of mediocrity, seeks to find the aristocracy which deserves to have put into its hands the responsibility of government. Democracy is opposed to privilege, but it does not stand for equality in a sense so foolish as to do away with leadership. A purely quantitative interpretation of democracy is unacceptable. Its ideal must be rephrased as the reconciliation of justice with inequality.

It is perhaps the mediocre man who reads with most pleasure a book like the one we have just summarized, for does not the mediocre man like to hear that most other men are mediocre? There is something more positive but less popular in the little book entitled "Toward a Morality without Dogmas." The moral dogmas that Ingenieros rejects are opinions imposed by authority, supposed not to be changeable or subject to experimental verification. His own opinion that not only are the duties of man realized in history, but also that our ideas change as to what those duties are, rules out at once any supernatural system of morality, for such systems cannot change. The philosophical systems go out too, for philosophers have given in to popular prejudice and made their ethical principles eternal and immutable. Rational systems have not gotten very far, for they have been almost entirely negative in their attitude, and essentially individualistic. They have thus been an imperfect substitute for the religious type of morality, which at least was a strong force back of social cohesion. The ethics of the future will trace the development of morality as a part of human experience by the genetic method and then modify the inherited codes of the past by taking counsel of science. Great care must be exercised to avoid letting the negation of dogmas lead to a relaxation of morality. Our aim is, in reality, to strengthen morality.

As it happened, Ingenieros had been invited to the United States in 1915, and had been much impressed by certain examples of "morality without dogmas" which he met there. Concord, he discovered, had in its great day fairly hummed with morality that eschewed dogma, and worked wholeheartedly to transform social reality in accordance with its ideals. Emerson is one of his heroes, one of his superior men persecuted in his time as a dangerous heretic. His "heresy" was, in reality, the most valuable kind of non-conformity and he was reaching out toward the type of social morality that the best minds of today embrace. As a result of his leadership, religion in New England moved in the direction of pure social morality, and the schools in the direction of character education and preparation for civic life. Even the most dogmatic of churches, the Roman Catholic, became in the United States in part an agent of Americanization and adjustment of the immigrant, social and not dogmatic in its attitude. Catholicism was lost, but something that Ingenieros values more was gained. He applauds even more the Ethical Culture society, which is the institutional embodiment of his hopes for the future transformation of religion.

In almost any one of the thinkers of the late nineteenth or early twentieth century, one finds that one object of thought is the men who preceded. Montalvo writes on Bolívar, Rodó on Montalvo, Rojas on Sarmiento, and González on Alberdi; Varona on Martí, Freyre on da Cunha. Their analyses and criticisms might in themselves make an interesting study. It is not here our object, however, and we shall pass over the most bulky of Ingenieros' works, the four volumes on the "Evolution of Argentine Ideas," as we do over some of the criminological and psychiatric works.

It is generally considered that his "Propositions Relative to the Future of Philosophy" is, in spite of its slender dimensions, a major work. For some curious reason, Ingenieros did not realize that a newly elected member of the Academy always speaks in praise of his deceased predecessor, and when he was elected, chose quite freely to speak of what was nearest to his heart. The mistake was detected in time and another speech was made, while the manuscript became this little book. Philosophers of the past do not stand in a very happy light; they have shown, thinks Ingenieros, a moral incapacity to rise above the opinion of the ignorant (i.e., mediocre men), and have concealed or disguised the opinions they had actually come to hold. This is the reason for our being plagued by so many philosophical problems which are not the most meaningful for our time.

Now and in the future we shall employ metaphysics to form hypotheses which will endeavor to explain that which cannot be put to the test of experiment; such hypotheses will have their legitimacy tested by whether they can be reconciled with the proved results of experiment where it is possible. In other words, the only difference between metaphysical hypotheses and scientific hypotheses is that the former deal with problems that are non-experimental in character. Their logic can be criticized; it can be pointed out that their terms are necessarily relative and imperfect; and the results of the hypotheses must live comfortably in the same mind that accepts the results of science. Ingenieros hopes for a growing tolerance (again from mediocre men) for philosophical opinions which are not mere rationalization of tradition and popular prejudice. More ideals, in this scheme of things, are hypotheses, too, and their value as principles of action is tested by their legitimacy and their harmony with what we know. With growing knowledge, our ideals will take on less and less the character of dreams or reactions against the imperfection of the present, and more and more that of a scientific prediction of coming reality, felt to be desirable and feasible. Each specialist will have an ideal in the field of his own competence, and each profession in the field of its interest, but all the ideals will move toward ends that are compatible and form a single, composite whole.

Even in a proposed address to academicians, whose average age is usually advanced, Ingenieros could not refrain from an appeal to his beloved youth, the hope of humanity, and, seeking a formula for his whole system of thought, he admonished them: "Respect the past in the full measure of its deserts, but do not make the mistake of confusing it with the present nor seek in it the ideals of the future." [71]

Having the ideals of the superior man and his independence in thinking which we have met, it need not surprise us that Ingenieros in publishing recollections provoked by the European war and the Russian Revolution claimed that they were the thoughts of a man who used his own head for thinking. We could have guessed that he would look for ideals in *New Times*, and would think that it was his business to communicate them to youth. With his determination to look into the future, he finds the sentiment which arises in our hearts as we contemplate the civilizations of the past and what is left of them likely to prevent our understanding the lessons of history. The sheer fascination of the past is an obstacle to dealing effectively with the present. Yet the scholar must not become a nostalgic; he must recognize the feudal régime for what it is, a transitory period in human evolution, and must not forget to work for the ideals of today just because he has fallen in love with the way certain ideals have been realized in the past. The ideals of feudalism, to take that example, were lower than those of the classic world, less respectful of the value of human personality, and less socially minded, so that clinging to feudalism in its colonial form is particularly unfortunate. Happily, in the century-old struggle between its old ideals and those we stand for, truth is on the side of the new.

The new ideals of self-reliance and personal responsibility, he says, have been preached most effectively by Emerson and Alvarez, and it is because she followed them that the United States in the nineteenth century became so powerful. It was natural, then, for Ingenieros to feel sympathy for the nations that stood closest to his ideals, and he took the side

[71] Ingenieros, "Proposiciones," *Obras*, XVIII, 116.

of France and Belgium and the United States, and with the
Revolution, of Russia. He could not, however, view the war
as one between two sets of ideals, and could not hope for the
wiping out of Germany. He was not jarred from his position
that the most important thing in the world was faith in the
future, ideals to fight for in the future, education to prepare
for the future. The world, to him, was divided into the men
of the past and the men of the future, and only a decided
break with the past and turning toward the future merited
the name of revolution. Real revolutionists know that they
are not working for the present nor for the happiness of those
who are now adults; they pin their hopes on children and on
their education for the world that will come. In any revolution, as in any reactionary movement, the impulse comes
from a minority, who are the revolutionists; the masses are
always neutral and an obstacle.

In a final chapter, Ingenieros proclaims the need for revolution as a result of the use of the state as a political instrument by plutocratic capitalism and of the loss of moral
quality under the heartless competition of the capitalistic
régime. He had given up his connection with the Socialist
Party in 1899, but never his socialism. Now, however, the
moral argument against capitalism is even more decisive for
him than the economic one. Idealism is not dead; even in the
United States, Wilson spoke in its name; everywhere a new
moral conscience is forming which rebels against parasitism
and privilege. Achievement of the ideals he has in mind cannot be expected from governments nor from the Leagues they
form; it must be for the people, and above all for youth,
which has no complicity with the past.

The forces that may be counted upon to work for the new
world form the subject matter of the lay sermons which saw
the light first between 1918 and 1923 and were collected
under the title "Moral Forces." These forces fluctuate,

sometimes seem quite gone. The present hour hath need of
them. First, we must rally "those who have no complicity
with the past." Youth must be defined more in such terms,
in terms of ideals and of the strength to go forth and conquer
the world, than in terms of years.

Gálvez, when he came to write "What This People Needs,"
also began with more youth; on some other points Ingenieros
and Gálvez are in agreement, as in the need for work and
discipline, but the whole spirit and aim is different, as different as Russia from Germany.

The whole book is a little too neat, a little too eloquent in
its unsupported assertions, but it is easy to imagine standing
and cheering when the chapters were first given as speeches.
The old master is speaking in the phrases that a lifetime of
writing has taught him to shape cunningly and well, and he
is speaking from the heights, like Rodó, to tell his cherished
youth that "the road to perfection is to live as if your ideals
were reality . . . sainthood is of this world, and those enter
into it who so live that their names are passed down as examples of the most perfect humanity." [72]

The fulfillment of personality demands that we live intensely. "Every hour, every minute should be used wisely
so as to extract from it as much as possible, whether in work
or pleasure." [73]

Every basic element in the thought of Ingenieros is here
reëxamined from the point of view of its usefulness in the
realization of his ideals. This is his "What Is to be Done?"
and what have we to do it with? The scientist has turned
preacher; the psychologist, moralist; the sociologist, revo-
lutionist. The patriot remains, but he is one with the inter-
nationalist. "Every people is an element of Humanity; the
desire for national greatness may be an aspect of faith in

[72] Ingenieros, "Las fuerzas morales,' *Obras*, XXII, 65–66.
[73] *Id.* at 83.

human dignity. Let each nation achieve its highest, and by the effort of all, the level of all Humanity will rise." [74]

The papers collected after Ingenieros' death and published as "The Treatise on Love" are an appendix and an anticlimax, but since scientific attention to the family has been as noticeably absent in Latin America as it is conspicuous in the United States, the work has its interest.

As he examines the evolution (of course, it would have to be evolution) of the family, Ingenieros finds a struggle (between two opposing ideals, to be sure). These two ideals are love, which is individual, and domesticity, which is social. The former is being sacrificed. In this case, Ingenieros cannot see the old value lost without shedding a tear. Nature has decreed that the Sexual Instinct should yield place to the Domestic, which insures that individuals learn to live in a family group able to provide protection for its children, and that good lovers should be sought only if they are good providers and good parents. The sacrifice of plural relations has been demanded for the same excellent reason, but incidentally sexual selection and the prolific reproduction of the fittest has been interfered with. Men and women endowed with such sexual instincts as they have can hardly be roped into so supremely social an arrangement without being told a "vital lie," which attributes a false value to matrimony and to monogamy, in addition to the demonstrable ones they possess from the point of view of the individual. Those who accept the lie, and find they were not made for the life, must suffer; those who exercise their freedom to love outside domestic institutions must be made to feel that they have violated a limitation set by society.

Seriously upset by this dilemma, Ingenieros asks if love is to disappear from the earth, and those who cannot be "domesticated" eliminated by natural selection. There is one

[74] *Id.* at 159.

hope. As the domestic family ousted the sexual family, so the social family may succeed the domestic. With everyone's duties being directed more to the state, and less to his family, he may find himself once more freer in his love-life, although never entirely free. The individual will certainly not be free to produce dysgenic offspring. It is possible that the objects of eugenics will be achieved by love, once love ceases to be interfered with by "domestic" considerations; instinct can be trusted to pick the right mate where social prejudice cannot. To love eugenically and produce the super-man is the last ideal Ingenieros leaves with us.

The work of Ingenieros was continued by his biographer, the even more forthright radical, Anibal Ponce, until the latter's untimely death in an auto accident in 1938. The *Revista de filosofía* survived only a few years; the absence of such an organ is much felt at the present time.

Alejandro Korn (1860–1936)

Korn was one of those who is greater as a man than as a writer. He wrote well although not prolifically in both the German of his parents and the Spanish of his own Argentina. But it was in his personal relations that he made the greatest impression upon his time. For his disciples he was a Socrates and would have been a great thinker if he had not written a single page. His love of the truth, his severely critical attitude, his wide learning, and his way of going to the bottom of every question and of relating every subject to the ultimate problems made him a Godlike figure to the young men who surrounded him. They are still carrying on his work. The most interesting philosopher in present day Argentina, Francisco Romero, whose work has not achieved any systematic expression, acknowledges the inspiration he received from Korn. "When you were with him you breathed a clear and stimulating air, the atmosphere of the heights." [75] Korn impressed all who knew him by his integrated nature. He was never the mere specialist so absorbed in one pursuit that he became a kind of machine. Even when he spoke of the idea of God he did not allow it to dehumanize him. He was not just the philosopher but the superior man philosophizing; not just a teacher but the teacher and exemplar of life and conduct. The result is that "Korn was the one who among us made the greatest contribution to a fundamental reconstruction of philosophy. His action in this respect constitutes one of his greatest services to American thought." [76] He combined as few people do a capacity for innovation with a profound understanding of the history of philosophy, and indeed of history in general. In the recent history of philosophy it has been the tendency we call positivistic which has prevailed. With this Korn had scant sympathy. It seemed to give man only a subordinate place in a world of blind and mechanical force; in opposition to its naturalism and determinism, he offers us a philosophy of personality, of freedom, of values. Science can give us only a mathematical interpretation of spatio-temporal reality. But man, although he lives in a world of space and time, is not defined by it; his personality is defined by the values that he freely chooses. Leaving to science the whole world of the external, Korn's philosophy goes straight to the subjective. The heart of the subjective is the reaction of the person before a fact, the value that he attaches to the fact. This definition of philosophy so influential at the present moment is the reason that Korn is regarded as more than an extraordinary personality — as the greatest purely theoretical thinker who has arisen in Argentina.

As Korn himself put it, in the last analysis reality is a

[75] Korn, *Obras* (La Plata, 1938?–1940), I, iii.
[76] *Id.* at xi.

psychic phenomenon. To exist is to be aware, and to know is to observe the contents of this awareness.[77] To enter into consciousness is to find values and the act of valuing. To apply to this world the methods of science is an error, for it involves a quite different kind of knowing.[78]

Axiology, or the study of values, takes us immediately into the philosophy of culture, the result of collective life. To value may be an individual and subjective activity, but it has no meaning for history unless the value becomes one held by the group. It is social values that constitute the norm for all; what is anti-social is the negation of culture, and that highest value that human culture has worked out — that of Justice — is the most eminently social, representing the ideal of living together, the desire to eliminate conflict and find a harmony of wills.[79] The relativity of the concept of justice, the diversity of ways in which mankind has conceived the right, does not worry Korn, for this relativity only means that what is right is the result of a complex historical process, and will always be part of a process of continual becoming.[80] If we must have a firm foundation for our values we can find it only in faith, for nothing that psychology, sociology, or history can contribute to their description can make them anything but precariously subjective; as a matter of fact men have always sought such supra-rational support for their values.[81]

There is something personal and subjective about ethical conduct at its best; mere imposition of duty can never lead to the heroism which is found at the heart of conscious sacrifice, the yielding of the legitimate individual goal to the higher supra-individual goal. One cannot prescribe the doing of this; one can only solve one's own ethical problem.[82]

[77] *Id.* at 65.
[78] *Id.* at 83.
[79] *Id.* at 113.

[80] *Id.* at 114.
[81] *Id.* at 116.
[82] *Id.* at 123–124.

Man as a rational being cannot rest content with false values; he struggles endlessly to rid himself of error, and for him Truth is the highest value, which tests all others.[83]

But beauty is also a highest value. In the esthetic experience man rises into a realm where there are no more antinomies and realizes his essential nature as creator. However, aside from the effort to subject matter to form and in the doing to realize one's freedom as a personality, history reveals no unity in mankind's esthetic values.[84]

Having found not one but several highest values, all supported by cogent reasons (some of his discussions are not reviewed here), Korn concludes that it is impossible to erect a hierarchy of values, that the act of valuing is an attitude, a psychological process, not a logical operation. The heart of the attitude is a turning away from an evil that we cannot endure toward its ideal opposite, whether that opposite be Well-being, Happiness, Love, Justice, Power, the ethical ideal, Beauty, or Truth.[85] We run less risk of leaving the real world if we define culture as an effort to free ourselves of felt lacks and pains rather than as the attainment of something that exists only in a world beyond the real. Both optimists and pessimists exhibit this non-acceptance of life as it is offered to us; one tries to create a better real world, the other resigns himself to the real world as he finds it and dreams of a better one, but both move toward liberation from what is.[86]

What we will do depends upon our will. We cannot borrow or import solutions; Argentina must find for herself New Bases (alluding to Alberdi), must affirm the values that she believes in and move toward them. In general terms, Korn is sure that the Argentine will is directed toward freedom realized by action.[87]

---

[83] *Id.* at 125.
[84] *Id.* at 127–129.
[85] *Id.* at 139.
[86] *Id.* at 142.
[87] *Id.* at 149.

In his "Philosophical Notes" Korn does not stray too far from the same topics. Here is the question of the relation of history to values. It is clear that history attempts to give us a coherent notion of the development of culture, and that it describes historic values for us as impartially and sincerely as it can. It cannot for all its impartiality be described as a science, for it deals with man acting, with man as subject and valuer, not with man as a mere object. It has not science's concern with the general, but is always occupied with the single, whether it be individual man, episode, or nation. History constitutes the most complete treatise of human psychology in existence, and its concreteness is infinitely preferable to the abstract psychology of the textbooks. It discovers that through the centuries men have affirmed ten classes of values, which recall the interest-sociology of Albion W. Small, the four wishes of W. I. Thomas, and many other formulations of the springs of human conduct. If some of these are so symbolic as to be mythical, that is not history's business; she can only note that at some time certain ones seemed more important than others, but that no hierarchy of values can claim any absolute and permanent validity. Primitive man was most concerned to solve his biological problems; his values were economic, instinctive, and erotic; he aimed at the distant ideals of Well-being, Happiness, and Love, and achieved those historic approximations we call technique, pleasure, and the family. Another group of values is the social, including the vital which aims at power, and the social in the narrow sense, which aims at Justice. Finally, the cultural values are classified as religious, ethical, logical, and esthetic, and their goals are holiness, the good, truth, beauty. All that has been reached is the half-way station of forms of worship, moral systems, and mores, such little knowledge as we have, and the art of our museums.[88]

[88] *Id.* at 214–231.

If this seems a modest contribution, perhaps because it is disfigured in the process of epitomizing, it is nevertheless the most valuable part of Korn's thought. In two other hand-some volumes of his collected papers we meet analyses of past philosophers, literary criticism, letters, useful information on the state of philosophy in the Argentine and the foreign influences that have been most potent there.

Of the historical part, the most interesting is that in which Korn indicates his reasons for dissatisfaction with the prevailing positivism of the late nineteenth century. Its great aim was to systematize science; science, eternally progressive, refused to stay within the bounds assigned it in the systems of positivism. The resulting crisis in thought was not just a matter for the epistemologists or metaphysicians; it was a general crisis of western culture. On the positive side the reaction against positivism can best be interpreted as a re-affirmation of the human personality, and unwillingness to have it treated as a mere cog in the machinery of the universe and as an insistence that the science in which personality played a part be treated differently from those where it was absent. We recognize old friends in this last statement; Korn knew his German philosophy.[89]

In spite of this debt to *Naturwissenschaften* and *Geistes-wissenschaften*, Korn is eager to see Argentina cease to be a colony of Europe, philosophically speaking, and seek within itself the solution of its own problems. He does not claim much in this respect, and tolerantly expects smiles when he entitles an article "Argentine Philosophy." Even Argentina's reading of foreigners, he admits, is not of the heavy-weights in philosophy; she prefers philosophic themes lightly treated by literary men or publicists, and takes philosophy *à la* Maeterlinck, Unamuno, Romain Rolland, Bernard Shaw, Valéry. He might have added that the better things of Ber-

[89] *Obras*, II, 215–216.

trand Russell and of Santayana are not much known to this day, and Whitehead hardly at all; Dewey is known only as an educator. Meyerson, Poincaré, Bergson, Croce, Ortega y Gasset have played a major part, however; Scheler and Husserl are getting to be known, and there is some return to Kant.[90] His own suggestion for an Argentine philosophy, in an article called "New Bases," is the subordination of that positivism which is neither quite acceptable nor yet possible to do without to a higher conception. This higher conception will find a place for determinism in the cosmic process and yet for the autonomy of the human personality without which there is no ethics. It is a basic and unavoidable problem. Has Korn solved it?

Manuel Ugarte (1878–   )

If Ugarte had not made so much noise in the world, and if the English translation of his book *The Destiny of a Continent* (New York, 1925) did not in its introduction call him one of Latin America's most brilliant thinkers and writers, an opinion in which many Latin Americans have concurred, the writer would follow his personal predilection and omit him. The historians of the short story will have to take him, in any case. To support commonplace thoughts with great vehemence and doubtful facts is hardly enough to make a *pensador.* To include Ugarte, and omit the glamorous figure of Alfredo Palacios, Senator and Rector of the University of La Plata, or those realistic economic analysts Adolfo Dorman and Alejandro Bunge, and such magnificent writers as Ezequiel Martínez Estrada and Eduardo Mallea, is a procedure I should not like to defend in debate.

Ugarte felt called upon to carry his message of warning against the United States throughout Latin America, and

[90] *Obras,* III, 259–280.

did so in the years following 1911 with a success that he is not slow to chronicle. There were plenty of hotheads ready to agree with him, for the same opinions are held and the same emotions felt, perhaps even in more extreme form, as by many today, although they do not rank among serious thinkers.

While Ugarte claims to admire the United States, and late in life he came around to expressing his admiration in more orthodox fashion, he does not in his principal book miss a chance to record an unfortunate boast or confession on the part of North American spokesmen or to uncover a shady diplomatic transaction, and he puts the least favorable interpretation on the overt actions of our political and economic imperialism. The high point of his thought is reached in his plea that Latin Americans cultivate love for their own countries and concern for their future rather than waste their energy in unproductive hatred of the United States, that they take their bearings and come to a realization of what they must do before it is too late. But even this is not enough to make of Ugarte a successor of Martí or Rodó.

Manuel Gálvez (1882–   )

Manuel Gálvez and Ricardo Rojas, the two most notable elder writers of Argentina now living, were born in the same year, and both began their careers as authors with volumes meant as homage to the country on the occasion of the hundredth anniversary of its independence. The strong nationalism which was entirely natural in these initial writings has continued to be the dominant note in the work of both Gálvez and Rojas; both have had distinguished careers in education; both have in addition to their ideological works produced major imaginative literature. There are, nevertheless, important differences in the direction their thought has taken, and in the following it has attracted.

Gálvez dedicated his first slender book to the memory of two great Argentines, Sarmiento and Mitre, for he, like Rojas, thinks of himself as continuing the work of the school-master president. The title, "The Diary of Gabriel Quiroga, or Opinions on Argentine Life," is a transparent device for presenting the opinions of Manuel Gálvez. Gabriel Quiroga is a non-existent person, and it is not even claimed that this is his real name. In an introduction bearing his own sig-nature Gálvez presents the diary as the severest judgment ever passed upon the Argentine Republic, a fact which proves its author to be a true patriot.[91] The most ardent wish of Quiroga-Gálvez is that his country should experience a spiritual rebirth and recover the life of the spirit that it lost with the coming of the materialistic epoch in which, he says, we now live, and from which, please God, we shall some day emerge. We have laid waste our powers getting and spend-ing, increasing our wealth and hastening the progress of the country.[92] The patriotism that Gálvez wishes to revive is a feeling so deep, so irrational, that it can only "exist really in peoples who have a soul of their own, peoples among whom the typical man is a genuine product of the soil, the race and the culture." [93] Instead of such men, Argentina has a lot of weeds that grow on the surface of her life, and that must be cast into the fire and burned.[94]

Cultures may be known by the cities they create. "A city is . . . the material expression of the heart of a people, of their social and individual culture." [95] If, with this truth in mind, we look at Buenos Aires, we find only a "repugnant materialism." From this slough there is no salvation through the Protestantism that some would propose; to adopt it would mean giving up the essence of Argentine nationalism,

[91] Gálvez, *El diario de Gabriel Quiroga* (Buenos Aires, 1910), p. 32.

[92] *Id.* at 51–52.

[93] *Id.* at 54.

[94] *Id.* at 58.

[95] *Id.* at 63.

for religion expresses in a peculiarly intimate and permanent way the very heart and soul of a people, and religions cannot be borrowed and bartered.[96] Materialism can endow us with civilization, but not with culture, and it is Argentina's sad condition to possess the former without the latter.[97]

There is nothing like a war to unite a nation behind a common ideal. Perhaps a war with Brazil would be Argentina's salvation, he suggests. Argentina would be defeated, for Brazil has some of the qualities Argentina lacks, and the defeat would be good for us.[98]

Gálvez made the same discovery made in very recent years by some of our North American intellectuals who were formerly focused on the negative, namely that his people lack ideas and faith for living.[99] To "arrive" is the limit of their ambition for themselves, for their country; it is their worst sin, their most characteristic quality.[100] To achieve this ambition, we have followed, he says, the teaching of Alberdi and Sarmiento, and have brought from the campagna of Italy hordes of peasants who have had a tremendous influence in denationalizing us. Then we have imitated English and French customs; finally, there have come the Jews and the Russian anarchists.[101] Sarcastically, he states the result: "Any one can see that we are completely civilized now." Then, in deathly seriousness, at the present moment "to govern is to argentinize." [102]

The guidance of past *pensadores* has not been all wrong. Sarmiento was the greatest of all, the most thoroughly Argentine, in spite of himself. "His most beautiful pages, written with love, with all his soul, are the biographies of those barbarians that he imagined he hated." [103] Alberdi, on the other hand, was only a mediocre thinker, out of touch

[96] *Id.* at 67.
[97] *Id.* at 71.
[98] *Id.* at 77.
[99] *Id.* at 90.

[100] *Id.* at 98.
[101] *Id.* at 101.
[102] *Id.* at 103.
[103] *Id.* at 114.

with reality, unequipped with scientific method, a rhetorician incapable of understanding the soul of America.[104] He was blind to the relations between society and its physical environment, and did not realize the importance of the racial factor.[105]

It is a bit unfair, he admits, to attack Argentina as if all parts of it suffered equally from the evils he excoriates. There are many Argentinas, and in some of them, in the provinces, the soul of the nation has taken refuge and still fights desperately against the cosmopolitanism of Buenos Aires. The provinces deserve the help of all men of good will, even if it be no more than the help of the water they so urgently need for irrigation.[106] Fatally, however, the authors of Argentina are attracted to the capital, which is not good for them; it is materialistic, cosmopolitan, it lacks the repose and the tradition essential to the flourishing of the intellectual life. And as a result, Argentina has no literature. "Most of the books which are published here are quite unrelated to the environment." [107] With no leadership from those who should lead, Argentina is anti-intellectual; even her intellectuals do not stand for intellectualism. Thinking of Rodó, and denying his thesis as a statement of fact, Gálvez exclaims, "Ah, Caliban, this decidedly is thy realm." [108]

Giving generous credit to Rojas for his emphasis on the word nationalism, Gálvez concludes the diary with a plea that his countrymen be Argentine, that they remember that they are Latins, Spaniards, Americans, and finally Argentines. This is but a pale summary of the glowing page that sings his love for the country, his appeal for its sake to follow high ideals of personal and social goodness.[109]

"Birth-place of Our Race" was written in 1910 and 1911,

---

104 *Id*. at 122.
105 *Id*. at 134.
106 *Id*. at 138.

107 *Id*. at 182.
108 *Id*. at 212.
109 *Id*. at 230.

but published in 1913.[110] In his introduction to the edition of 1936 Gálvez disclaims having exactly the same opinions as when he wrote it, says he is less combatively hispanophile. The difference is not great, for he goes on to note the decay of Spanish influence, the growth of Yankee influence, the increase in non-Latin immigration. Today, he says, we feel more Latin than Spanish, and we must cling to this loyalty, for it defines our essence and is our defense against the United States.

The ancestral mansion which gives the title to the book is of course Spain, admirable Spain, Spain where there is still an intense spiritual life, Spain that is profound and marvelous.[111] Enough progress in right thinking has been made in Argentina so that many have accepted as axiomatic the necessity of spiritualizing the country. This means a hard fight, in books, newspapers, universities, everywhere, against the "Caliban," the materialism that thrives among us. "We have to preach like madmen, preach love for our country and its land, its writers and great men; reveal the idealism and the originality of our past, show how these qualities of a romantic and poverty-stricken past can still save the land of today, without prejudice to its material greatness." [112]

Now, possession of the same or similar languages is the source of the same or similar modes of feeling, thinking and even of acting. Development of the right attitude toward ourselves is closely related to what we think of the one European country where our language is spoken. "I aim also to spread affection for Spain, from which will result love for our race, which so many snobs put in second place after the Anglo-Saxon race, and love for our language, the most beautiful, most sonorous, richest and most living of all mod-

[110] Gálvez, *El solar de la raza* (Buenos Aires, 1913; new ed., 1936).
[111] New edition, 1936, p. 7.
[112] *Id*. at 12–13.

ern tongues." He proclaims his enthusiasm for Spanish literature and art, and proposes to construct an Argentine idealism out of elements derived from "our race, that is to say from the Spanish and American elements that we bear in our bosoms." [113]

From this point, the book is a kind of "Ground We Stand On," surveying Spain and Spanish characteristics for the elements out of which to form ideals. Whereas modern industrial society lives for money and sensual pleasure, the Castilian has another concept of life. "The soberest of men, he has no excessive love for material pleasures. He does not love effort for its own sake, nor is he convinced that happiness for mankind lies in commerce and industry. . . . In short, he has the Christian concept of life."[114] Spain is willing to stand out against Europe and to seem eccentric or unique in these qualities. The Spaniard has seen absurd legends grow up about his qualities; defects he never had have been attributed to him: avarice, indolence, cruelty. This last Gálvez labels frankly a lie; never has he known a people more compassionate, more generous, less egoistic.[115] Such legends arise because history writing has been in the hands of the Protestant English, who naturally have had little sympathy for Latins and Catholics; and Spain has had the misfortune not to be a nation of historians.[116]

The truth is that Spanish land has "engendered the noblest and most heroic, most chivalrous people that ever lived . . . together with artists unsurpassed down to our day, extraordinary saints, lives almost superhuman in their heroism, writers of genius. . . . Such lands can teach us much about energy. . . . The dryness, austerity, sobriety of the Castilian are results of the dryness, austerity, sobriety of the land." [117]

[113] *Id.* at 15–16.
[114] *Id.* at 28–29.
[115] *Id.* at 30.
[116] *Id.* at 31.
[117] *Id.* at 47.

It is a land that produces nothing, or without water would produce nothing. In this extraordinary land an extraordinary people has comforted itself with the spiritual, with a fixed belief in a few fundamental truths. Progress has never seemed very important to the Spaniards; they have known that all is vanity save Stoicism, and they have shown how poverty and pain can produce a virile race.[118] Gálvez' eloquence is here more moving, because more deeply felt, than anything in the novels he rather patently and artificially constructs to illustrate his ideas.

The lesson of Spain is taught in various chapters, various accents by her different cities. We cannot follow Gálvez through them all, but must say a word about the love which he, a citizen of a new country, feels for the age, rich in tradition, ideals, nobility, of the city of Segovia, most serious and profound of cities. "Segovia makes us think of death; of death coming peacefully, bringing translation to a life beyond, death that frees us finally from misery." [119]

In the modern world, Spain is sad, for she is at odds with its ideals, and knows that her ways are not the ways of this new and powerful world. Why can we not in a world of industry preserve intact some examples of the past "to serve as places of refuge for incurable dreamers, for those who have lost the fight, for those who are tormented by spiritual problems"? Nothing could be better for such men than to sojourn a while in so spiritual a city as Salamanca and to be bathed in its mysterious, divine influence.[120]

Depth has spoken unto depth, and heart to heart in this book. Gálvez has told the story of the ancestral home of Argentine men, for he believes that we shall never know where we are going if we do not first know whence we have come. Fortified by this knowing, we may expect his guidance

[118] *Id.* at 47.
[119] *Id.* at 50–52.   [120] *Id.* at 59.

through the Argentine cities where the soul of the race sleeps, through landscapes that are Argentina's own and like no others; his help toward understanding the Argentine soul, the spiritual physiognomy of the Argentine people.[121]

"The Spirit of Aristocracy and Other Essays," published in 1924, hardly fulfills this promise, and yet it does contain some interesting observations and shows in what direction he is beginning to look for salvation.

Aristocracy and democracy should not be thought of as incompatible. An aristocrat is a man with distinction, and the greatest democrats have been such. They are not only intellectually superior, but possess some innate quality, the result of history and tradition — something that is more a matter of the spirit than of intelligence, and that manifests itself in manners and in delicacy of sentiments. The historic aristocrat has been given to follow fashions; he has been too much the passive spectator of life to make good revolutionary material. The truest union of the ideals of personality and love, or aristocracy and democracy, is that furnished by Christianity and realized by the greatest figures in its history.

In another essay Gálvez analyzes the cultural crisis of the day and finds its cause in the utilitarian character of education, with its insufficient emphasis on the humanities. If he must choose between life and art, he is on the side of life, but he cannot help noting that it is only works of imagination that last, and that nothing is more perishable than so-called social science.[122]

Still another paper grapples with the problem of freedom of thought. Really such freedom does not exist, or exists only if the thinker is in accord with the predominant, official doctrines. Other and more real freedom than this does not exist because most men do not want it to; being themselves incapable of such thinking, they hate it in others. Ideally,

[121] *Id.* at 60–69.   [122] *Id.* at 171.

the spirit of man should be free, without limits, for there is in it something divine that does not abide bonds.[123]

In the preface to the 1935 edition of "Argentina in Our Books" (the second part of which deals with Argentina in everyday life), Gálvez again says that he has left the book as he originally wrote it, but would like it understood that if he were to rewrite it now he would modify certain of the views. The Eucharistic Congress in Buenos Aires has taught him that he was too harsh and pessimistic in his judgment of Argentine psychology.

Even in the original form of the book there is flat contradiction of his earlier statement that Argentine books do not deal with their country. "If we consider our literature as a whole, we shall observe that the great majority of us, the authors of these books, have done nothing else than occupy ourselves with Argentina. . . . The country, every inch of it, has found its way into books." [124] His own "Tragedy of a Strong Man" is a case in point. This novel deals with Buenos Aires, but more with its moral than its material side. The way he wrote it appears baldly in his own account of its contents. "Politics and political parties, women and modern love, changes in moral ideas, the Jews, and other matters of equal importance, all are there, nothing is lacking. All these matters are presented novelistically, in action. And I am not the only novelist who has taken into account moral aspects of the country." [125] There does exist, as a result of such writing, a clearly defined Argentine spirit. The sad thing is that the writer still finds little true understanding. Society, except for little groups insignificant in numbers, "is indifferent to intellectual production. . . . Which might not matter so much if we only had freedom to produce. . . . But even for the gathering of factual material and local color we are

[123] Gálvez, *El espíritu de aristocracia y otros ensayos* (Buenos Aires, 1924), p. 103.
[124] *Id*. at 137–141.
[125] Gálvez, *La Argentina en nuestros libros* (Santiago, 1935), p. 9.

handicapped. . . . The fact of the matter is, we writers have not succeeded in getting together and so strengthening our position." [126]

The young fellow who has the inner urge to write has no one to tell him what to read: "He does not study; he has little interest in classic literature, philosophy, history, or religions. Nor does he put his heart into the effort to learn foreign languages. . . . The books he can afford to buy are cheap, fraudulent editions, nearly always incomplete, and inaccurately translated." [127] "It is only in Argentina that the writer counts for nothing, absolutely nothing." [128]

Argentines still do not seem able to distinguish clearly between the social significance of writing and its value as art. Gálvez has the audacity to speak slightingly of two treasured classics of his country, *Martín Fierro* and Sarmiento's *Facundo*. Both are social documents, but their artistic quality is inferior. "*Facundo*, except for the introduction and a page of brilliant description here and there, is a truculent, vulgar feuilleton, written by an ill-equipped journalist." [129]

The country has everything needed to develop a great literature: "individual ability, a characteristic environment, landscapes, customs that have never been described, a history rich in great personalities, magnificent newspaper coverage, intellectual curiosity, esthetic sensitivity." Ambition and work are what we need; he would not even blame an excess of French influence, as some have done, for it is only technique that is borrowed from the French, while the themes of Argentine writing grow more and more domestic.[130]

Some who write of these themes (he means himself) are clear-eyed and civilized, and would import the best European methods to solve local problems (we shall soon see what these

[126] *Id.* at 13.
[127] *Id.* at 21–22.
[128] *Id.* at 26–27.

[129] *Id.* at 30.
[130] *Id.* at 43.

methods are).[131] In straightforward first person singular he recalls writing the first really literary Catholic book of recent decades, in "The Diary of Gabriel Quiroga," and points proudly to its political reactionary quality.[132]

Such is the situation with regard to culture, books, and the intellectual life. What is the spiritual situation? "Among us there is no spiritual life. . . . There is no interest in the things of the soul. In general, we lack a religious sense of life. We care little about philosophical problems. Money and good living are our aims. Religion, in most cases, is vulgar routine, or politics, or mediocre devoutness. Such idealism as there is, is directed to aggrandizement for the country, material improvement for the individual. There is nothing spiritual about it, and it had better be called aspiration, rather than idealism." [133] The spiritual poverty of Argentina shows in its literature, rich in other things, but the poorest in ideas that he knows. If man reaches the heights through his striving for moral, spiritual, and intellectual values, then Argentina is headed straight in the other direction, that is, for barbarism.[134]

No wonder he feels, not only in himself but in many others, an enormous discontent with the kind of life his compatriots are living, with their character and their country. But the people who feel thus are cut off from each other, and live in spiritual solitude; every man is alone in Buenos Aires. A few years after the first edition of this book was published came another called "The Man Who Waits Alone" — a title Gálvez apparently wishes he had thought of.[135] Vanity keeps men apart and is responsible for the lack of spontaneous and friendly living.[136]

He has not exhausted his reasons for anger. The modern

[131] *Id.* at 64.
[132] *Id.* at 76.
[133] *Id.* at 85.

[134] *Id.* at 121.
[135] *Id.* at 150–152.
[136] *Id.* at 161.

apartment is an enemy of culture. It has no permanence, no place for books or pictures, writing or family life. A city of apartment houses is almost as bad as communism; in neither can one find the needed "order, hierarchy, discipline." [137] Fortunately, one can flee from Buenos Aires to the provinces; tradition and culture live there, and some religion, although he exclaims with a finality that the Eucharistic Congress made him regret, "There is not on the face of the globe a less religious country than ours." [138]

"What This People Needs" has ten chapters on as many separate needs. You could fill them in without looking. Seven of the chapters were published serially, and went no further than a general discussion of moral questions, without indicating the remedies Gálvez considered useful. Even when he does preach remedies he considers himself still a writer rather than a man of action and leader of campaigns. This view may be rationalization of his disappointment, for he has had hankerings for enthusiastic disciples.

The first need treated is Argentina's need to be young. It is full of old men, men who never were young, never had the "heroic ardor, the impatience, faith, enthusiasm, aspiration to create" that are proper to youth. Wisecracking is mistaken for youthfulness; its essence really is affirmation; youth "curses shouts and strikes." Argentina needs to be youthful in order to "awaken from its native siesta, to shake off the colonial drowsiness which still persists." Gálvez repeats that his countrymen think only of material pleasures, and are sapped by skepticism about ideals; they exhibit motivational mollification. They have been governed by old men or young men with old ideas.[139]

Second, Argentina needs patriotism. We think we have

[137] *Id.* at 167–168.
[138] *Id.* at 171–172.
[139] Gálvez, *Este pueblo necesita* (Buenos Aires, 1934), pp. 7–12.

patriotism, he says, but it is not so. We want our country to
occupy an important place among nations whether it deserves to or not. We talk about our country. "But what
have Argentines done for their country? Is patriotism shown
by spending one's life in Paris? . . . In the United States
rich men build universities and museums. . . . Here they
have done nothing. Even in the case of industries, they have
founded only a few here and there." Loving one's country is
not enough, nor working for its greater place in the world,
nor building schools, founding industries, governing hon-
estly, or being the perfect employee. No, beyond all these
is the necessity of defending the country, saving it from the
threatened catastrophe resulting from corrupt systems of
ideas. And Gálvez, who since the day when he wrote his
thesis on the white-slave traffic has been the enemy of
pornography, even when his own novels got into trouble on
that score, launches into a diatribe against the scandals of
North American films and their "pernicious paganism." [140]

Third, Argentina needs an heroic sense of life. Once it was
heroic and proved it by great deeds and in war. The austerity and strength of those days were connected with their
poverty. With wealth has come decay. Not that making
money is bad in itself; Gálvez believes it to be a fine thing.
The evil is to have no enthusiasm for one's job, one's profession; to work only with the thought of money and the com-
forts and pleasures it will buy. "Are not the new work
camps of Germany where young men practice the most rigorous and austere kind of life a magnificent thing?" To develop
anew the heroic sense of life much must be destroyed, purified, corrected; we have tendencies, customs which grow out
of an unhealthy concept of life. Vanity, the worst of our
vices, must be fought, and also the tendency to leave things
for another day. It will be seen, he says, that my idea is

[140] *Id.* at 19-28.

tant soit peu religious. During peace times we shall not change much; the needed reaction will come with the approaching struggle, the social war against communism. Salvation will come from men of the people or of the middle class, perhaps from some socialists converted to belief in order.[141]

Fourth, moral reform is a necessity. "The strong, normal, patriotic man . . . seeks, above all, to do his duty." The task of government is to cultivate this desire, is, in a word, to spiritualize. In the process of becoming good we shall find it necessary to do away with our vast estates; our Catholic women will have to cure themselves of their vanity. Such preachments still seem quite unacceptable to most people. Gálvez takes occasion to defend himself against the accusation of extreme rightism. A reactionary in politics, yes, for he is against the lies of universal suffrage and the parliamentary system. But socially he stands for a program more radical than that of the socialist party, and believes that only the state should be rich. The mere mention of socialists sets him off on a tirade against the murderers of Russia and his old enemy pornography, while for contrast he turns to the Italian of today, who is a new man, austere, idealistic, a man of order.[142]

The fifth need is ideals and idealism. The generation to which Gálvez belongs grew up in an atmosphere of materialism. It came to them from above. Their gods as university students were materialists, determinists. There was no spirituality, no religious feeling in the university. That can all be corrected if priests will teach Catholics, and rabbis Jews, and pastors Protestants, the essential respect for the spiritual and the ideal in which all are more alike than might at first be thought. This is one more thing that has not been accomplished under that "stupendous failure," democracy.[143]

[141] *Id.* at 31–40.   [142] *Id.* at 41–53.   [143] *Id.* at 55–64.

The sixth need is order and discipline. We have never been strong for discipline, he says; instead, we have a tendency toward rebellion against moral and social values. He dares raise his voice, as very few will do in public, against the vaunted University Reform movement, with the power it puts in the hands of a rebellious student body. In other parts of the world "youth attends the university to learn and to obey; professors go there to teach and to command," but here, of course, it must be different! [144]

Seventh, Argentina needs hierarchy. With a kind of twisted Platonism, Gálvez tells us that hierarchy cannot be where the material is allowed to usurp the first place, which belongs to the spiritual. It cannot exist in society unless each man first practices it in himself. Democracy and yellow journalism have obliterated it with such follies as asking the man on the street his opinion. In Argentina only General Uriburu has had a sense of hierarchy. Gálvez begs his readers not to misunderstand; he is not opposed to the ideal of equality: we are equal before God and the law. The country, however, cannot function without hierarchy; a people without hierarchy is only a tribe, a mass of humanity. To have hierarchy, we must accept authority; a new type of authority must be created. It has been done in Italy, where Mussolini attends to everything, without forgetting the improvement of morality, in which he has accomplished "the incredible."[145]

Eighth, results, not politics are needed. All politics is condemned, as Argentina's greatest evil. Parties, committees, the whole rigmarole of democracy are powerless to accomplish anything. Only a state that is strong can unite a nation, a state that is above all divisions, all self-seeking. This doctrine may sound like communism, but whereas communism destroys, this state will preserve family life, religion, social, historical, and cultural traditions. This is what our country

needs, he cries, and what we will never get from the men who
live by the vote. Communism is its worst enemy, and for the
"epidemic" of communism in the country he sees no solution
but suppression by official violence.[146]

Ninth, Argentina needs social justice. One practical
achievement of the new order will be the solution of the
social problem, a practical socialism, with no nonsense about
class struggle, with none of the sad consequences of party
politics.[147]

Tenth, authority is needed to carry out the program. Both
for spiritual and material reasons the country needs a strong
hand at the helm. It needs to abandon the constitution it
erected in 1853 in imitation of North America. As he writes
he is not too hopeful, for what fascists there are in his country
emphasize the military and dictatorial aspect of their theory,
and fail to realize that fascism is first of all moral, and that
the iron hand that rules must first exert its pressure through
a severe censorship of theaters and movies, the radio and
books, nudity; it must save the Christian family and morality. More applause for Mussolini, Hitler, and Dollfuss.
Curtain.[148]

Ricardo Rojas (1882–   )

The "Prince of Argentine letters" is one of the few men of
his country whose life has been given wholly to the humanities. The fact that he held the first chair devoted to Hispanic-American literature has permitted him to make the
literature of his own country his primary object of investigation, and thus he has to a remarkable extent fused the
literary and nationalistic interests. Thus his scholarly work,
like the inimitable "History of Argentine Literature," is not

[146] *Id.* at 87–97.
[147] *Id.* at 101–102.
[148] *Id.* at 113–132.

merely accurate spadework chronology and bibliography, but a creative synthesis, which asks what Argentina has to say about itself, what is the soul that expresses itself in books. No denial of the importance of such work is intended if we turn from it, and from the biographies, poems, and plays which only a writer with Rojas' ideas could have written, to the volumes in which his thought is most explicit.

These volumes are "Glory of the River Plate," which appears as the first volume of his works, "Argentinism," "The Restoration of Nationalism," and *Eurindia,* in which the very title expresses his thesis of the two sources, European and Indian, of the national culture. Rojas himself points out how the same essential ideas have found application in these writings, application to the ethnic formation of Argentine stock in the first, to the process of winning freedom and setting up democracy in the second, to education in the third, to esthetics in *Eurindia,* and to the evolution of the national culture in his literary history. They are alike not only in the steady bass of the national theme, but in the fact that without neglecting the methodology of historical scholarship he has sought to clothe each argument in the language of poetry and eloquence. What might be plodding and pedantic has wings. The noble passion of the author made an immediate appeal, and critics spoke of a place on the bookshelves between Sarmiento and Alberdi. Rojas has always felt that he was continuing the labors of Sarmiento, with modifications which did not in any way diminish his reverence for the great civilizer.

Gálvez hailed *Blasón del Plata* as fundamentally a book of ideas and yet as the work of a true poet; perhaps the poet is more evident than the ideas in most of Rojas' work, "The Restoration" being the chief example in which the reverse is true. The nature of his thought is fundamentally political; it touches on all the great social problems, the destiny of nations, education, collective psychology. Gálvez, writing in 1912,[149] in spite of his admiration for Rojas noted a tendency to romanticism, even mysticism and exoticism, which takes him off into regions whither it is difficult to follow. Reduced to simple words, *Blasón del Plata* teaches that there is something about the very land of the South American continent which infects its inhabitants with the desire for freedom. Those born of this land have always fought for it, the Indians against the conquistador, the Creoles against Spain, the federalists against the unitarians, and today the same fight is being fought to proclaim spiritual autonomy and throw off the rule of the foreign and imported. Independence was the reconquest of the land by the spirit of the Indian. It is only because we have the white man's prejudice against the Indian and the patriot's mistaken view of the Spaniard, he says, that we fail to see the thread that ties all our history into one.[150] In reality, there is something of the Indian in all of us, whether it be his blood or not. The same landscapes have bred in us the same emotional responses. The native and the exotic are the forces that are contending on Argentine soil, not as Sarmiento maintained, barbarism and civilization. The problem of their fusion in happy proportions is a problem that every Latin American country faces.

The origin of "The Restoration of Nationalism" was a trip Rojas made to Europe at the request of the government to study methods of education. The report that he made proposes no copying of the latest thing from *outre mer*, but a greater emphasis on what is Argentina's own. His object is "to awaken Argentine society out of its coma." [151] Our task, he maintains, is "to learn again to cohere, to do something to preserve that strong native spirit that gave us our inde-

[149] *La obra de Rojas*, pp. 140–150.
[150] Rojas, *Blasón del Plata* (1910), p. 235.
[151] Rojas, *La restauración nacionalista* (1909), p. 13.

pendence. . . . There is no other road than that of education.
. . . A modern liberal education which will teach about our
land, our language, our tradition, the way men of this nation
should live and act, this is the proper instrument of the
needed reform." [152] Rojas goes on to map out the studies, by
years, by hours per week; it is curriculum-making from
above, with the single clear object of fostering nationalism.
The need for it is clear; we may be a people, he says, but we
are not a nation. "Cosmopolitanism in men and ideas, the
breakdown of the old moral principles, indifference to what
is the business of all, increasing forgetfulness of traditions,
corruption of the language in the mouth of the people, ignorance of our own geography, lack of national unity, desire to
get rich quick, social prestige of the wrong elements in society, disdain for high and noble undertakings, lack of passion
in our struggles, venality in politics, the fad of the foreign, a
destructive individualism, lack of respect for the other man's
ideals, constant simulation and cynicism of the gutter — all
that defines our time — these things prove beyond a doubt
the necessity of a powerful reaction toward nationalism and
loyalty." [153] Education can take even the son of the immigrant and make him deeply, passionately Argentine. The
melting pot has not worked; it must be made to, or else we
shall be forced to adopt a less liberal policy in regard to
immigration.

In "Argentinism," we have a lyrical history of a period
when national spirit was vital, dynamic, and led the people
of the colony in the direction of a distinctive and superior
society. Back of the few individuals whose names every
schoolboy knows lay the strength of a truly Argentine spirit,
deeprooted in the people. The people knew their goals: freedom and national greatness. In this book Rojas is once more

[152] *Id.* at 123–124.
[153] *La obra de Rojas* (Buenos Aires, 1928), pp. 120–121.

the philosopher of history or the historical sociologist, giving a rational explanation of Argentine history, with due attention to historic fact and to spirit, and then projecting the process into the future.

Rojas is perhaps on more congenial ground for his thinking in *Eurindia*, for here the question is esthetic. In recent years there have been many arguments about the necessity of a national music, about painting or dramatizing "the American scene." They move in the same area as this *Eurindia*, but no other has the mighty music of Rojas' style. Neither the barbarism of the *gaucho*, he argues, nor the cosmopolitanism of the port city is the answer to the problem of Argentina's culture. That culture must be national, compounded of the two elements. What will be the nature of the art that adequately expresses it?

The subject of *Eurindia* is an esthetics based on history; its moral is the recommendation to the artist that he love Argentina's history, that he paint her landscape lovingly "as a nude," to use Archibald MacLeish's phrase, that he dwell upon her men and problems. The recommendation can be extended to other lands of South America, for Rojas feels that their problem is similar, and he embraces them all. All have had the problem of achieving a fertile union of Indian and "exotic" elements, and all have failed by overemphasizing one contribution to the exclusion of the other — Buenos Aires cutting its own roots for the sake of "progress," Jujuy becoming only a living museum; neither finding the desired creative life with traditions, aware of its historic mission and the future to which it is called. All have "a certain organic unity between territory, race, tradition, and culture," a unity of interacting influences. "Culture is . . . the organization of traditions into a body of political institutions, philosophical doctrines, and emotional symbols which create national self-consciousness. When this process occurs, the nation has reached maturity, and takes its place as an actor on the world stage." [154] Only the artist who accepts these conditions of his expression can achieve full satisfaction for himself and the highest function for his art.

[154] Rojas, *Eurindia* (Buenos Aires, 1924), pp. 332–333.

CHAPTER VI

Rebellion on the West Coast

Juan Montalvo (1832–1889)

THE CONDITIONS that faced Ecuadorian and Peruvian thinkers after Independence, and indeed down to recent times, were such as to remove all possibility of their spending much hate on the Spaniards, like Lastarria, for they hated the present even more than the past. Before, like Bello, they could sit on one end of a log and educate South America sitting on the other end, there was much fighting to be done. With none of Bello's timidity, they were the men to do it.

The first of them, Montalvo, was the incarnation of protest, the great fighter for justice and liberty in Ecuadorian history. Justice and liberty are fighting words, but a bit vague for science, and it must be confessed that Montalvo's strength was in attack rather than in definition. He shared the faiths and hopes of civilized men in his time, but was no farther advanced as a thinker than many others. Perhaps one may follow some of his Latin-American critics farther and say frankly that he was less advanced, his idea of freedom naïve, and that there are few thinkers in whom one has to search longer for an original idea. It is the style and the energy of Montalvo that make him a towering figure; not, we may note, a popular one. The magniloquent, mannered language, the power of invective, the union of passion and learning (the best of Sarmiento and Bello, Rodó said) have not contrived to rescue Montalvo from dust and neglect. Everyone knows him, but who reads him? When Spain finally awoke to American literature, it was to become inter-

ested in the contemporaries, not in this lover of archaisms
who dared to imitate Cervantes and ape his style in "Chapters that Cervantes Forgot." In Latin America his books,
with the exception of two anthologies, have become extremely difficult to lay one's hands on; the biographies have
not been distinguished or numerous. Even Ecuador does not
find inspiration in him today. To be fair, however, let us
remember the classic of liberty in the English language, and
ask our friends or our classes if they have read the *Areop-
agitica* or Locke on *Toleration* or Mill's *Liberty*.

Not finishing the University, Montalvo went to Europe
for the first of his three visits, worshiped dutifully at the
shrine of Lamartine, but take it all in all, was not happy.
At least one Latin American has been homesick and wanted
to leave Paris. After his return he grasped his pen and became the implacable foe of tyranny and obscurantism. Feeling as Varona did that the explanation of tyranny is the
vileness of a few and the cowardice of many, he flagellated
his people, too, arguing that if there had been a conscience
of the Ecuadorian people no such government as they toler-
ated would have been possible. But he was at his terrible
best when he could attack individuals rather than the state
of morals in the nation. As to morality, he has been called
austere, and it is certain that he could write against alcoholism, but it is a surprise to turn over the page from his austerity to his illegitimate child and the manner in which he
lived up to the Don Juan of his name.

The individual who drew his fire for the longest time was
the theocratic despot of Ecuador (1860–1875), García
Moreno. This was an enemy worthy of him, equally sincere,
also learned and brilliant, a moralist in his way, and personally incorruptible. The contest was waged in savage articles
by Montalvo — soon, naturally, from exile — and finally by
four disciples of the writer, who killed García Moreno in a

particularly gory assassination. Montalvo is said to have exclaimed: "My pen hath slain him!"

Freedom was not won, however, and when a few months later Veintimilla came to power, Montalvo would have willingly had García Moreno back. Fiercer invectives had to be found, more derisive laughter.

The clergy were part of it, too. They blackened Montalvo's name with the tar of heresy, but the truth seems to be that he was profoundly religious, a deist who could not stomach religion as the accomplice of tyranny, or as a tyrant in its own right. Falsity in religion, hypocrisy, fanaticism are the things he flays. Like a Hebrew prophet, he inveighs against tithes and ceremonies when there is neither love nor justice.

He is *par excellence* the censor, attacking the evil that he resents, rather than the scientist, explaining why it exists. For those of us who believe that it is futile to expect the evil to vanish at a word, Montalvo's passion is no substitute for patient analysis. For those who find the scientist irresponsible, with his talk of objectivity, that passion is God-given and without it nothing great is accomplished in this world. For some he is only a negative figure, perpetually attacking; for others there is no gulf between hate and love, but those who love tolerance, charity, justice, and freedom most are in the nature of things those who hate most bitterly those who would banish these things from the world. The man who believed that no one merited the esteem and affection of his fellow men unless he had in him something of Don Quijote was not a *Geist der stets verneint*.

The masterpiece of Montalvo is his "Seven Treatises," essays somewhat in the manner of Montaigne, on nobility, beauty, and other topics. It is in the second of these that he makes one of his few references to the United States in a passage which gives a faint idea of his style and shows what license he takes to roam abroad in these loosely constructed essays.

But a nation so extravagant and fantastic as the United States of America, where the customs run contrary to the laws; where the latter summon negroes to the Senate, and the former refuse them entrance to restaurants and inns; where democracy reigns in institutions, and aristocracy in the form of pride and scorn excludes from the common society those whose color is not light enough; where neither talent nor wealth is of the slightest avail if the individual is stigmatized as quadroon or mulatto . . .; this nation, I say, in the midst of its liberty, its liberalism, its progress, must inspire terror in the breast of South Americans.[1]

He has no desire to inspect this land, and if any artist should have the bad taste to do his portrait, let it stand in the contract that his face is not to be exhibited in New York, although, to the best of his belief, he is no zambo or mulatto.[2]

These are fairly straightforward statements and have their interest for North Americans who would see themselves as others see them. In general, however, if you dip into the hundreds of pages of the "Treatises," the "Chapters," the "Moral Geometry," or the various polemical journals reprinted in book form thanks to the pious care of Gonzalo Zaldumbide, you will find not clear and bald ideas, but a prose as richly embroidered as that of Sir Thomas Browne, which will entice you ever farther into its labyrinthine charm, and will be as much its own excuse for being as any esthetic experience can be.

Manuel González Prada (1848–1918)

González Prada is a kindred spirit to Montalvo, although more serene than that tormented soul, and to Martí, although he is more negative and less the man of action. If we would place him in the stream of liberal Peruvian thinkers alone, he finds his predecessor in Francisco Vijil. This priest was born in Tacna in 1792 and died in Lima in 1875. González Prada on one occasion, in 1890, told his story, that of a liberal

---

[1] Montalvo, *Siete tratados* (Paris, 1912), I, 121.
[2] *Id.* at 124.

member of parliament who never rose to a position from which he could exercise any real control over the trends of his country, a Christian who favored the power of the state as against that of the church, a man fated to attack fanaticism in a land of fanatics, and fated to fail, partly because erudition and dignity are as insufficient as good intentions, and he was beyond a doubt a bore. González Prada deplores the fact that he had no successor to carry on the work, at the very moment when he was Vijil's and Montalvo's most brilliant successor.

González Prada stands out as Peru's most distinguished writer, although his qualities are most un-Peruvian, and his countrymen who preferred to be amused gave first place to Ricardo Palma, author of the many volumes of charming *Tradiciones*. No later figure can rival don Manuel. The elegant cosmopolites, Francisco and Ventura García Calderón have their enthusiastic admirers who think the mantle of Rodó has descended upon Francisco's shoulders and call him the Orienter, or "our advanced thinker," for the way in which he has mediated the intellectual atmosphere of France to Latin America, or promote Ventura out of all recognition by a comparison to Remy de Gourmont. González Prada was also at home in things European and there is more substance in him. But there is no reason why we should not say with cordial inclusiveness that all three were among the initiators of the new era in Peruvian literature.

The life of Manuel González Prada has been written by Luís Alberto Sánchez, and it is less like a campaign biography than most Latin-American biographies. Sánchez had previously chosen to eulogize González Prada when he presented himself for his doctorate at San Marcos — that can be done, whereas at least the pretense of impartiality is demanded of graduate students in North America. A faculty member did object that the object of the eulogy "had been a mediocre poet, a pompous prose writer, a man of questionable conduct, a failure in politics, an ideologist without an ideology, and in general an imitator." Undismayed, Sánchez continued to eulogize, and he still does. The data he presents will help us form an idea of González Prada.

He was born into a good old family; "born sincere," Ventura García Calderón puts it. Sincerity is perhaps a weak word for the character that soon showed its mettle when the boy threw ink at a teacher who struck him unfairly. No discipline found him very docile, and least of all discipline plus unfairness. Passing the years from seven to nine in Chile, Manuel was sent to the English school in Valparaíso, where his timid arrogance was a foretaste of the man to come, perhaps always a little insecure at heart. Here the boy dreamed of growing up "so that he would not have to say his prayers." The auguries for a successful adjustment in a Seminary were bad, but he was sent to one nevertheless, and told to stick it out when he begged to leave. That ended in running away. Somehow he did get his bachelor's degree, in 1862, which is early enough, even when one remembers that the *bachillerato* comes at the end of secondary school. Trying the law, he found that he hated it, and finally gave up the attempt to complete the course.

By this time he was alarming his aristocratic family by hiding its light under the democratic form Manuel G. Prada, and was writing the poetry that was always a consolation and the most intimate expression of his personality. Eight years of isolation on the family estate gave him opportunity for wide reading, and according to his biographer, hardened his character.

In the war with Chile, González Prada acted as an officer under the dictator Piérola, and seems to have done very well, but he got into trouble through his refusal to confess before going into battle.

It was only after the war that his leadership of groups began, with his presidency of a literary circle which discussed anything and everything. He began to make an impression as an orator, more through the boldness of his ideas and his irreverent treatment of the sacred cows than through voice or manner, which did not lend themselves to addressing large audiences. He was more apt to cite the forbidden Renan than to indulge in glorification of all that one is supposed to admire in the past; he defended this attitude by saying that if one is to leave his own time and its problems it should not be to disinter the dead but to prophesy the future. The liberty that he claimed in this respect is part of a general attitude that demands unlimited liberty in all things, and allies itself with anarchy. Mere political freedom did not satisfy him, if writers were to be bound to the language and literary forms of the Madrid purists, and if the substance of their thought was to be dictated by the Syllabus of Rome. It is easy to see how this literary group turned into the beginnings of a political party, and the social function of literature came more and more to the fore in its discussions.

In 1887 González Prada married Adriana de Vereuil. He was almost forty and had done nothing he had planned; she animated him to return to the struggle.

It was a struggle. The articles of this period are called "Propaganda and Attack"; the great speech shouts, "Old men to the tomb, young men to work!" The question that agitated him was, under present circumstances, what are the duties of a Peruvian writer? He answered his own question by attacks on the church which pained his sisters and mother, who typically remained devout Catholics, and by ventilating the Indian question, to which Montalvo had devoted scant attention. "We are accomplishing the miracle of killing in the Indian something that dies hard in man, I mean hope." In spite of the death of two children, which for some reason is supposed to bring people closer to God, González Prada attacked orthodox dogma in his "Death and Life."

In politics, he and his group stand for issues, rather than men, and are flatly opposed to the personal rule which has been so dominant in Latin-American politics.

The year 1891 brought a long-dreamed-of trip to Europe, with worshiping at the feet of Renan and Guyau. It was in October of this year that was born the son, Alfredo, who has continued for years the task of rescuing his father's work from oblivion in radical journals long since dead, and has published volume after volume of poems and polemical articles. The death of Renan was marked by a renewed attack on Peruvian clericalism, an appeal for the emancipation of education from clerical control, and a eulogy of the master who delighted while he taught. The eulogy sounds one note of criticism: Renan had the wings of an Ariel, but they were weighted down with the dust of libraries, and he was not the man of action he should have been. In Paris, González Prada published one of his best books, "Free Pages," rubbed shoulders with Verlaine in the crowd, and shortly afterwards went to that poet's funeral. From Paris, he eventually went on to Barcelona and to Madrid, where he knew the men who have gone down in literary history as the generation of '98. It was in the beginning of that year 1898 that he returned to Peru, via Bordeaux and Panama, and began once more those "Hours of Struggle" that constituted another of his best books.

An attempt to make a public speech on free thought led to government prohibition and student and worker support. An attempt at a radical journal, *Germinal*, taking the side of the people and attacking the clergy, led to its closing and the inauguration of a substitute, "The Independent." The article "Politics and Religion" argues, in the face of a president who personifies clericalism, that liberty and Catholicism

cannot exist side by side. Burned in effigy, attacked in the
pulpit, González Prada continued the fight in the renewed
Germinal, and moved closer to the working class, seeing in
their support the only hope. The social question occupied
him more and more, and the poet wrote an article against
poetry that is mere entertainment.

There was talk of Don Manuel for president in 1903, but
that honor was destined never to be his, and it may be that
he lacked the qualities for the office. He might have com-
promised his principles and received one of those diplomatic
posts with which Latin America rewards her literary men
and women; but though it was his only hope for returning to
Europe, he would not, and continued wedded to his propaganda. Putting his truth before everything, he incurred the
serious anger of his sister Isabel by a speech on "Women, the
Church's Slaves." In politics he continued to lash out at the
pseudo-democracy of Peruvian public life, and in literature
(in the preface to Chocano's poems) to insist that poetry be
judged by its social and political aims and results. Forsaking
his own social class, he proclaimed his discovery that the
proletariat would solve the social question in the only way
possible, by revolution; the wind of rebellion, which came
from solitary thinkers, as always, was beginning to stir the
masses. He was still weak as to program and much better at
anti-conservatism than at socialism. Not thinking freely
enough to refuse the label "free-thinker," he was an enthusiastic officer of a league of that most evangelical of sects,
presided over — believe it or not — by one Christian Dam.

There were several attempts to find a government position
which would provide for him and symbolize his rank as a
writer, but he was difficult. Refusal to head a boys' school
was motivated by the fact that he could not participate in a
régime that required the boys to go to confession and take
communion. What then would he take? Would he never co-

operate? He replied that he refused only posts for which he
did not have the qualifications or the requisite knowledge.
A library post was the obvious answer to that, and when in
1912 Ricardo Palma resigned from the National Library for
the third time, González Prada was offered the directorship
and accepted, only to find himself in difficulties with the intransigeant who thought he had sold his soul. Palma, although busybodies tried to stir up a quarrel, admitted that
Don Manuel was the only man fit to take his place. It was
not long until the coming of President Benavides meant the
loss of the post and a period of silence. González Prada was
appointed once more as librarian in February, 1916, and died
in July, 1918. By 1922 the People's Universities bearing his
name were founded, and the doctoral thesis that has been
mentioned was attacked and defended.

A little later the tendency seems to have been to make him
innocuous by official approval, although carefully without
the honor of a collected edition of his works, and to drive a
wedge between him and revolutionaries by insinuating that
his ideas were not theirs. Mariátegui had to come out with
a clear statement that there was something deathless, eternal
in the rebellious spirit of González Prada as well as something
contingent and temporary, that he represented revolution in
his time, in his way, we in our time, in our way; we can salute
his memory and be like him in protest.

Although it is true that the books of González Prada give the
impression, in the clever words of Ventura García Calderón,
"of miscellanies of an admirable writer whose chief books
have been lost," the ensemble constitutes a keen and mordant
analysis of a country handicapped by a colonial tradition, a
stratified society, and considerable exploitation by her own
politicians and foreign capital. González Prada is not profound either in his philosophy, his understanding of science,
his sociology or his economics or his psychology, but he is

civilized in the great tradition of Greece and of France. He judged what he saw about him in the light of that tradition, and it was not good. Just how bad it was he said in a style that he created as one forges a sword, and for the same purpose. If he is something less than sophisticated as judged by the standards of 1943, we must remember his environment and what he was trying to do in it. Blanco-Fombona, the Venezuelan literary Jack-of-all-trades, who is also a fighter, sums it up:

All that caste system, all that egoism of the few top people, all that submission of the lost Indian population, all that lack of foresight on the part of the governing group, all those civil wars, all that ignorance of the people, all that extravagance on the part of the master-class, all that literature in imitation of foreign models, all that religious fanaticism, the whole history of half a century of organized disorder, was about to culminate in the disastrous war. . . . Peru was certainly a country in a condition of disorganization like . . . the Argentina of Rosas and Facundo Quiroga, without a high political morality, without much willingness to make sacrifices for the sake of the country: a country burdened with Quechua blood and divided into castes; a fanatic, ignorant country whose leaders were behind the times, sensualistic and weak-willed.[3]

That Peru has changed, is changing, is largely due to the virile voice, the electric style, the social criticism, and the very real love of González Prada.

Anti-clericalism is something that North America knows very little about, for the happy reason that it knows very little about what causes it. And so some of González Prada's paragraphs will seem crude and sensational:

What the priest does to children is even more pernicious than what he does to women. . . . We see the effect of religious education all the time, we feel it constantly. All those perverse, crooked souls, all those dry, selfish hearts, all those men who with one hand

[3] Rufino Blanco-Fombona, *Grandes escritores de América, Siglo XIX* (Madrid, 1917), p. 294.

cross themselves while they stick the other in their neighbor's pocket, show plainly enough where they come from, they bear the stamp of religious education.[4]

The trouble . . . comes from religious doctrine. You can imagine a Protestantism that you can talk reasonably to; not a Catholicism without dogma and intolerance: the Catholic, if he cannot convince his adversary, suppresses him.[5]

With very rare exceptions, from time immemorial, priests have been the more determined oppressors of Humanity, especially of the underprivileged classes. In the past, they did nothing to abolish pauperism and improve the social condition of the masses; in the present it is the same old story. . . . They perpetuate the grossest superstitions and live petrified in an atmosphere of errors and lies. They constitute a force hostile to civilization. . . . They have no reason to exist.[6]

Catholicism in this country has not gone a step beyond idolatry. Properly speaking, we do not have religion, but only religious practices. From the depths of the peoples to the surface of the ruling class, we find no men animated by a spiritualized belief, but rabbles sunk in the grossest superstitions. . . . Our Catholicism is clericalism, worse still, it is rule by friars.[7]

In Peru there exist two great lies: the republic and Christianity. We talk about civil rights . . . and most Peruvians have no security in their freedom or their lives. We talk about Christian charity . . . and stand by consenting to the crucifixion of a race. Our Catholicism is an inferior paganism, without greatness in its philosophy or magnificence in its art; our form of government should be called an extension of the Conquest and the Viceroyalty.[8]

The question, rather than being pedagogical, is economic, social. . . . The Indian will be saved thanks to his own efforts.[9]

The physical decay of man inspires much less pity than his intellectual and moral poverty. . . . What mental hygiene can we

[4] González Prada, *Prosa menuda* (Buenos Aires, 1941), p. 20.
[5] *Id.* at 48.
[6] *Id.* at 81.
[7] *Id.* at 92.
[8] *Id.* at 156.
[9] González Prada, *Horas de lucha* (1902; 2d ed., Callao, 1924), pp. 337–338.

use if we desire to keep to the last a youthful spirit in our think-ing?[10]

The reader can turn to the prose of González Prada and find much more of the same kind of thing. It is easy to criti-cize, but does not much credit belong to a literary man who pinned his hopes on science, to an aristocrat who learned to look forward to the proletarian revolution, to the Spaniard of old family who gave the Indian first place among his coun-try's problems, to the poet who accepted economics?

José Carlos Mariátegui (1895–1930)

A more consistent, systematized, and if you like, more scientific radicalism is found in Mariátegui, the mestizo lad who in his short life took Peru farther on the road to Moscow than anyone else. He did not only arraign the evils of his country; he knew, or thought he knew, their causes and their cure; he was, or thought he was, the doctor to a sick society, a doctor who expects no miracles, indulges in no sentimental-ity, but does everything that science can do. Like a physician with a pet remedy, he attempted to cure nearly everything with economics; but, after all, it is a good drug and many believe in its efficacy. Student and intellectual, Mariátegui is the theoretician of a movement and the analyst of a con-dition, whereas his better-known friend (until they drifted apart), Haya de la Torre, lays little claim to being a writer and thinks of himself as a man of action, achieving his results through organization and speech.

It is not necessary to belittle González Prada, as Mariá-tegui's biographer Bazán does, belaboring the matter of his sentimentality, his romanticism, his political incapacity, in order to bring out the difference of Mariátegui.

A poor boy, José Carlos knew what it was to eat too little

---

[10] González Prada, *Nuevas paginas libres* (1931), pp. 112–113.

and to wear clothes he was ashamed of; and he had to go to work at twelve, in a printing shop where he soon had an accident to his right knee that brought him lifelong suffering.

For Mariátegui reading was an escape, an intoxication; it was apparently an escape in depth, for he wanted knowledge rather than daydreams. Bazán claims that at sixteen he was making corrections in the manuscripts sent in by famous authors, and that eventually his mental equipment was one of the best of his time. The next step was writing. By the time he was eighteen he had attracted favorable attention, had been taken up by Valdelomar, was petted and spoiled. An experience with the army brought him back to earth; he did a sort of *New Yorker* profile on the army officers and got beaten for it. But life went on agreeably after the incident. He played around with theater people and newspaper men and took part in the famous scandal of the Russian ballet dancer who exhibited her art to a small group in the cemetery, as the most fitting setting for Chopin's Funeral March. He knew congressmen, and covered the legislative sessions as well as the horse races. Valdelomar's influence on him was literary, D'Annunzian; on his left, however, was César Falcón, a journalist of advanced ideas, anxious for a link between intellectuals and workingmen, coöperating with radical students in protests against the medievalism of the university and its control by a few rich families.

These activities seem a strange way of leading up to a government grant which enabled the two young men, Mariátegui and César Falcón, to go to Europe to study, but the fact is that their ability was thus recognized, and that their acceptance of support from the Leguia government was criticized as abandonment of principle. No such abandonment appeared in Mariátegui's behavior after his return from Europe.

The trip took young Mariátegui through the Panama Canal, and the experience impressed him tremendously.

Here man and the machine were fused in something of breathtaking magnitude. Judging by this, he concluded that "the people, product of Quakers and rebels, smugglers and Nordic exiles, has carried the capitalist system to its highest point. . . . They will have their period of world leadership."[11] In comparison, England was decadent.

The few days in New York waiting for a boat, on the other hand, appear to have meant little. Mariátegui was handicapped by lack of English, and was trying hard to learn some French. Arriving in the Latin Quarter in 1920, he was just in time to suffer the influence of Barbusse and the Clarté group.

Up to this time, he came to feel, he had been only an intellectual, and like intellectuals highly individualistic, unamenable to discipline, to following a program. Now he became firmly convinced that no decent person could remain outside the revolutionary movement, and he added the cause to his intellectual interests. Eagerly, he studied "sociology," tramped the museums of Italy, followed Italian politics of the hectic days before facism, set up a communist cell of four members, as well as housekeeping with his Anita, in a little isolated house on the campagna. "Up to this time," he said, "Marxism had been for me a rather confused, boring theory, and one that lacked warmth; but in those days I saw the light, I had a revelation." [12]

After six months of museums, the German language, and the sanguine expectation that Germany would soon be a second Soviet Republic, Mariátegui returned to America. He returned rich with four years' experiences and study, to find that America too had changed. There were new things in the poetry of Gabriela Mistral and Juana de Ibarbourou; labor was in ferment, and the universities had fought for

[11] Armando Bazán, *José Carlos Mariátegui* (Santiago, 1939).
    Id. at 79.

their reform movement; Vasconcelos and Palacios were great leaders of youth; Haya de la Torre was emerging as a noble, devoted character with a promising program, and there were others who had drunk the heady wine of Ingenieros and Prada, as well as Tolstoy and Victor Hugo.

In this ferment, Mariátegui began to play an important part with endless speeches and articles which, apparently harmless, never stopped sowing the seed of political and economic change. His activity was interrupted by the amputation of the leg injured years before, and Luis Alberto Sanchez came forward to lead a movement of sympathy and to provide material for his convalescence.

In 1925, Mariátegui published his first book, a collection of papers called "The Contemporary Scene." Contemporary happenings fall into their place in the historic scheme of things which the Marxist always has ready. "The United States with its imperialistic attitude is just accomplishing its historic mission. Imperialism, as Lenin said . . . is the final stage of capitalism. The United States, rather than being a great democracy, is a great empire." [13] It is all according to prophecy, so let it go on.

The book contains analyses of fascism and democracy, portraits of leading personalities. Like the "Defense of Marxism" which followed, it reveals a keen intelligence which follows trends all over the world. Or rather, all over the world, except in Hispanic America. After the publication of this book, Mariátegui founded his journal *Amauta*, applied his new method of analysis and knowledge to the problems of his own country, and became the first — perhaps the best — of those who have made this application of Marxism.

The year 1928 saw the publication of certain papers from *Amauta*, under the title "Seven Essays Interpreting the Realities of Peruvian Life." Mariátegui does not depart

[13] Mariátegui, *La escena contemporanea* (Lima, 1925), p. 102.

from the usual pattern of Latin-American thought in one respect; he goes back to the Incas and the conquest. Indeed, his revolutionary thought turns out to be in a way reactionary, for he seems to tell us that the conquest interrupted a state of affairs, or an evolution, to which we must return. To turn back the clock four hundred years is odd doctrine for Marxism, and more careful students of Inca government and economics would question Mariátegui's interpretation — accuse him of wishful thinking and sentimentalizing. He claims that the problem of the Indian, when people have thought of it at all, has been considered as an ethical one; but we must be concrete and see it in economic, social, and political terms. You cannot propose an education for the Indian which runs counter to the economic interests of the dominant class, for education only reflects class structure. Change that first. "We are a people in which there live together, without assimilation, without mutual understanding, aborigines and conquistadores." [14] It is the living together, as a cultural problem — one of customs, sentiments, myths, spiritual elements, residues and derivations in Pareto's sense — that is important; race is a fiction; the question is not one of skin color, but of psychology.

Again and again in this meaty and well-thought-out book, Mariátegui comes back to the economic question, although he handles literature, religion, and education also in a mature and realistic manner. The system of the *latifundio* acts as a deterrent to white immigration, which sees no future in it; it also plays directly into the hands of foreign capitalism, with Peruvian landholders standing in a feudal relationship to it, acting as its agents and tools. The Spanish inheritance was not only, as has been said *ad nauseam*, psychological and intellectual predispositions, but also an economic and social

[14] Mariátegui, quoted by Bazán, p. 120.

system, and that system has persisted to this day, in spite of
revolutions. It is not enough to explain the lack of economic
development in terms of religion; there was even more religion in New England, and it did not prevent the growth of
industry. Later, he admits, like Max Weber, that there is a
close relation between Protestantism and capitalism. South
American religious liberalism is too weak to play the same
role, and while South American countries cannot stop Protestant missions, their expansive force seems to have been
exhausted. The possibility of a religious atmosphere congenial to industrial development is therefore slight. It is the
necessity of getting intellectual support for the growth of industry which has led to the importation of North American
methods of education. Other writers have argued that
French Canada must change her methods of education if she
is to compete economically with English Canada; Mariátegui
merely says that the same motivation is at work in Latin
America, and that it is more a question of economics than of
pedagogy. In the case of the Indian, to emphasize education
is to put the cart before the horse; primary schools will not
save the Indian, morally or socially; the first step is to abolish
his state of servitude.

None of the factors that he has discussed — religious, educational, racial, spread of ideas through literature, or what
not — is likely to bring modern industry in any very short
time. Peru will necessarily continue to be a producer of raw
materials.

Something must be said of Mariátegui's relation to other
radical movements. In a footnote to the "Seven Essays" he
wrote: "After having finished this book, I found in Haya
Delatorre's (sic) book, 'Toward the Emancipation of Latin
America,' ideas that are in agreement with my own on the
agrarian question in general and on the Indian community

in particular. We start from the same point of view so that necessarily our conclusions must be the same." [15] But when APRA [16] was organized, Mariátegui demanded a clarification, as many have done since, from Haya de la Torre. The program of APRA was Latin-American, Mariátegui was decidedly international, and refused to exclude from coöperation the exploited classes of the imperialist countries themselves. Undoubtedly, temperamental differences contributed to the split between the two leaders, which took place in 1928. Before that Mariátegui had founded the Peruvian section of the Third International and had been imprisoned for a time.

Neither were Mariátegui's relations with the Third International always happy. He had insisted upon making an application of Marxism to the conditions of his own country, and in doing so had made the point that industry, and therefore an industrial proletariat, was not to be expected for a long time in sufficient force to perform the revolutionary function. The contradiction in Peruvian economic life and the struggle that must ensue is between an agrarian form of communism practiced by the indigenous inhabitants and liberal-individualistic economic principles as practiced by the white bourgeois landholders and their foreign superiors. He was revolutionary in wishing to eliminate exploitation and injustice, but until the end of his brief life did not satisfy the leaders of communism with his formula explaining privilege and exploitation as being due to the superposition of the Spanish colonial régime on a glorified, non-violent, communistic Inca régime. This was mere romantic nationalism, in

[15] Mariátegui, *Siete ensayos* (Lima, 1928), p. 60, note.

[16] The APRA Party (Alianza Popular Revolucionaria Americana) was formed when the old political parties practically disappeared from Peru as a result of the 1930 revolution. With branches in several Latin-American countries, it was composed of younger intellectual and middle-class followers, and formed the principal opposition to the Union Revólucionaria. In 1936 the National Electoral Board declared the APRA to be an "international organization," and denied to it the right to have candidates in the 1939 election.

spite of Mariátegui's statement that the best of European technique would have to be used to solve Peru's problems. He depended too exclusively upon the tradition of the Indian and his natural aspirations together with the collectivistic instinct of the Peruvian peasant, and did not understand the historic role of the proletariat, which he made into an unimportant appendage of his four million Indians. Thus, until the period when he saw the light and joined the Communist International, Mariátegui was no more advanced than the ideas of old-fashioned *petit bourgeois* "socialism." [17]

This is the interpretation of a critic who appears to speak with authority and express the party line. For those who do not follow that line, the question of Mariátegui's conformity to reality is more important than that of his acceptance of an official theory.

[17] V. Miroshevesky, "El populismo en el Perú," *Dialéctica*, vol. I, no. 1 (1942), pp. 41–59.

CHAPTER VII

Three Thinkers of Brazil

E VEN IF WE LIMIT our survey to thinkers of the republican
period, it seems hardly less than criminal to name only
three Brazilians. The intellectual and artistic world of the
Portuguese-speaking republic is so vast and so effervescent,
so various and so modern, that it deserves many books in
itself. It is at the same time less known to us, and even to
its Hispanic-American neighbors, than can be unblushingly
admitted. We have not found in any of the Hispanic-American lists of "continental men" and great "maestros" a
single mention of Brazilian writers. If the dial that measures
space given to Hispanic-American thinkers in our histories
of social and political and economic thought, and philosophy
as well, did not indicate zero, we should argue that Brazil
receives even less attention.

It is with regret that we pass over the attractive figures of
Joaquim Nabuco, finest flower of Brazilian civilization, abo-
litionist, admirable writer of prose and poetry, beloved diplo-
mat, and of Machado Assís, classic and Olympic artist,
gentle satirist, and perfect stylist. Ruy Barbosa (1849–
1923) cannot be dismissed with a sentence of eulogy. He was
a world in himself, and amazes his disciples, as loyal and
lyrical as those attracted by any South American thinker;
for them he was the greatest writer, the greatest orator, the
greatest linguist, and the greatest lawyer of his time.[1] Paren-
thetically, and just because one should never neglect mental

[1] Baptista Pereira, *Vultos e episodios do Brasil* (São Paulo, 1932), p. 8.

hygiene, it may be good for the sense of security of those who have spent weary and unproductive hours over foreign languages to consult the two printed speeches which the "greatest linguist" delivered in English; but it will bring them down a peg again to see the perfection with which he handled French in his address to Anatole France.

Ruy (for Brazilians love to use the first name, and disconcert the foreigner by arranging indexes with the first names in alphabetical order) was tirelessly active in politics. He had principles to guide his political activity; the key words are law and liberty, the category conservative liberalism. In his first speech, at the age of nineteen, he was already attacking unprincipled politics. "Politics . . . in our country . . . instead of being ennobled by its association with liberty, instead of identifying itself with public opinion, has almost always been a spiteful violation of our representative institutions, a systematic betrayal of the public conscience, a constant defiance hurled at the national sovereignty." [2]

England was always for Ruy the chief home of the law and liberty he adored. His father had taught him as a child to admire England, and not to be fooled by mere forms of government; England, a monarchy, could be the most democratic of governments. When he had a chance to see for himself and wrote his "Letters from England" he agreed. The United States, for which he later felt great friendship, exhibited inner hatreds, chronic evils, a spirit of restlessness and revolt. But England! No people so lives its religion. No people expects of its politicians such light, such spirit, such ideals. There politicians are statesmen. He seized upon the appearance of Balfour's *Foundations of Belief* as an important social fact, an example of what occurs habitually in England. When he thinks of his own country, he says, it is with discouragement. "We pass our lives boasting about an

[2] Barbosa, *Collectanea literaria, 1868–1922* (São Paulo), p. 27.

infinity of things that we do not have — credit, inexhaustible resources, republican institutions — while the whole fabric of our politics and our society leaks at all the joints. The foreigner smiles at our fatuity, has no faith in our so-called civilization, stigmatizes our character." [3] He adds that "our great evil, at present, is militarism." [4] The English rule is that of capacity, and he quotes the English phrase, the right man in the right place. The Brazilian seems to be the opposite and by hunting places for men rather than the man for the place, his country generally gets the wrong man.

An early phase of Ruy Barbosa's thought took him through a crude anti-Catholicism that turned out to be transitory, for he came back with "his soul sweetened" as Baptista Pereira puts it. The reputation of atheism clung to him, and he had to reject it in decided terms, pointing out that in maturity he had only fought Jesuitism with the word of Christ.[5] In reality, it is the lack of religious feeling in society that worries him. "All the influences of the present day seem bent on nothing else than destroying it, transforming liberty into disbelief, converting the legal neutrality of the State into support of atheism." [6] More generally, "the true crisis is the crisis of character, of conscience and of modesty, a moral, social, human crisis." [7]

In such utterances he may not have carried every one with him, but in politics his passion, his eloquence, the very exuberance and lack of moderation in his nature, made the spokesman of an era. His credo he once defined in these words:

I believe in omnipotent liberty, creator of healthy nations; I believe in law, which is derived from it, its chief organ, the first of its necessities; I believe that, in this régime, there are no other

[3] *Id.* at 285.   [4] *Id.* at 441.
[5] *Id.* at 428.
[6] Barbosa, *Ruinas de um goberno* (Rio de Janeiro, 1931), p. 76.
[7] *Id.* at 188.

sovereign powers, and that the sovereign is law interpreted by the courts; I believe that popular sovereignty needs limits, and that these limits are the constitutions created by the sovereign itself in its hours of highest inspiration, as a safeguard against the impulses of disorderly passion. . . . I reject absolute rule; I abominate dictatorships of all kinds, military or scientific, by crowned heads or by the masses.[8]

In international affairs, Ruy became the great and successful spokesman of small nations at the Hague, and the earnest advocate of an American federation modeled on the United States. "Law and liberty made North America. The United States are good examples of law and liberty; their superiority is based on them. In their liberty and their law South America can find models." No isolationist, he hoped the United States would enter European politics prepared to fight for its ideals, and that the nations of Latin America would cluster around in their enthusiasm for the ideal.[9] Another source of the arbitration which he thought would be the mark of the twentieth century was the Papacy, unrivaled and immeasurable in its power to help solve international and interclass problems, and he noted the prestige of the Papacy even in Protestant countries.[10]

Euclydes da Cunha (1868–1909)

It is curious that the book we in the United States are waiting for is the Great American Novel, rather than any other form of literature. Brazil waited for the Great Brazilian Book, and found it in da Cunha's masterpiece about the frontier country of the interior. The country is mirrored in a book that becomes scientific without ceasing to be literature, that is accurate and yet vivid, that captures the geography and the psychology of Brazil and explains both. *Os sertões*

[8] Barbosa, *Collectanea literaria*, p. 127.
[9] *Id.* at 290.   [10] *Id.* at 164.

immediately challenges comparison with Argentina's book, *Facundo*. Both begin with the land, and relate life to the land; both deal with the inevitable conflict that emerges between city and country; and both are unique and highly personal books, unclassifiable and almost untranslatable. But English readers will not accept that judgment when they read the excellent translation of Samuel Putnam.

Euclydes da Cunha was a traveler, engineer, and professor of logic, who wrote his chief works in quarter-hours stolen from work, sitting in a tiny "zinc" hut at the end of a bridge he was constructing. The hut has since been enclosed in a larger structure and made a kind of shrine by admirers of the author. Da Cunha wrote other books, and his letters have been published. In these books he deals with various problems and questions of Brazilian life; he is the clear-headed, ironical, rather melancholy journalist, but hardly the thinker or sage. He finds South American union a very beautiful ideal, but absolutely impractical. He would like to see Brazilian statesmen cultivate some of the strenuous virtues of Theodore Roosevelt's Ideal American, although it is an ideal that has scant attraction for him personally. But whatever the statesmen do, the course of history will be the same; social Darwinism decrees that strong nations will expand along the lines of least resistance, and that weak ones cannot stop them.[11]

An enemy's revolver ended the life of da Cunha at a comparatively early age. Strangely enough, his two sons were also shot.

Let us follow da Cunha into the *sertão* of Canudos, if not into all the distressing details of the minor military campaign that resulted in the total extermination of the rebels of that region. Canudos is an epitome of the *sertões* of the north, exhibiting on a reduced scale their characteristics, chief

[11] Da Cunha, *Contrastes e confrontos* (Porto, 1923), p. 221.

among them repeated droughts. These dread phenomena seem never to have allowed man a respite of more than thirty-two years.[12]

Because of these droughts, this region constitutes a geographic category which Hegel did not see fit to describe in his three-fold division of geographic setting for human life. At different times of year it seems to belong to different categories, passing from complete sterility to marvelous exuberance. The change from desert to fertile valley — vast ownerless orchard — challenges da Cunha's descriptive powers and luxuriant vocabulary.[13]

"The martyrdom of man here is a part of a greater, more extensive torture, that embraces a whole life economy. It is born of the age-old martyrdom of the earth." [14]

Turning from nature to man, da Cunha considers in a state of chemical purity the three constituent races of Brazil. The very word, purity, reveals him as a man of his age, holding theories of race that have been criticized out of lecture halls and off the printed page wherever science is free. He is aware of the fact that history has played tricks with his abstract, mathematical crossings of races, and that the result is complex.[15] "The truth is, there are many ethnic types. We do not have racial unity. Perhaps we never shall have it." If we are to form a new race in some distant future, he says, a peaceful social evolution must provide the setting in which the slow biological process can work. "We are condemned to civilization. Either we progress or disappear. The affirmative is sure." [16]

Society has turned out differently in the northern and southern frontier regions; with the same colonizing elements, different results occurred where nature strengthened and

[12] Da Cunha, *Os sertões* (1902), ed. cited, 1940, pp. 32–33.
[13] *Id.* at 50–51.
[14] *Id.* at 61.
[15] *Id.* at 68.   [16] *Id.* at 70

vitalized, and where she enervated.[17] All through the seventeenth century we find the men of the South energetically spreading through the whole country as *bandeirantes*. The northern colonist met unfavorable natural conditions, lost his *élan*, and became practically a different sub-race.[18] Isolation and mixture with the conquered native peoples is the subsequent story of a wild, rude society, in which life was a school of courage.[19] Because of isolation from the coast, race mixture had here different results. "The fusion was accomplished in circumstances more favorable to the inferior elements. The dominant ethnic factor while transmitting to them civilizing tendencies, did not impose civilization upon them." [20] The whole society remains in close contact with nature, dependent upon her and drawing strength from her. The man of this region "is a retrograde; he is not a degenerate. . . . Although his psychic development lags, he has now the guarantee of a strong, well-built physical type." [21]

There follows a magnificent anthology piece on the frontiersman, "who is above all a strong fellow" — not like the neurasthenic mestizos of the coast. From his appearance you do not expect this strength, for he has not the carriage or the grace of the athlete, and he seems permanently tired. But that is only the appearance; put him in the circumstances that test his skill and endurance, give him a horse he can ride, and this man whose childhood was a series of catastrophes, who hardly had a childhood, will show you that his whole life was a preparation for struggle. "He reflects the nature about him. . . . He is inconstant as it is. It is natural that he should be. To live is to adapt oneself. Nature molded him to her image: barbarous, impetuous, abrupt." The landowner, who lives far away on the coast, has reason to trust

---

[17] *Id.* at 82.
[18] *Id.* at 85.
[19] *Id.* at 99.

[20] *Id.* at 111.
[21] *Id.* at 112.

these men: "He knows their matchless fidelity, and does not check up on them. At the most, he knows their names." They carry out their part of the bargain, report accurately on the number of cattle, take only what they are entitled to.

What does the drought do to such a man? He smells it from afar. "It does not frighten him. It matches his own tormented life, is its tremendous back-drop. He stands up to it, stoically. In spite of the sad experience of an endless series of terrible episodes, he cherishes through the anguish the hope of possible resistance." But if there is no sign of rain by St. Joseph's day, March 19, he knows that all his hopes are down. The drought is inevitable.

"He faces inevitable fate and reacts." He is transfigured and his stature is heroic. All is in vain; finally he yields, resists no longer, flees the country. After months, the scourge has passed. He is homesick for his frontier region and returns. "He returns gaily, invigorated, singing; he has forgotten misfortune and comes back to find the same fleeting hours of impermanent pleasure, soon lost, the same long days of anguish that try men's souls."

"His religion is like himself, mixed. . . . It would not be far wrong to call it a hybridization of creeds." It contains the anthropomorphism of the Indian, the animism of the African, the emotion of the superior race as it was in the period of discovery and colonization. From the standpoint of that race, it is a clear case of atavism. These people are a prey to freak religious movements, to strange messiahs, ascetics whose fanatical followers they become, allowing themselves to go practically crazy.[22] When the crackpot religious leader has military ambitions, is an "undisciplined hero," the situation is ripe for one of those rebellions that the campaign of Canudos put down with such cruel finality in the years 1896 and 1897. The rebel leader in this case was

[22] *Id.* at 114–140.

Antonio Conselheiro, who was not just "a pathological case, for this figure of the little great man is explained by the rare circumstance that he epitomized in the most striking and suggestive way, all the delusions and superstitions which lie in our temperament." [23]

José do Manoel Bomfim (1868–1932)

The depth of Manoel Bomfim's interest in his country is attested by the long list of books in which he discussed her history and place in the world. He was also a physician and experimental psychologist, but it is the social and political thinker that will occupy us.

The scant or unfavorable attention that Latin America received from Europeans worried him. Like many others, he decided to examine the situation afresh and for himself. The results were at first most disheartening. Instead of making the rapid progress that they should because of their connection with Europe, these countries were in a condition which hardly gave them the right to be called civilized. (He wrote this at the beginning of the present century.) But he did not stop with the fact; its causes puzzled him, and he tried to relate them to a broader background of bio-social theory which included the idea that societies are organisms, and that they have their relations of parasitism and degeneration. Much of this is an old story, and not one listened to with much patience in these days. It need scarcely be repeated. The more original part of his work — at least in "Latin America," he repeated a good deal in subsequent books — comes when he applies the borrowed theories to South American realities.

The colonies of South America were born and lived under a régime of parasitism, the influences of which did not cease to affect them even after independence. Every aspect of

[23] *Id.* at 619.

their life — economic, political, social and moral — was
touched by the necessity of adaptation to exploitation by the
home country. The most immediate effect was economic,
and was destructive in the highest degree. It was impossible
to found a society with habits of peaceful work. Slavery
came with its special evils, not the least of which was that
working, producing, became associated with slave status, and
therefore vile and demeaning. Parasitism was made policy
by the prohibition of industry and of relations with the rest
of the outside world.

The bloodsucker technique in economic life led to evils in
political life, the more understandable when one remembered
the poor, or rather decadent organization of politics in the
mother country. Spain and Portugal could do no better for
their colonies than for themselves, and they actually did
worse. Favoritism on the one hand and oppression on the
other were the rule. Political employment was not service to
the country, but to a distant king or to the ideal of quick
wealth. The state existed exclusively to do ill, and performed
none of the functions for the public good which the modern
service state performs.

The social life that developed in the colony was characterized by "a heterogenous population, unstable, divided into
groups, possessed by internal hatred, from the first formed
into what were practically distinct castes." [24] As for morality, neither humanity nor chastity could long survive under
the conditions of colonial life. "Populations were born in
disunity; they grew, and hate grew with them. Life was one
long conflict, a confused conflict with episodes of violence
and barbarism, of bestial cruelty and stupid perversity. This
struggle began on the day when the first adventurer stepped
on American soil, and it is not over yet." [25] "A mixed, brut-

[24] Bomfim, *A America latina* (Rio, 1905), p. 149.
[25] *Id.* at 154.

ish population which is formed out of the dregs of all classes combines in itself all the vices and hatreds of the peoples who formed it by their mixture." [26]

Bomfim has no inconvenient doubts about the inheritance of the distinctive qualities of any social group, for social heredity is just psychological heredity writ large. He admits that because of the scant development to date of ethnographic psychology, we find it impossible to distinguish the part of behavior that is due to heredity in the group from the part that is due to education and imitation, and frankly gives up the attempt as far as South American peoples are concerned.

Certain it is that their education leaves much to be desired, and Bomfim adds his stone to the pile that critics have hurled at an education that is too purely bookish and produces men who are slaves of formulas, fetichists of the absolute.

No Brazilian can close his eyes to the problem of race mixture, and Bomfim involves himself also in a discussion of the traits of Indian, Negro, and white, and the results of their mixture. The first two had to curb their own impulses, pattern themselves on the master race (not through natural imitativeness and recognition of cultural superiority, but through force). "They lived at the service of the white, and governed themselves by the wishes and sentiments of the latter." Still they had some influence; certain traits of the Negro — his passivity, "unconditional submission, weakness of will, servile docility," whether innate or effects of the situation — have entered into Brazilian culture.[27] The Indian, on the other hand, was characterized by "a violent love of liberty, truly remarkable physical courage, and great intellectual, or I would even say spiritual instability." [28] His

[26] *Id.* at 155.
[27] *Id.* at 271.
[28] *Id.* at 272.

love of liberty is organic rather than founded on tradition or personal dignity, and his courage is based on indifference to pain or death, a kind of fierce obstinacy or impassivity.

Bomfim is chiefly interested, however, in the question as to whether these races have any capacity for progress, whether they can be bearers of civilization. The assumption that they have not or cannot is pure ethnocentrism or pooled egoism masquerading as science.[29] There are more rational explanations, from history and from technology, for the Spaniards' defeat of the Incas and Aztecs than the complacent conclusion that they were inferior races. On the positive side, Bomfim appeals to the development, progress, and culture of the American Negro, in spite of his disadvantageous position, as an eloquent proof of a real capacity for civilization in the case of the Negro.[30]

There is nothing in Latin-American history to demonstrate that mestizos have degenerated in character as compared with the qualities of the races that produced them. "The ✓ defects and virtues which they possess come from the inheritance that weighs upon them, from the education they have received, and from their adaptation to the conditions of life that were offered them."[31] They are accused of being cruel and perfidious, but Bomfim would hate to have anyone make the comparison with the whites on these counts, for the mestizos would appear saints. Are they rebellious to discipline? Possibly, but how do they get along in their remote, unpoliced societies, with so little crime?

Latin America, he concludes, is not doomed by its racial ✓ make-up to continue retarded. Let us have a serious, long-continued effort on the part of the classes that direct our societies to vanquish the influence of the past and adopt a policy the opposite of that which has been followed; let them

[29] *Id.* at 278.
[30] *Id.* at 303.   [31] *Id.* at 310.

seek the causes of social problems and eliminate them; let
them think in social rather than in narrowly political terms,
and raise the level of the population in health, in material
well-being, in ideals; let them give up the folly of making
free and prosperous nations out of stupid and ignorant
masses, and you will see, he argues, that Latin America can
proudly take her place in the world.[32]

With a loyal effort to carry out such a program as he has
advocated, it would no longer be necessary to look to the
United States for protection and guarantees of security
against European aggression. "Such protection is already
half conquest, and a people or nation can consider itself free
and sovereign only when it provides for its own security." [33]

The nations of Latin America cannot be dismissed as decadent, he holds, for they never enjoyed a more prosperous
state than now, never were more advanced or cultivated.
Rather the opposite is true: they have progressed, although
slowly, and nothing prevents their looking forward to continued progress.[34] They have the intelligence to understand,
admire, and adapt to their own needs the scientific and intellectual progress of the rest of the world, and they have the
social-mindedness to coöperate in ever wider unions. One
vital difference between biological and social parasitism is
that the latter is not irreparable; causes of decadence can be
recognized and combatted.[35] The present picture is black
enough, with no interest in work or beauty, no will to correct
the evils inherited from the past, but with education something can be done. So, like most wishful thinkers the world
over, he ends with an ode to education; let him make the
curriculum and he cares not who makes the laws or the songs.
He claims there is no mysticism in his attitude, but only a
recognition of the role education has already played in the

[32] *Id.* at 333–334.
[33] *Id.* at 342.
[34] *Id.* at 367.
[35] *Id.* at 378.

history of civilization. Utopianism there is, but it does not frighten him, for the only bad thing is to expect Utopias to bring themselves into being; "let us by all means be Utopians, and remember to work for our Utopias." [36]

In his later book, "Brazil in America" (Rio, 1909), "Bomfim returns to the same themes, again to combat hopelessness based on acceptance of racial inferiority. Mixture is an ineluctable fact, and Brazil cannot hope for purity of blood; from its earliest period it has not had that, and certainly today it cannot untangle its strains. It can hope, however, that a new racial type of relative stability will emerge from its mixture, and it can point to much progress achieved in the past century by its people, mixed though they are.

Gilberto Freyre (1900–   )

Among our contemporaries in Brazil there are many interesting figures: the esteemed Afrânio Peixoto; versatile Roquette Pinto; Oliveira Viana, author of the thoroughgoing "Southern Peoples of Brazil"; Carneiro Leão, rural sociologist; and Fernando de Azevedo, principally interested in educational sociology; the specialist on Negro matters, Arthur Ramos; the economist Simonsen, the brilliant critic Sérgio Milliet; Azevedo Amaral, apologist of the *Estado Novo*; and many others, without including those represented in an amazing flowering of the social novel in the 1930's. To toss off a book any morning before breakfast seems to be nothing to any of these men. Such men and their enormous production constitute a living disproof of the severe judgment of Nelson Werneck Sodré in his recent "Directions of Brazilian Thought": "The picture we get is one of an élite of literary men, with a leaning toward facile discussion, the cult of the word, rather than to the study of our own problems, the investigation of our own peculiarities. That is the

[36] *Id.* at 429.

source of the tendency, so pronounced among Brazilians, to have a superficial view of things, to be seduced by the spoken word, the well-constructed phrase. . . . The restriction of intellectual life to the coastal area, hand in hand with the exaggerated urbanization of Brazilian life, would naturally have the effect of putting this élite in closer contact with foreign centers of culture than with the reality of their own country." A century of such pernicious tendencies has made "deep wounds in the mentality of the nation, wounds from which we are only now beginning to recover." Brazil has been a prey to a pessimism which stood ready "to proclaim our own bankruptcy, our incapacity to carry out our mission in the world . . . an acceptance of all the teachings which humiliate and lower us in our own eyes, including the doctrine of racial inferiority." By reaction, nationalism was bound to arise, and that suddenly; on the intellectual side it was marked by a great curiosity about Brazil, veritable soundings into Brazilian peculiarities, and an attempt to explain them.[37]

Of this last tendency there is no better example than Gilberto Freyre. Of all the thinkers treated in this book, he is the only one educated in the United States. A graduate of Baylor University, he went on to Columbia, where he took a master's degree, studying with Boas and Giddings. Not only did Franz Boas' method in anthropology become a part of him, but he frequented the circles of Randolph Bourne and Van Wyck Brooks. Frequent visits to the United States in later years have kept Freyre thoroughly informed as to intellectual and social-science trends in this country, but without in the least denationalizing him. The center of his interest is always Brazil, its past and future, its culture and its race, its relation to the rest of the world. He is Brazilian,

---

[37] Nelson Werneck Sodré, *Orientações do pensamento brasileiro* (Rio, 1942), pp. 1–11.

too, in his desire to avoid such tags as "sociologist" and his preference for being called a writer, or possibly a social historian. Certainly no one would remark of a North American social scientist, as a friend does of Gilberto Freyre, that he is great not because of his science but because he writes so poetically. When he returned to Brazil in 1925, says José Lins do Rego, he began to talk "in his articles of subjects entirely new to Brazil, to mention people quite unknown to our literary folks, revealing to us a Joyce, a Meredith, the neo-Thomism of Maritain, the Brownings, Ganivet." [38] The curious juxtaposition is revealing to us.

When, after European travels and variegated journalistic and teaching experience, Freyre reworked the topic of his master's thesis into a full-length work at the suggestion of H. L. Mencken, he was mature enough to achieve at once a book that "was born a classic," and that aroused hot debate wherever coffee was drunk and ideas discussed. This solid volume, "Big House and Slave Quarters," combs little-used historical sources for materials to picture the life of the colonial patriarchal society under the plantation one-crop system. It is to be noted that this is the new history, with an emphasis, unusual for Latin America, on the family. The over-all view and the desire to generalize are not lacking, but Freyre believes that it is only by loving and careful study of the social institutions of a particular region that generalizations can be safely made.

The social history of the plantation manor house is the intimate history of practically everything Brazilian: of its domestic, conjugal life, under a polygamous and slave-holding régime; of the life of the child; of its Christianity reduced to a family religion and influenced by the superstitions of the slave quarters. The study of the intimate history of a people contains something of a Proustian introspection. . . . It is as if one were meeting oneself. . . .

[38] Freyre, *Região e tradição* (Rio, 1941), p. 15.

And one remembers things one never knew, but which were there inside.

It is in the plantation manor house that Brazilian character achieved its best expression down to our days: our social continuity is in its story. In this story the political and military part is minimized, and instead of the striking things it offers us, we are given the routine of life; but it is in routine that one can best feel the character of a people.[39]

The story of routine, in any case, is not boring when Freyre tells it, perhaps in part because of his emphasis upon the sexual.

To tell the story he uses inventories, wills, pastoral letters and relations, travel books which reveal the impact Brazil made upon the mind of the stranger, and material dug up in a thousand unlikely places; cook-books, etiquette books, folk-lore, novels, all aid him in picturing and interpreting the significant aspects of the formation of the Brazilian family.

Even a "new historian" must have some aspect of the social process that interests him more than others. In Freyre it is certainly not agriculture, economics, or intellectual history; these he has not dealt with to the satisfaction of all critics. The angle that attracts him is the problem of race mixture: is the mongrel character of his people that was pointed out to him on Brooklyn Bridge, as he passed a group of Brazilian sailors, something that dooms Brazil to an inferior place at the feast? He reacts to the suggestion by a glorification of certain qualities of the Indian and Negro, by finding in them a dynamism that is lacking in the European stock of his country, and by defending them against the charges commonly made. There is nothing commoner than the assumption in story or entire seriousness of a heightened sexuality in the Negro, the point of which is his more "animal" nature; there is also more than a suggestion of envy in the way

---

[39] Freyre, *Casa-grande e senzala* (Rio, 1933), p. xxii.

whites refer to it. But Freyre, instead of explaining such alleged facts biologically, that is racially, is modern enough to look for causes in a social situation. He analyzes the sadism of the slave-owner and its counterpart, the masochism of the slave:

As a result of the persistent action of this sadism, of the conqueror over the conquered, of the master over the slave, it appears to us the fact, naturally linked with the nature of our patriarchal economy, that woman has so often been in Brazil the helpless victim of the domination or abuse of man; a creature repressed sexually and socially, living under the all powerful domination of father or husband. But we must not forget either the sadism of the woman, when she is a great lady, exercised toward the slaves, especially the mulatto girls, and having its roots in jealousy or sexual envy. This sadism on the part of the master and corresponding masochism on the part of the slave have extended beyond the sphere of sexual and domestic life and have made themselves felt throughout our history in a broader area: social and political. We think we can find it in our political life where the dictatorial tendency has always found ready victims on which to exercise its sadistic qualities.[40]

The oscillation of Brazilian political life between the opposite poles of authority and order or liberty and democracy is the natural consequence of having lived through a régime of slavery and slave ownership. We still find a balance between these age-old, deep-rooted realities:

sadists and masochists, masters and slaves, educated and illiterate persons of a predominantly European culture and those whose culture is in large part African or American Indian. And not without certain advantages: the duality has not been at all harmful to a culture in process of formation, enriched on the one hand by the spontaneity, by the freshness of imagination and emotion of the great bulk of the people, and on the other hand, through the élite, with the science, technology, and advanced thought of Europe. Probably nowhere in the world is there proceeding so

[40] *Id.* at 54.

freely the meeting, intercommunication, and even harmonious fusion of diverse traditions, formerly at daggers' points, as in Brazil.[41]

Freyre does not claim perfect intercommunication between the two extremes of culture, but certainly progress has been made since the time when the difference exploded into that armed conflict in the region of Canudos which gave da Cunha his excuse for writing his great book. Brazil can congratulate itself on being the scene of such an adjustment of culture as has been very rare in the history of European colonization of the tropics in modern times. The primitive culture, whether American Indian or African, is not isolated in Brazil in the form of hard, dry, indigestible lumps in a social system that is predominantly European. It does not constitute a mere museum piece or ethnographic curiosity. It is not merely picturesque, but living and creative. The two races are not arrayed against each other as enemies as they are in all countries colonized by Anglo-Saxon protestants. The contact has been lubricated by very extensive race mixture, whether blessed by the Church or not.[42]

Even without race mixture, the profound influence of the Negro has made itself felt in Brazil. Every Brazilian, no matter how blonde, bears in his soul something of the Negro. "In the tenderness, in the tendency to mimicry, in a Catholicism in which our senses delight, in music, in our way of walking, in our speech, in the lullabies of little children, in everything that is the sincere and immediate expression of life, we find the unmistakable mark of the Negro influence." Freyre goes on to tell lovingly all that the white Brazilian owes to his black mammy, from whom he first heard ghost stories and animal stories, to the colored boy who was his first playmate, and the mulatto girl who made a man of him.[43]

This book has gone through several editions, but its author

[41] *Id.* at 55.   [42] *Id.* at 127.   [43] *Id.* at 197.

has not been content with its fame. In a book about "Mansions and Huts," Freyre described brilliantly the state of Brazilian society at the beginning of the nineteenth century, and then the shift of power from the rural aristocracy to the city. One society has broken down and a new one is in process of formation. Its leaders are young men with a university education and no interest in plantation life. Freyre's friend the outstanding novelist Lins do Rego had told the same story in his "Sugar Cane Cycle."

Freyre himself deals specifically with the sugar cane régime and its effect upon the life and landscape of the northeast of Brazil in his volume entitled "Northeast." The result of his North American studies appears in the first line, in which he calls it an attempt at an ecological study of the northeast of Brazil, or at least of the agrarian part of it.[44]

This agrarian Northeast was for a time the center of Brazilian civilization. It was a type of life based upon a single thought, large plantations and the slave system. It was a man's civilization, and in a way an aristocratic one. The sociologist urged to generalize appears in various contentions that what happened here happened also in other parts of America wherever European colonization established itself upon a basis of sugar. He is writing the history not only of his own land, but of all those cultures which live on a single crop, employ slave labor, and divide the land into huge estates.[45]

It is clear that the triumph of sugar in the far Northeast was favored by group circumstances and not by one alone: by the nearness of Europe as well as by the easy communication with Africa, source of slaves; by the quality of the European colonists . . . and also by the agricultural experience and relatively sedentary habit of life of the Negroes who were brought in.[46]

[44] Freyre, *Nordeste* (Rio, 1937), p. 9.
[45] *Id*. at 12.
[46] *Id*. at 26.

The very nature of the soil attracts his attention. If the history of Brazil was during the decisive period of its formation the history of sugar, this fact depended upon mud and clay and humus. Our essentially serious author yields to the temptation to make a pun with which nothing can be done in English. He has been accused of undue regionalism in his treatment of Brazilian history. In this case it is not regionalism (*bairriso*) but "mud-ism" (*barrismo*).[47]

It is not only this one physiographic factor that interests Freyre. The very closeness of this relation, the "furious" nature of the one-crop system, had in the end unfortunate results.

The monoculture of sugar cane in the Northeast ended by separating man from the very water of the rivers; separating him from the very animals, wild beasts that he despised or thought of only as enemies of the sugar cane, that he has to keep a distance from the mills, as he did the oxen also when they were not pulling carts. And let us not speak here of the enormous social distance which this system produced, as no other force can, between two groups of men — those who work in the sugar mill and those who live badly or in luxury on its product.

The natural web of life was broken and

with the destruction of the forest to make room for the sugar cane alone to grow on the black or red soil, the nature of the Northeast, its whole life, ceased to be an harmonious whole in its interdependence, and instead there developed relations of extreme or exaggerated subordination: of people to other people, of some plants to others, of some animals to others; of the whole world of vegetation to the lordly and all powerful sugar cane; of all the variety of human and animal life to the small group of white men — officially white — who were the lords of the sugar cane, of the rich land, of the beautiful women, of the race horses.[48]

This last type, the lord of the sugar plantation, came nearer to being an aristocrat than any other Brazilian. And it was

[47] *Id.* at 28–29.   [48] *Id.* at 68–69.

the one-crop system of sugar cane that made him. He is the product of a sedentary system, of endogamy, of regional specialization which affected even domestic architecture and diet, and of a restriction which limited sexual selection to the families of the manor houses.[49] At the other end of the social scale, the importation of Negroes into the Northeast did not follow esthetic or amorous criteria, but conformed almost absolutely to the requirements of sugar cane agriculture and industry.[50]

Freyre concludes that the civilization which took such an exaggerated form in the Northeast, especially in the neighborhood of its focal point, Pernambuco, with all its defects "gave to Brazil some of its greatest cultural values, today characteristically Brazilian. These values have fused with other cultures, have spread to other areas, have suffered dilution by other ways of living, but the mark of their origin is still visible to the naked eye." A civilization that was the most pathological, socially speaking, that Brazil had known, enriched that country with the most characteristic elements of its culture.[51]

The enthusiasms with which Freyre's books were greeted suffered a diminution when he published a biography of "A French Engineer in Brazil." Why should a social historian bother with Louis Vauthier, who left a diary covering the years of his stay in Brazil (1840–1846)? The answer is that Freyre is still on the track of social processes, in this case the impact of a more advanced culture, through one of its technicians, upon a less advanced South American country:

Less interested in the purely historic study of facts than in the historico-social and whenever possible sociological study of processes in attempting to bring to life the figure of Vauthier, and see what was its impact on a Brazilian environment, I have been try-

[49] *Id.* at 121.
[50] *Id.* at 169.   [51] *Id.* at 219–220.

ing to establish the characteristic influence of a clearly defined and advanced culture — in this case French culture of the early nineteenth century considered in its less grandiose and most matter-of-fact aspects — on an embryonic, and as it were green culture; the Brazilian of the same period.[52]

Vauthier himself had used the phrase "technical agents," and apparently had some insight into his cultural role in the Pernambuco of 1840. Certainly for us he represents a characteristic or typical case, and this book may be considered a sociological case study, the first of many, Freyre hopes. It teaches us the lesson that the French influence was in many respects a most beneficent one, a fact which no criticism of the excessive French influence in art, literature, and philosophy should be allowed to obscure.[53]

At the time, the activity of imported technicians caused rivalries, hard feelings, and even hatred. It was a shock to the traditions and routine of the region and came into conflict with vested economic interests. While preserving their enthusiasm for French culture, the inhabitants of the region exploded in resentment against the expansion of French commerce and technology.[54]

In the course of the study, Freyre examines minutely the data as to French books arriving in Pernambuco and the extent to which they were bought and read. There was perhaps a certain lag in the arrival of the latest thing, but the French influence through the printed page was undoubtedly great. The most enlightened Brazilians, desirous of promoting the material progress of their country, had been sufficiently impressed by French technological books as early as 1827 to begin calling for the importation of French engineers.[55]

[52] Freyre, *Um engenheiro frances no Brasil* (Rio, 1940), p. 9.
[53] *Id.* at 14–15.
[54] *Id.* at 37.
[55] *Id.* at 98.

Vauthier when he arrived analyzed the situation and concluded that the great problem of engineering and economics was that of means of communication. He pointed out that the enormous difficulties in the way of land transportation considerably increased the cost of goods, whether imported or exportable, and presented a tremendous obstacle to the development of the interior of the country and of agriculture.[56]

Criticized for his innovations, for the mere fact of being a foreigner, and because he worked for a government that was under attack, Vauthier continued a most active career which proves him to have been a man of imagination as well as a simple technician. If he found much ill to say of the country in his diary it can be forgiven him in view of his laborious investigations and the extensive improvements which he carried out or planned. His vision included the socialized use of the rivers of the territory both for agricultural and urban use, the conservation of the forests, and the whole question of land use. He was, in other words, a public-spirited man who did not forget human values. Means of communication meant for him not merely the transportation of goods but the diffusion of ideas. He was also a man of courage who fought for the administrative reforms which would make it possible to carry out the technical changes he proposed. He is for us a typical case of French science put to the service of one of the oldest provinces of Brazil and there encountering a resistance and an inertia that made the contact a little painful on both sides.

The relations of Brazil to Europe occupy Freyre in another book consisting of one lecture delivered in London and three in Portuguese universities. The title of this volume in its final form is "The World that the Portuguese Created." Speaking to Portuguese audiences, Freyre addressed himself to the problem of the adaptation of the Portuguese colonists

[56] *Id.* at 118.

to the conditions of life in America, and laid emphasis upon
the fact that the Portuguese was a special case, belonging as
he did to both Europe and Africa.

Again it is the social process that interests Freyre. "In
the last analysis an individual becomes Brazilian in the same
way or through the same process as he becomes Catholic . . .
under the pressure of the social on the individual." [57] He
has no doubt that this pressure will make good Brazilians
out of Italians, Poles, Hungarians, Jews, Japanese, Austri-
ans, Ukrainians, Spaniards, Syrians, and even Germans.
"We are the beginning of a vast plural culture," he says.[58]
He pauses, as we need not do, to explain the anthropologist's
definition of culture and then to point out that when he
speaks of a plurality of culture he does not intend to deny
the primacy of the original culture of the country, which was
predominantly Portuguese and Christian. As he sees it, that
culture has been modified by a race mixture which was not
unnatural to the Portuguese, since he had from a very remote period been in contact with colored peoples. Race
mixture took place for sentimental as well as purely physical
reasons.[59] Portuguese colonization was for this reason more
humane than that of other countries, and Freyre even finds
in it an element of ethical creativity, for it leads in the direction of democratization. There was even in this negation of
racial theory something that transcended national boundary.
The result is that the Brazilian is a natural enthusiast for
cultural or perhaps even political union. Many have viewed
the process of hybridization with alarm, but he finds that its
advantages are greater than its disadvantages, and that it
constitutes one of the major victories of man as creator.[60]
Brazil has had its purists in racial theory and those who have
resented the contamination of their culture, in its language

[57] Freyre, *O mundo que o portuguez criou* (Rio, 1940), pp. 33-34.
[58] *Id*. at 36.   [59] *Id*. at 44.   [60] *Id*. at 56.

or religion, by African and Indian influence, but Freyre is happy that their point of view has never been influential enough to prevent the rise in the social scale of the mestizo, which has nearly always taken place under the approving eye of the government. Himself a user of Brazilian as it is spoken, he resents the imputation that that language has moved in the direction of the primitive; on the contrary it has been enriched under the conditions of culture contact.[61]

It is precisely because of the importance of the Indian and the African contributions to Brazilian development that he insists upon the use of a methodology generally associated with studies of primitive peoples, namely that of social or cultural anthropology. The situation of our population even today, he says, approximates that of primitive peoples with practically no race history. To the excessively literary methods which have predominated in Brazil he opposes the new and more scientific methods of investigation which he learned from Boas and Herskovits, methods which involve field work and a mental flexibility unacceptable to the academic mind. He musters at length the names of those who are on his side, for he knows that they will have a hard fight to secure recognition. At the end is a goal worth fighting for, "for the truth exists: no kind of literature does more to separate nations one from another than political, military, dynastic history, with its often exaggerated insistence on the heroic or patriotic note; no branch of social science — at times extended into literature or social philosophy — does more to bring nations close together than social and cultural history." [62] An example would be the kind of comparative study of sugar cane civilization in Cuba and Brazil that he hopes to see made.[63]

Under the key words "Region and Tradition," Freyre

[61] *Id.* at 64.
[62] *Id.* at 92.
[63] *Id.* at 123-124.

assembled in 1941 scattered writings which give us the story of his intellectual life. They go back to a valedictory oration delivered at the age of seventeen. They are bound together by the conviction, as his friend Lins do Rego puts it, that "to be of one's own region, of one's corner of the earth, is to be more of a person, a living creature, closer to reality. One must belong to one's own house in order to belong more intensely to humanity." [64] It is necessary to say this kind of thing because the "traditionalistic regionalism" which has flourished in Recife since 1923 has had its troubles with the official modernism of the two greatest Brazilian cities, in spite of its agreement with that movement in its reaction against the conventions of the classical, the academic, and of linguistic purism.[65] The regional in his mind was never separated from the human, and the traditional was never meant to inhibit experimentation. It was looked at askance because it had its own roots, its own contact with Europe, and never asked a blessing of the master of modernism in Rio, Graça Aranha, whose disciples tried to make a Houston Stewart Chamberlain out of his confused and confusing thought. Regional studies have been historical, cultural, ecological, in opposition to the universal kind of sociology that amounted only to armchair philosophizing. Freyre feels that he approached his region after years of absence with a fresh understanding, and was able to see it both critically and with human sympathy. This explains the apparent contradiction of his traditionalism and his modernism, his romanticism and his realism. His withdrawal for a time, followed by return, constitutes really the optimum condition for sociological research.[66]

Those who attempt to break with the past and find purely verbal or legal embodiment for their ideals fail to appreciate

[64] Freyre, *Região e tradição* (Rio, 1941), p. 20.
[65] *Id.* at 26.   [66] *Id.* at 38.

the solid accomplishments of the past and the high qualities which were required to make even systems that were no longer approved of work and persist through the years. To be the owner of a sugar plantation meant "a superior tension of the will and also a constant direct action." [67] Thinking did not make things happen for the women of the house, either; they were real executives, wearing themselves out in ceaseless assumption of responsibility. He almost sheds a tear for the ruin that abolition brought to many plantation owners of the Northeast, as well as for the decline of regional architecture and cooking; imitation is the order of the day, when a noble and distinctive architecture had been achieved at the height of the sugar cane culture; even Recife does not offer a good regional meal any longer, and when that happens it is a sign that something is very wrong.[68]

An architecture of city planning the "solutions" of which depend upon denationalizing a people or destroying in them all their temperament, all the peculiarities of their character and their national tradition in order to strengthen them, is an unhuman technique, and not a science, much less a social art, which must if it is good social planning harmonize with the desires, tastes, attitudes, first of a group or a region, and only later — if, spontaneously, it finds it possible to expand — with the desires, tastes, and attitudes of the so-called universal whole.[69]

[67] *Id.* at 175.
[68] *Id.* at 210–211.
[69] *Id.* at 216.

CHAPTER VIII

The Cubans and Hostos

Félix Varela y Morales (1787–1853)
José Luz y Caballero (1800–1862)
José Antonio Saco y López (1797–1879)

IN ADDITION to the revered revolutionary leader José Martí, Cuba can point with pride to a number of distinguished thinkers and with pious care has studied them. The incorruptible Father Varela not only was the first modern teacher of philosophy in Cuba, apologizing in 1824 for finding himself under the necessity of attacking scholasticism, but is credited with having taught Cubans to think and having aroused them to the realities of their social situation. In the Cuba of his time these activities eventually led to difficulties, and Father Varela spent the last half of his life in the United States, editing his review *El Habanero* until 1826, and later, with Saco, *El Mensajero Semanal,* and becoming a well-known figure in liberal ecclesiastical circles. His inability to separate his religious principles from his respect for human freedom make him a memorable figure of colonial Cuba, and his mission to innovate bore fruit that he did not live to see.

With something less of revolutionary zeal, Luz has been attacked in some quarters as less than a true patriot. He was, in any case, a great educator and trainer of teachers. His successor in the chair of philosophy, the more versatile and influential Varona, had only high praise for his teaching.

Saco, too, is a figure around whom controversy has centered. Soto Paz, with some vehemence, lists the reasons for regarding his glorification as excessive, and calls him slave-

owner, anti-abolitionist, defeatist, and opponent of separation from the mother country; man without a country. With
more reason, his followers in the respected Economic Society
— which has always stood for realism, industry, and progress
— applaud his solid merits, his magnificent writing — less
rhetorical and better informed and documented than was
customary in his period — his sincerity, balance, powers as
an analyst and historian, his energy as a thinker and polem-
ist. Impossible to classify except by applying the elastic
term sociologist, Saco knew his country, thought through her
problems, looked into her future, and recorded her past. One
of his own statements, made in 1862, shows that he knew
himself, too, and reveals the reason for his curiously mixed
reputation. "I cannot reconcile myself to the political
maxim, all or nothing; instead, I am guided by its contrary,
if not all, then something at least." [1] He did want the best
for his people, but he knew the difficulties and was less sanguine of quick success than more enthusiastic but less informed thinkers. He wrote the history of slavery and desired
its abolition, but knew that abolition would bring problems,
and that the time had to be ripe. He chafed under Spanish
misrule, but thought an adjustment with Spain might be
made, and admitted that complete independence would be
difficult to achieve unaided and in view of the apathy of
many Cubans; so in a famous paper on annexation he held
the whip of possible annexation to the United States over
Spain's head. Not desiring incorporation in the American
republic, he still knew that it might become necessary and
was prepared to make the best of it. In the meantime, judi-
cious mention of the possibility might help secure a solution
more to his liking. Reform, but peaceably and within the
limits of proved possibility, is his aim. Such reasonableness,

[1] Fernando Ortiz, "Valoración cubana de Saco," *Revista de filosofía*, XXX (1929),
361.

in 1848 or any other year, is not calculated to rouse the wild enthusiasm of Latin Americans.

Enrique José Varona y Pera (1849–1933)

If Varona is not better known to us and to all of Latin America, it is for interesting reasons. Except in literary criticism, where his interest was catholic, he limited himself almost entirely to Cuban matters. His solutions for domestic problems were not always followed, however. Varona was so superior in his culture, so austere in his political morality, so much a man of balance and *mesure* that he perhaps missed the following and the political success we would wish for him. He rose to be vice-president of the Republic, was to an incomparable degree the teacher of his people, provided a rationale and a goal for their social and political course. To lead a people forward on the path of civilization one must be more than a specialist, and Varona multiplied himself and his activities to an astonishing degree, teaching, admonishing, and writing on a wide variety of subjects, and so prolifically that his bibliography swells to 1880 items. All of this makes him one of the highest specimens of the intellectual life of the island; but note the word, "specimen," and remember that Latin America does not use anything so colorless or inactive for its great heroes of the sword or pen.

Varona is credited with having introduced Positivism into Cuba, with being one of its great exemplars in the whole of Latin America. True enough, he did admire many things about Comtism; he did distrust metaphysics and believe that Latin America had suffered from excess of theology and "literature"; he did call for the development of the scientific spirit and for investigation. But although his thought was orderly, he was not seduced by systems, and was enough the independent thinker to reject parts of Comte's teaching and to follow other guides as well: Spencer, Schäffle, Lilienfeld, Ward, Giddings, Tarde, Durkheim. There is no question that the name of Positivist has stuck to him, however, and one reads between the lines that this fact is not unrelated to the bogging down of the project to publish his collected works at the end of the fourth volume.

For us, Varona refuses to be forcibly adjusted to the Procrustean bed of Positivism, or any other. No single label describes the man. No single sentence sums him up, unless it be one that Rodó wrote him: "You might be the Próspero of my book." Even within the realm of his philosophy alone we must distinguish two Varonas, two periods or modes of thought. In one aspect he is "academic, systematic, optimistic"; in the other "vital, fragmentary, organic, skeptical." [2] When we step over the boundaries of one discipline to attempt a summary of his whole evolution we find useful guidance in Entralgo's chronological scheme. In his first phase, say from 1879, he is liberal, positivistic, reminds us of Lastarria; after 1885, the influence of Spencer is dominant, and he is in all things the evolutionist and the psychologist, but more pessimistic than the English writer. Utilitarianism and economics attract him after 1899, and we conclude that he has been reading a good deal of John Stuart Mill. With the coming of the World War his pessimism and skepticism reach new depths, and it is the pacifist, the nihilist, the admirer of Montaigne and of Anatole France who speaks to us in aphorisms as bitter and disappointed as any we can find in Latin-American books.[3]

Such a summary helps us to picture Varona. The Cuban sociologist, Agramonte, contributes another, according to which the master emerges as anti-metaphysical, an evolutionist, an advocate of a philosophy based on science, a

[2] Varona, *Obras*, I (1936), p. 77.
[3] Elías Entralgo, *El ideario de Varona* (a lecture).

negator of religion who sees in it only a consolation, not a
system of truth; a sympathizer with Rousseau and with the
newer trends in education — empirical in his logic, physi-
ological and sensualist in his psychology; a relativist and in-
dividualist in ethics; in sociology one who has a clear and
penetrating vision of the social whole; a persistent doubter of
the possibility of history; in literary taste fundamentally
intellectual and romantic in spite of the polished classicism
of his form.[4]

Medardo Vitier adds to the picture a note on Varona's
tolerance, his remarkable ability to summarize the ideas of
others and present them sympathetically, his lifelong intellectual curiosity, which resulted in a vast and varied erudition, his sunny southern clarity, his love of the truth, even
when it led to frank heterodoxy.[5]

When one remembers that Varona's eloquence impressed
his hearers as overwhelming, and that as the presiding genius
of *La Revista cubana* he shaped its policies and spoke to the
mind and conscience of Cuba's élite, it is evident that we are
dealing with a figure of the first magnitude, one of the glories
of Hispanic American thought and writing.

In the *Homenaje* to Varona, unfortunately delayed in appearing until after his death, Vitier applauds the position
taken by Varona, eminently a man of the humanities and of
philosophy, toward the university. Cuban youth, he held,
should look less exclusively toward the university and more
toward industrial and mercantile life; he pled for natives of
the island to go into business and industry, to show more
ambition and exploit the resources of their land by hard
work and enterprises started and managed by Cubans. The
reaction against a purely literary education has started, but
the fruits of the reaction ripen slowly.[6] Asked to summarize

[4] Varona, *Obras*, I, 188.
[5] Medardo Vitier, *Varona, maestro de juventudes* (La Habana, 1937).
[6] *Homenaje a Enrique José Varona* (La Habana, 1935), pp. 65–66.

Varona's civic teaching, he stresses the demand for civic virtue and criticism of its lack; Cubans have too much tendency to appear publicly satisfied with their government, and to grumble in private. Another unfortunate trait is their love of ostentation and of living beyond their means, which is related to the desire to make profits quickly and by any means whatever — their preference of gambling to the painfully slow results of hard work.[7] Varona not only preached against such stumbling blocks on the road to national greatness; "his whole life was the incarnation of an attitude . . . toward the various problems of his country," [8] and he was the mentor and consultant of two generations.[9] Consultants, to be sure, do not speak with clarion voice, are not agitators or inciters to rebellion; Varona is apollonian, not dionysiac; he failed to communicate and to arouse, and so he is respected, but not popular — a potential Próspero, who for some reason failed to write the great works and lead the great movements; and he is more likely to lie in the cold hard bed of the "classic" than to lie in the hearts of men.

It is the "philosophy" that creeps into his brief articles on a thousand and one varied topics that is most likely to speak to our hearts. A few samples will not be amiss.

A lying press spreads the spirit of the lie. No other agency can do more harm to a people. I love liberty, above all because it teaches a man to be a man . . . to have a heart up to the level of his thinking, to be able always to call the good, good and the bad, bad. To deceive the people and give them the false for the true is worse than poisoning their bread and water; it infects the moral atmosphere in which they live.[10]

Nature is horrible in its indifference. . . . Every organism to live must destroy other organisms. This is the terrible law which we call the law of life, and which is really the law of death.[11]

[7] *Id.* at 70.
[8] *Id.* at 71.
[9] *Id.* at 523.
[10] Varona, *Obras*, vol. III: *Desde mi belvedere*, p. 48.   [11] *Id.* at 50.

These thoughts, like so much in Varona, are not new, but he has reworked them and made them his own, has felt them and desired others to feel them again.

He puts himself in the place of the obelisk, and imagines her reflections on history. "I have seen millions of men in thousands of years; I have seen changes in their clothes, their dwellings, their gestures, language, ideas. But never have I seen their appetites, their passions change." [12]

Looking at his country: "We are in need of popular education, but also of education all along the line. . . . We are, in fact, a pretty badly educated society. . . . Education does not come with precepts, but with examples. . . . What works upon men's conscience is action they see repeated and that they repeat. Especially action of those whom we esteem. . . ." [13]

Externals and internals concern him, as for instance the problem of the individualistic artist in an age when all is being socialized; he must reproduce in his work what he sees about him, even if it clashes with his own temperament.[14] "It is useless to change the form of institutions if men's hearts are not changed. Equality, before being written on the statute books, should be written on the heart." [15] The world needs badly more humanity and tolerance, and at one point he admits that they seem to be increasing in the cities of the United States; [16] at other times he indulges in a literary *tour de force* by writing the diaries of two visitors to New York who get quite contrary impressions,[17] and in his own person he criticized Americans at the St. Louis Exposition for amusing themselves with the spectacle of human unhappiness.[18] In his most discouraged moments he finds no

[12] *Id.* at 65.
[13] *Id.* at 82–83.
[14] *Id.* at 87–88.
[15] *Id.* at 127.
[16] *Id.* at 126.
[17] *Id.* at 194.
[18] *Id.* at 200.

diminution in human cruelty with the passing years:[19]
"Man must be tamed, and taught to feel pity for the ass
that bears his burdens, for the ox. . . ."[20] A meliorist, he
hopes for such improvements, but as a student of history he
doubts his own hopes. "To be sure, man is being humanized.
We still sacrifice animals because we need them for food,
just as we sacrifice criminals, because we don't need them
for anything. But we do it more secretly, in a cleaner way,
more quickly, and we hide the blood. . . . Bloodshed has not
stopped, but the sight of it. . . . Day by day in every way
we grow more sensitive to pain."[21] We cannot all sympa-
thize with everything. "There are some of us who sympa-
thize with men and human affairs; others feel pain or pleasure
wherever they discover life; and some experience as it were a
fellow feeling with the whole of existence."[22]

In a letter to Plutarch he seeks advice and asks a favor.
The making of great men has become a business in these
days; we turn them out in series. "We Cubans are few in
number, but we are all illustrious. Our history is not just
history, it is an epic. Nothing that we do is a mere fact, it is
a doughty deed, a fiery feat. Except for our stature, everything about us is great and admirable." Please, Mr. Plutarch,
can't you send us some mediocre men? They seem to be the
one article we are short of.[23]

The same writer who found human nature unchanging in
another article gloomily sets down his conclusion that "the
human obeys the inflexible law of change, as does the non-
human. All is transitory. . . . Nothing persists, not even
ideas. Beneath the same lying labels of words, my thoughts
are quite different from those of the men of yesteryear.
What I call justice, what I call right, what I call liberty, have

[19] *Id.* at 151.
[20] *Id.* at 154.
[21] *Id.* at 208–209.
[22] *Id.* at 159.
[23] *Id.* at 186–187.

only the name in common with what was so called by our ancestors. Not even in their passions are the men of different periods the same." [24]

He is disillusioned about men's love of truth. Writing to a French history professor who got into trouble by talking freely about Jeanne d'Arc, his irony is exquisite: "You seem to take as your starting point the idea that nothing is better for us than the truth, and that men are drawn by a natural inclination to pursue and possess the truth. In a professor of history that is perhaps a respectable delusion, but a very strange one. Everything you told your indignant students is the veriest common sense. But you must have had your head lost in the clouds to think you were authorized to say it." The myths men accept may be necessary; they are certainly as indestructible as the Jungfrau.[25]

It is so commonly maintained that we must not confuse lowly origin with present lack of validity, say in religion, that the forthrightly negative attitude of Varona has a certain originality. "Whether new or old, the manifestations of the religious spirit always contain, in reality, a considerable number of elements which bring us into contact with the most remote past, with the timorous infancy of humanity. Even in those that are most refined, most imbued with the spirit of rationalism, . . . there are formulas, rites, and ceremonies which correspond to primitive beliefs and to the primitive manner of interpreting man's relations to the universe. . . . And so we have the curious phenomenon that the higher parts of religious belief have been transformed, and it is possible to trace their evolution, while deep below a basis that corresponds to savagery persists, changeless through the ages." Through time and space, religions transmit the same basic state of mind. [26]

[24] *Id.* at 202–203.
[25] *Id.* at 205–206.
[26] *Id.* at 215–217.

Even in his comments on single figures, Varona manages to express his general ideas, examining them in the light of their social situation and the role they played in analyzing or transforming it. Thus he seeks the heart of Ibsenism in the environment, physical and social, in which Ibsen's moral attitude took shape. He shared with others the Lutheran concern for "the torturing enigmas of man's fate and of his attitude toward life." His genius was his own, unique; his fight "against routine, against hypocrisy and lies and the shame of spiritual compromise and weakness of character" is his lasting claim to glory.[27]

Varona's own predecessor Luz is another hero of reform, whose work is "apostolic" and splendid. Living in a society where indifference and egoism reigned, he dedicated his whole life to the task of raising, through education, the entire moral and intellectual level of Cuba. He saw clearly that in such a society culture in its highest form is important, "but will always flourish as an exotic plant and in constant danger of death if it does not have its roots in a broad program for the education of all, carefully thought out and intelligently directed. From that conviction flowed the great and ceaseless effort of Luz to train teachers for Cuba." [28]

To this day we must look to Cuba for the best book in Spanish on North American literature. Years ago Varona led the way by his "Survey of the Intellectual Movement in America," which answers an ignorant Spanish jibe by listing at length the accomplishments of Yankee science and literature, which he knew well, and in which through likeness of temperament he felt always remarkably at home.[29]

[27] *Id.* at 219–222.
[28] *Obras*, vol. II: *Estudios y conferencias*, pp. 189–194.
[29] *Id.* at 81–105.

José Martí: A Life

It is significant that even in the *Homenaje* to Varona about half of the pages are devoted to the man who in a spirit that was all flame and a life that was given single-heartedly to Cuba and to freedom summed up the most generous aspirations of his people. In spite of the forty-two volumes of his collected works, "the most extraordinary work which Martí left was not books, but his own life." [30]

José Martí (1853–1895) was born in Cuba, the son of immigrants from Spain. In Cuba he passed the first seventeen years of his life; to Cuba he dedicated all of that life, most of which was passed in other lands; and at the end on Cuban soil he gave his mortal life for independence; in Cuban hearts he is not dead, but "goes marching on."

Martí's parents were poor, but in spite of poverty he secured the beginnings of an excellent education under Mendive, who also inspired in the youth those liberty-loving ideals which soon got him into trouble. We find him condemned to military prison for his writing at seventeen, and then at the end of 1870 exiled. On the boat to Spain he delivered a scorching harangue on the cruelties of the prison he had just left, and ended his portrait of the butcher who was its director by pointing an accusing finger at him, for he happened to be a fellow traveler, and from that day a traveler ostracized by his ship companions.

In Spain he found friendship, understanding, and greater sympathy for the cause of liberty than the colonial administration had led him to expect. It was the love for Cuba among his Madrid associates that led him to undertake his burning tract on the Political Prison of Cuba, a story that won him immediate fame. With an insatiable desire for knowledge, he also triumphed over rules to enter the uni-

[30] *Pensamiento de América*, II: *Martí*, p. x.

versity with only three years of *liceo* training. In the universities of Madrid and Zaragoza he had a meteoric career, astonishing the jury and audience by the brilliance and originality of his treatment of the theme — drawn by lot, as the custom is in most Latin universities — of Roman forensic oratory with special reference to Cicero. A grade of "distinguished" was the natural result, and foreshadowed the career in which he was to prove unequaled. But his efforts were not merely academic; the eager attention and affection which he met fortified his faith in the freedom of Cuba and his belief that he was born to achieve it.

By way of Paris, Mexico, and New York he returned to Havana, four years after leaving it for exile. The situation had not improved; right-thinking elements were scattered, and there was a work of organization to be done. It had to be done, however, from outside the country, by articles, letters, and personal contact, and he settled for a time in Mexico, making his living as he might, but living for the ever-present end, the freedom of Cuba. Cuba was, indeed, only a step to something larger, for Martí dreamed a dream of America. This became clearer to him in Mexico, where the difference between Europe and America was driven home, and he became, like most of our thinkers, a thoroughly American figure. He was hurt by the imitation of decadent Europe which he saw in some quarters, and advocated the development of American art, and life, and thought, American types of government and economic institutions, and an education adapted to American needs. Out of these, he held, would come the new man who should dwell in these new lands. The vision that never left him took shape in these years, and he began to express it in a vibrant style that lifted Latin-American journalism to new heights.

With the triumph of Porfirio Díaz, Martí felt that his dream for America was postponed. His parents, who had come from Cuba to live with him and struggle along doing military tailoring, were shipped back to Cuba, and Martí himself turned to Guatemala, where he added teaching to writing. He had many things to teach to a land that needed instruction and inspiration, and the ideas for several books were fermenting in his brain. The ideas were ideas for doing things, too, "teaching much, destroying the concentration of power in the hands of the few, restoring to men their personalities which have been trampled under foot or ignored."

In 1878 there was another brief stay in Cuba, where he learned at first hand of the forces that prevent successful revolution, the apathy that retards it. He planned to overcome the causes of failure, correct past mistakes, and execute a coup which would be victorious before the Spanish could summon reinforcements. The wife whom he had married in Mexico in 1877 accompanied him, and their son was born in Cuba. The boarding house in which they lived was used by Spanish army officers; Martí chatted in friendly enough fashion with them, but without concealing his opinions. His revolutionary opinions inflamed his hearers in a series of public addresses, Varona speaking on the same program at least once and getting those impressions of the young patriot which later he molded into the best of all orations on the significance of Martí's political career. Deported once more on September 29, 1879, Martí left for Spain, to be followed by reproachful letters from his wife, who felt abandoned, asking why he cannot be as other men are, why he must always sacrifice personal relations to the cause. He, in turn, felt abandoned, meeting no more understanding of the imperatives that guided him.

Soon he was again in New York, where so many years of his life were passed. Those who imagine that cultural relations date from 1938 may do well to thumb the pages of some seventeen volumes that Martí wrote about the men and doings of the United States, from Congress to high-school commencements, the new books and art exhibits, and horse-racing and the trivia of everyday life. With universal curiosity and sensitivity he examined the life about him and described it to the readers of Latin-American periodicals for which he was a correspondent. It is unfortunate that of all he wrote one sentence primarily seems to stick in the minds of Latin Americans: "I know the monster, I have lived in its entrails." He was often sympathetic and well-informed, and his first impression was one of breathing the air of a free country where everyone was his own master and respected the equal rights of others. He determined to study the North American people, indeed thought he had done so in a month, and was not afraid to generalize.

For a time he lived in Caracas, where he found work as a teacher of French and French literature. Here he met Venezuela's grand old man and typical *pensador*, the respected and neglected Cecilio Acosta. Although Acosta was more the steadfast than the flamboyant type, Martí made a hero of him in the pages which now figure as an introduction to an anthology of Acosta's writings. Acosta had found a way of living under Guzmán Blanco; Martí, more impatient, could not restrain himself, and was summoned to the presence of the tyrant. The interview was stormy, and Martí saw that he had no other course than to leave the country.

Back in New York and Brooklyn he tried to pump enthusiasm into a Cuban colony profoundly discouraged by the failure of "the little war." He maintained his own convictions and hopes unshakably.

By this time his fame had spread through America. Sarmiento, in spite of certain differences of ideas, admired the torrent of his writing, but curiously seemed not too certain of his nationality: "A Cuban, I believe," were the words that accompanied his mention of Martí.

The febrile excitement of the "Apostle" grew in 1890 as it became apparent that the moment for striking in Cuba was approaching. But there were still years of pain, of anguished planning before on January 29, 1895, Martí gave the word for the uprising, then hastened to the Dominican Republic and from there to Cuba, to die on May 19 and become the Martí of legend and liturgy.

These are, in brief outline, the facts of his life. To one outside the tradition the bald recital hardly justifies the language that is used to express the adoration Cubans feel for Martí, and the reader must remind himself that it is unfair to tell even the story of Lear in brief, unadorned prose as Tolstoy did — that any life of man might be made to sound commonplace by telling the trains he took and the merely human episodes in a life that is more than human. If our word liturgy seems strangely strong, take for example the way in which Rodríguez-Embil refers to the mystery of Martí's conception, and adds, "Blessed be the parents of Martí." [31] The same writer apostrophizes Martí, evoking his immortal spirit, professing to put himself and his readers in the proper frame of mind to receive it.[32]

Called to a messiahship, Martí was more the man of action, less the man of science than Varona; there were no hesitations, no reserves, no qualifications in his affirmations and negations. But he was also an artist and an intellect fertile in ideas. Ideas were for him weapons in the fight for a better world, in which freedom for Cuba was the first step. To preach this gospel and to redeem America, this was his obsession and his mission.

The wealth of ideas in Martí is almost entirely related to this central theme; he had little patience with literature with-

[31] Luis Rodríguez-Embil, *José Martí, el santo de América* (La Habana, 1941), p. 12.
[32] *Id.* at 7.

out a social message. The characteristics of man and message have led to no little controversy among worshipers and students of Martí, who have called him now romantic, now the least romantic of leaders, have tried to claim him for Marxism, and have denied the similarity of his views to orthodox socialism or communism. These followers have used him to bolster their anti-United States emotions, and have found in him support for friendly collaboration with the northern republic.

While the imposition of system upon a body of thought that was not systematic would be an error, it seems possible to find a statement which will convey the essential attitude of Martí. He was a mystic, but a practical one; a utopian but at the same time a realist. He took up again the dreams of freedom and union that had been dreamed by Bolívar and inspired others with them. He hoped for a benevolent attitude on the part of the United States, and eventually for some kind of union in the whole Hemisphere, but never for a situation in which Latin America would be the vassal. The United States and Latin America represent two differing, and incomplete, conceptions of life; each can learn from the other. As they learn to know each other, each will come to understand and even to incorporate in its culture what the other has to offer. Martí would have welcomed the coöperation of the present moment, and would have rejoiced that it includes cultural elements as well as military and political. He distrusted the materialism of the United States and taught that rapid growth, when it is without firm spiritual foundations, is likely to be followed by rapid decline. For some eleven years, themes based on life in the United States occupied a major place in his writing, and his observations were often perspicacious and open-minded. Empty hatred had no place in them; it would not have been realistic, given the special situation of Cuba, and it would not have aided in the accomplishment of the great task. Cuba necessarily must seek cordial relations with its neighbor, but cordiality does not mean dependence, either economic or political, and it will be an empty cordiality until the heirs of the Puritans, racially intolerant, profiteers of the slave system, ignorant of the best of Latin America, learn to know and to respect the culture of the other American republics. A sincere and useful union is an ideal, but only under these conditions.

What Latin America has to learn is indicated by Martí's statement that he had never been surprised by what he saw in any country he had visited until he came to New York. Here he was amazed, and said goodbye forever to the idle life and "poetic inutility" of European countries. North America still showed that it owed its founding to men who had abjured feudalism and were seeking to establish a liberal way of life; Latin America too plainly revealed that it had been peopled by men who had no ideal beyond transplanting medieval customs and institutions to a new setting. After less than a month in the United States he understood all this, or thought he did.

On the question of his economic ideas, it behooves us to remember that Martí was no follower of another man's system, and that the keynote of his own thought was love, for love, he said, is the only force that builds, and the only ethical justification of force. What he took from other ideologists was assimilated and made to fit in with this principle and with the emotional, inspirational character of all his thought. When it is accepted that economics is a branch of ethics, Martí may be claimed as an economist, not before. If he urged a less bookish and more industrial and agricultural type of education, it was in his own special way, for teachers and county agents were to sow the seed of love and tenderness quite as much as they were to explain new fertilizers and cultivators. He did give a practical attention to forest conservation, the introduction wherever possible of modern industry, better salesmanship of the natural products which Latin America possesses in abundance. Mother earth, he held, in one way or another can of her bounty provide for the independence of the individual, and through him for the greatness of the nation, if we will work hard and avoid the suicidal folly of mono-culture. Laborers are needed in the vineyard, but let them bring their families and some skill and training, or they will prove enemies within the state.

Economics was important to him because without economic justice there can be no liberty for all. The sure road to colonial status is to permit oneself to be seller rather than buyer, and seller to a single customer.

Martí's economic program had a few simple planks: the division of the land, the education of the Indian, the opening of means of communication, dropping useless literary education on the elementary level and substituting a scientific type of training — then sitting back and watching the nation grow.

These practical suggestions have received less attention in the myriad lyrical meditations on Martí than the high-sounding phrases that sing and shout his final goals — liberty, happiness, justice, or the anti-imperialistic patriotism which made him insist that it was better to sink or swim by one's own efforts than to contract a debt of gratitude to a powerful neighbor, and the criticisms he pointed at that neighbor for its failure to solve its own problems of unity and well-being.

Whether his own solutions are not sometimes ingenuous or verbal is a question. It is all very well to agree with the finding of the anthropologists that there are no races and never have been, but to jump from that assertion to the conclusion that there can be no such thing as race hatred seems an exercise in logic rather than in social observation. To solve the population problem with the line, "There are no contradictions in nature; the earth will know how to feed all the men it creates," seems a bit less than adequate.[33] It is perhaps unfair to judge him by single utterances; it is certainly unfair to forget that he grew and changed his ideas, was more individualistic, more the lover of beautifully linked sounds in his romantic and idealistic youth; more scientific, more materialistic, more revolutionary in his attitudes toward capitalism and imperialism and religion, more the tactician of an historic movement in the years after 1887. In the earlier period his reading, and to some extent his friendships, revealed the sentimental and romantic tendency. Later, in North America, we find him supplementing the pomp and circumstance of Victor Hugo with the writings of Spencer and Darwin, Marx and Henry George. He never became the disciple, and never ceased to emphasize spiritual factors in a way that to say the least is not predominant in Marx. He does epitomize the progress of Latin-American thought from enthusiasm for the ideals of the French Revolution, the rights of man, to the ideals of socialism, which he understood to mean an emphasis upon man's duties. His life was given in the struggle for political liberty, but he would believe he had failed utterly if salvation from one tyranny ended in our being delivered over to another, that of a class which exploits those below it in the social order. Only so close does he come to being a precursor of Lenin.

Eugenio Maria de Hostos y Bonilla (1839–1903)

Latin-American countries have a laudable custom of organizing commissions, sometimes with the excuse of an anniversary, and doing homage impressively to the great writers who are the glory of their people. The works of the great man are collected, rescued from the oblivion of being out of

[33] Martí, *Obras*, XXIII, 59.

print that is so frequent in these countries, and given condign publication by decree of the government. Bibliographies, critical introductions, funeral orations, and a chronology of the events of the celebration complete the picture. To such proceedings we owe the many handsome volumes of our thinkers, the most recent of which are the sets of Hostos and of Martí, which facilitate the task of the student enormously. Some contemporaries, one can guess, are predestined to the same glorification; some great figures of the past still lack this consecration, and outcries at the injustice of it all are raised by the faithful and enthusiastic, as in the case of Manuel González Prada.

Rescue was needed for Eugenio María de Hostos. While there have been few men of his stature in Latin America, he has missed wide acclaim. A much more systematic thinker than Sarmiento, more deserving of the title sociologist, he was also much more of an introvert, with less of the inborn talent for being his own publicity man. The consequence is that Hostos and his works have suffered a neglect that it is difficult to justify. Even on the ground of political activity, Hostos is notable; in time he learned to discipline the rebellion that was in him, but he continued to fight for freedom, and in its behalf made so great an Odyssey through Latin America that it was only natural that the first locomotive to cross the Andes should be given his name.

Born in Puerto Rico, Hostos belongs to America, but especially to the Dominican Republic, where during ten years he labored to reform the educational system, and to Chile, where he was a university professor. Cuba, strangely enough, he never visited, although he once was wrecked on the way there. His secondary and university education in law he acquired in Spain, and somehow there he learned the devotion to humanitarianism, education, liberty, and reason which marks his life and all that he wrote. Liberty for his

beloved island was the goal that sent him on his four-years'
trip through South America in 1869, and that years later
took him to Washington to plead with President McKinley.
The method of reason, the faith in education, and the love of
his fellow man which no one can help mentioning when he
describes Hostos, permeate even the most schematic of his
work. That his writing can be not only grave and severe but
also brilliant is illustrated by his prize-winning "In the Exposition," in which he draws the lessons from Chile's exposition commemorating the winning of independence and
demonstrating subsequent progress. The transformation of
the country in every respect is his theme, and his masterly
handling of it established him as a writer and as a sociologist.
He yielded to the temptation to look into the future, as sociologists often do, but with better luck than most of them
have. Thus, to take another instance, he predicted revolution in Russia, and great distress in Puerto Rico if his program were not adopted. The revolution came fourteen years
after his death; the distress is with us to this day.

Although Hostos settled down to the teaching of sociology
and law, his life refuses to be told in terms of courses, for always he was, and in many ways, a "benefactor of America,"
a living proof of the fact that one may be a professor and still
have a great deal of talent. He taught by his life and through
the periodical outpourings of the press, for like most of our
pensadores he was a journalist of the kind that is not for hire,
but uses journalism as an instrument for the uplift of a
people.

Uplift would seem to be the keynote of an early work, a
kind of novel in the form of a diary, "The Pilgrimage of
Bayoán." Hostos introduced it with these words: "This
book, more than a book, is a desire; more than a desire, an
intention; more than an intention, a thirst. Thirst for justice
and truth; intention to prove that there is another happiness

greater than that men seek: desire that the example bear
fruit." He addressed it only to "pilgrims"; let no others
read it, he says, and let no one merely turn its pages, which
is profanation. Pilgrims through life will find that it strengthens their courage and teaches that the very lack of happiness
in their lives is something they would not willingly exchange
for the "useless happiness of the happy." [34] Dreaming and
thinking of America, of "our islands," Cuba and Puerto
Rico, is the ceaseless occupation of the characters, and the
book ends with an embarkation for America.[35]

Nine years later we find him explaining to the Chileans the
simple facts of the geography of the West Indies, with Cuba
and Puerto Rico "queens" among them, natural paradises
converted by Spain into hells, their native sons treated as
foreigners while Spaniards monopolized the best of everything. A new day, he insisted, was dawning; Cuba was poor,
but heroic, ready to die if need be, but determined that the
tyrants should go.[36]

Once free, he explained to readers of Spanish in New York,
the West Indies could do their part to carry out the four
great positive progressive steps which modern history reveals. These began with the discovery of America, which
"was the most resounding demonstration in the whole life of
mankind of the superiority of science over ignorance," as
well as the chief cause of that intellectual revolution which
brought with it the growth of modern science. History will
some day see a second great step in colonization, which
marked a break in the age-long struggle of races for national
superiority and substituted "the coöperation of all races in
the work of civilization." Not all the colonizing nations, to
be sure, recognized in the New World a new environment for

[34] Hostos, "La pelegrinación de Bayoán," *Obras*, VIII, 33.
[35] *Id.* at 286.
[36] Hostos, "Temas cubanas," *Obras*, IX, 176.

something new in the moral and intellectual order; the contrast between North and South America is so striking that it will lead to an intellectual awakening, and out of it will come "a new moral and intellectual world which with the native virtues of the Latin race will perhaps combine those that make of the Anglo-Saxon the part of humanity that is most useful to civilization." The fourth step is also in the future: the transition from irrational to rational government of society. For any part of the New World to remain unfree is to handicap fatally the forward movement that Hostos finds so natural and desirable.[37]

In spite of its desirability, Hostos recognized obstacles, chief among them the nature of society in Puerto Rico and Cuba, made up as it was of suffering Negro slaves, of white slaves who managed to make a good thing out of their slavery, of a greedy "dominant minority" that exploited them to retire satiated. Where were the right mental and moral conditions for directing the work of reconstruction to be found? He answered that the very struggle for freedom would create them, for struggle purifies and makes virile; but they would be produced even more by education, "educating reason in accordance with a system of education that is common, universal, and includes women and children, the freedman and the free, the rich and the poor, an education that will include enough acquaintance with scientific method to free the mind from fanaticism; an education of the conscience in the unlimited practice of all the liberties which affirm and strengthen human personality; an education of the spirit of nationalism through laws which will immediately prove favorable to economic reconstruction through work," through commerce and industry.[38]

In 1874 he explained to the people of Buenos Aires that the Cuban revolution was not the work of a single class, and

[37] *Id.* at 204–208.   [38] *Id.* at 216–217.

could not hope for success if it were. All Cubans were behind it. Moreover, it was not revolution looking toward annexation to the United States; nothing could make that annexation acceptable. "The United States has been almost as cruel and stupid with us as Spain," he says, and we detest the wrong when committed by the strong so much that "we are sure they can possess us only after destroying us, but with our will never." [39]

Hostos continued to dream of more inclusive unions. "Federation was the goal of the ideals of the New World; the union of all nations." [40] Certainly, however, imperialism is not the road to union. Imperialism it will be unless the peoples of his beloved islands rouse themselves from their dreams. Either "they organize themselves for civilization, or civilization will sweep them into its maw; the process of absorption has begun. . . . Civilization or death." And so we find him quoting with approval Alberdi's "To govern is to populate," calling for an immigration program that will bring selected *families* and establish them in agricultural colonies, and even condescending to argue about whether the streets are too narrow for street cars. [41]

The mental grasp of Hostos, indeed, permitted him to comment enlighteningly on the most diverse topics; and without attempting to impose any unity on this diversity, we should like to offer a few samples.

The proof that peoples fit for democracy do exist is the history of the United States, of Switzerland, and off and on since 1863 of Colombia. These nations approach being true peoples, with clear common interests, well defined political and national aspirations. But elsewhere in Latin America he finds instead those "vicious social classifications which corre-

[39] *Id.* at 290–291.
[40] Hostos, "La cuna de América," *Obras*, X, 19.
[41] *Id.* at 387–393.

spond to forms of government absolutely opposed to democracy," and diversity of education, of mentality, of hopes and
aspirations.[42]

"When you cannot be just through virtue, be so through
pride," he says. "If you would know what justice is, let
yourself be persecuted by injustice." [43]

"There are complete men and incomplete men. If you
would be a complete man, put all the strength of your soul
into every act of your life."

"The better I know men, the more appalled I am at the
difference between what they are and what they ought to be.
Consider men to be children, so that your countenance may
shine with benevolence. All men are good when they are not
influenced by passion, interest or error." [44]

"Fools are not free creatures because they are not reasonable creatures." [45]

"Ignorance is as harmful as wickedness itself."

"Love is an instinct, a passion and a virtue. As instinct,
it makes sick; as passion, it weakens; as virtue, it strengthens.
Almost all rational beings love; almost none knows how to
love. Almost all men love as animals; some love as wild
beasts; only a few love as men." [46]

"The most fruitful of words is the spoken word, for it is
closest to action. The word is the action of a thought." [47]

And surprisingly enough, in the philosopher of duty and
work: "Why is dying sad? Because living is sad. And why
is living sad? Because it is work." [48] But he adds that work
may be a delight, life may be harmonious, death may be
serene.

There is something higher "than being a great man in the
eyes of history, and that is to be a man useful to one's time.

[42] Hostos, "Hombres e ideas," *Obras*, XIV, 360–361.
[43] *Id.* at 290.
[44] *Id.* at 291.
[45] *Id.* at 293.
[46] *Id.* at 294.
[47] *Id.* at 296.
[48] *Id.* at 298.

The thoughtless world and history itself have preferred the so-called great men to those who are useful: one of the innovations the New World is called upon to introduce is putting the second ahead of the first." [49]

It was this "man useful to his time" that Hostos aspired to be and was. In time he became convinced that although war and revolution might be necessary, they were not for him, and that his usefulness lay in education. If we are to find a core to his teaching it is in such works as the treatises on Morals and on Sociology, which demand at least as much analysis as will send the reader to the originals.

Most of the former book is naturally devoted to social morality, but there is briefer consideration of those moral principles that Hostos calls natural and individual. Natural morality includes those duties that grow out of our recognition that we form a part of the physical world, that we owe nature gratitude and admiration, that we should respect ourselves as part of nature (and so refrain from homicide and suicide), that we should cultivate knowledge of nature, and recognize the limits beyond which our knowledge does not reach, spreading the scientific knowledge we have acquired but showing tolerance for those who differ from us with regard to the Unknowable, or as yet Unknown.

Man's relations to himself give rise to the duties that constitute individual morality. These duties he classifies as those toward the body, the will, the affective and rational sides of our nature. Self-preservation and self-development along physical lines, avoidance of agitation, education of the will to carry out necessary action energetically, and its training for a life which is certain to require abstentions and sacrifices, development of our rational factors and even more of conscience — all these are defined and defended as imperatives of the good life.

[49] *Id.* at 328.

The thesis presented in the section on social morality is that duty is no austere, repulsive ideal, but is at the same time the purest source of morality and the natural mode of development for individual and society; that man is most a man when he does his duty, thus proving his rationality and worth; that to be civilized and to be moral is the same thing, and that morality and civilization are both attained by fulfilling one's duty in every relation of life.[50]

Hostos develops at length the nature of our relation to the groups of which we form a part, and the debt of work and obedience that we owe them; thoroughly socially minded, he preaches the duty of being useful, of coöperating, of finding a way to reconcile what is useful to the we-group to what is useful to the they-group. As Royce is the philosopher of loyalty, so Hostos is the philosopher of duty — of the duty of being dutiful, not with the impulsiveness of heroism on grand occasions, but to the level of every day's most quiet need. For the solution of conflicts between duties, he proposes the primacy of the "most immediate, most extensive, most concrete." [51]

In an extensive section that belongs to social science as much as to speculation, Hostos examines the relation of morals to other social institutions, such as the Church. In this instance, his emancipated conclusion is that Protestantism is more advanced than Catholicism, and that religious evolution is farther advanced in the United States than anywhere else, especially when religion takes the form of unitarianism and universalism. As a good positivist, he also holds that men of science live more conformably to the moral order than any others, and that their names are in general the purest and most honorable that humanity can point to.[52] Of art he is more fearful, thinking of the vanity of the artist,

[50] Hostos, "Tratado de moral," *Obras*, XIX, 106.
[51] *Id.* at 184.   [52] *Id.* at 247–248.

his corruptibility by applause, and he can only hope that
artists will be true to what they glimpse in their moments of
contemplation, will find their mission within the larger framework of civilization, moralization, humanity.[53]

It is not, however, only social institutions that Hostos
analyzes in relation to morality, but individual men, for he
concludes the volume with a series of case studies of virtue,
taken in part from the history of Hispanic America but also
including Franklin, Washington, and Peter Cooper. The
Sunday-school tone is avoided, and an approach is made to a
inductive ethics.

The "Treatise on Sociology" is also based on student notes,
but while the "Morals" dates from 1884, the lectures on sociology were given in 1901 and the book was first published
posthumously.

There are critics who would say that there is something
about sociology which ruins writing. At any rate, it seduces
Hostos into a series of barbarous neologisms hard for a purist
in things Hispanic to accept. Sociology is divided into soci-
onomy, sociography, sociorganology, and sociopathy.[54] Under the first heading fall the laws of society in general, which
are seven: the law of sociability, without which there would
be no society; the law of work, without which it could not
function and survive; the law of progress, by which he seems
to mean rather social continuity, for it includes death and
decay as well as genesis and growth; the law of the ideal of
the good, which ideal exists in direct proportion to the development of morality, inversely to the individual and social
lack of capacity to comprehend religious and moral goals; the
law of conservation, which points out that the continued life
of societies depends on the vigorous functioning of their organs; and last, the law of means, according to which societal

[53] *Id.* at 254–259.
[54] Hostos, "Tratado de sociología," *Obras*, XX, 61.

agents are modified by the means they use, the circumstances which surround their operation; this last is Hostos' curiously roundabout way of recognizing the importance of environment and culture.[55]

Sociography for Hostos means a rather sketchy account of the State and other social institutions through history; sociorganology, a description of the organs of society and their role in the body social, for Hostos is in a loose sense a social organicist, who does not insist on the detailed comparisons of a Lilienfeld or Schäffle; his sociopathy makes the idea of sickness its point of departure, and diagnoses, especially in the countries of Latin America, pathological conditions of economic life, of the political system, those that he calls intellectual and moral, and deficiency or excess of attention to the immediate environment. Social hygiene, which has a more limited connotation with us in North America, is used to designate the whole application of our knowledge of healthy functioning to the prevention of these social ills. One must not expect to find in the skeletal twenty-five pages on social pathology that complete account of Latin-American social problems and the movements to combat them which to this day constitutes a glaring gap in our libraries. Hostos has written the sociology of his day, which is the day of Spencer and Ward, and it is a sociology without benefit of charts, tables, or photographs of housing conditions. Perhaps we can do without them and remain grateful for a life that was noble and devoted, for "truths that contained quite a lot of truth" as Blanco-Fombona remarks, and for two or three seminal books.

[55] *Id.* at 62–78.

CHAPTER IX

The Mexicans

I N DR. JOSÉ MARIA LUIS MORA (1794–1850) Mexico had perhaps her greatest political thinker, certainly the outstanding one of the period immediately succeeding the revolution.
He faced much the same problems we have already met, gave
a solution that in its emphasis on freedom and education was
not fundamentally different, and felt at the end of his life the
same profound discouragement that has affected many Latin
American thinkers from the days of Bolívar's exclamation,
"We have ploughed the sea!"

Dr. Mora was a historian — of not quite modern standards
as to documentation; an author of essays, portraits and
aphorisms — not quite of the order of genius; an educator —
who naturally enough did not solve all the educational problems of his country; and a political writer — who did not
have to live to see the class in whose name he had led the
fight for freedom and against dictatorship itself impose on
the country the long dictatorship of Porfirio Díaz. His less
polemical writings are charming, his central ideas lucidly expressed, his essential message a clear one that all times need
to hear; his social analysis rises at times to the height of
prophecy. Why, then, is it that the two volumes of stray
"Works" which he published in Paris to defend the part he
had played in political life between 1822 and 1834 are so
little known by the present generation? [1]

A liberal, oscillating between Adam Smith and Jeremy

[1] *El Dr. José Maria Luis Mora, 1794–1850, Homenaje de la universidad nacional
de México* (1934), p. 45.

Bentham (and so illustrating that the English influence was potent in this period), Mora was the spokesman of freethinking and anti-militaristic middle-class elements in post-revolutionary Mexico. They had been through revolution: what now? they asked. Like his contemporary Auguste Comte, Mora seemed to feel that it was time to establish order. He wanted both liberty and order, but unlike the more hotheaded Ramírez would choose the latter if the option were forced.[2]

Dr. Mora was not without courage, and if he preferred to attack institutions rather than persons, he stood his ground and fought steadfastly against the two privileged classes of the clergy and the military that were dominant in the nation. His liberalism had a place for them as servants of the people; as oppressors, never. The result was that Dr. Mora saw his work attacked in turn with unparalleled vehemence. With the passage of time, his confidence in the inevitability of progress and his positivistic optimism declined, and he exclaimed: "Nothing has been accomplished. Our efforts have been in vain!"

Besides formulating the principles that guided the liberal party, in the six months of his *El Indicador de la federación mexicana* and other writings, Dr. Mora played an important part in developing the culture of his country. He established the first course in economics; in 1824 he became professor of philosophy in San Ildefonso, and the voice of doubt was heard in Mexico for the first time.[3] He proposed and obtained supervision of educational establishments by the national government.[4] Spain's policy was to keep us ignorant, he said; we can make no better use of our freedom than to cultivate our minds. Out of freedom, truth. As he phrased the classic argument for liberty: "Opinions on doctrinal points

---

[2] Leopold Zea, *El positivismo en México* (Mexico, 1942), pp. 78–106.
[3] *Homenaje*, p. 17.   [4] *Id.* at 28.

should be entirely free. . . . The surest way, or better the only way, to arrive at the truth, is by free discussion." [5] At the same time, wisdom rather than excitement is Mora's characteristic quality, and he is well aware of the need for a middle-of-the-road course. On the one hand, "after a revolution nothing is more important than to minimize the real or apparent motives which may lead to the accumulation of great authority or power in the hands of a single man, giving him sway and ascendancy over his fellow-citizens." [6] On the other hand, "a people that has lived under a régime of oppression will not think itself free when it has thrown off the chains that bound it to the despot's chariot, but will desire to break all the bonds which unite it to authority." [7] In the process, the people may easily be misled, and surrender their rights to a demagogue who leads them to his own ends, but in the name of liberty. "The word liberty has often served for the destruction of the substance of liberty." [8]

Rewarded at the end of his life by being named Minister to England (1847), Dr. Mora died in the land that better than any other exemplified the orderly liberty and progress he desired for his beloved Mexico. He would have agreed with Alvarez and many other Latin American thinkers in criticizing the naïve expectation of achieving the English results just by borrowing the English political institutions; the way to improve the human lot, he recognized, is rather by improving the morality and industry of the citizenry. It would be wrong, however, to leave the impression that Mora had the modern *indianista's* concern for all that citizenry; he represents rather the last generation that cherished the ideal of pure European blood and feared the Indian, who neither as human being nor as symbol aroused any great sympathy

---

[5] Mora, *Obras sueltas* (Paris, 1837), II, 64.   [7] *Id.* at 70.
[6] *Id.* at 68.   [8] *Id.* at 78.

in this liberal statesman, heart and brain of the Reform of 1833.

Ignacio Ramírez (1818–1879)
Manuel Ignacio Altamirano (1834–1893)
Justo Sierra (1848–1912)

It is possible to trace a living connection between the three thinkers who bridge the gap between Dr. Mora and the twentieth century. Ignacio Ramírez was revered as teacher and friend by Manuel Ignacio Altamirano, who in turn looked at the young Justo Sierra and his brother, and exclaimed in 1868, "These boys are the glories of the future!" Sierra, looking back on "El Nigromante," or Ramírez, called him a sublime destroyer of the past and a workman of the revolution, and did not hesitate to call him Mexico's own Voltaire. If his writings do have some of the bitter brilliance of Voltaire, he was a Voltaire who was permitted to have some of the personal pleasure that comes when one has authority to *écraser l'infame.* In the most brilliant period of his life, Ramírez passed from the club and the salon, the newspaper and the professor's chair, to the seat of the legislator and finally to the portfolios of Justice, and Public Instruction and Development. The same man who had thought, written, and preached Reform, who in the name of these thoughts and writings had suffered persecution and imprisonment and won the name of martyr and apostle, now could execute the laws he had fought for, and was the agent who closed the monasteries and convents and at one blow put an end to a monastic empire three centuries old. Altamirano tells the story with unction and delight in the biography of Ramírez which introduces his Works.

Altamirano himself marks an important stage, for he was of indigenous stock, a poor country boy, who became not only a novelist but an orator capable of drawing the souls of

men out of their bodies as he talked in congress and on the
public platform of his twin ideals of liberty and learning.
The making of citizens, the formation of new men, new
minds, were his lifelong aims. But while his admirers think
of him as sowing new ideas, it is not out of place to emphasize
something simple, almost bucolic about Altamirano — a
patriotism that is of the soil, a love of the earth and "airs of
Mexico" which is perhaps related to his non-Spanish race
and culture.

The name of Justo Sierra, founder of the National University in 1910, ambassador to Spain, loyal worker for realiz-
able ideals during the régime of a president whose principles
he could not accept, occupies an honorable place in the history of Mexico. Of his writings, the novels are of the style of
another day, and do not concern us. His historical studies
perhaps entitle him to be considered a *pensador*. We shall
give only a sample, from his "Political Evolution of the
Mexican People" (1910), handsomely republished recently
by the Casa de España.

Society, maintains Sierra,[9] "is a living being, and as such
grows, develops, and undergoes transformation; this inces-
sant transformation is more intense just in proportion to the
inner energy that the social organism uses in the process of
assimilating elements external to itself, and putting them to
the uses of its own progress." The influence of the social
organicists is evident in the phraseology, and that of one in
particular, Herbert Spencer, comes to mind as we read: "Colonization, labor and capital to exploit our great riches, means
of transportation to enable wealth to circulate, these were
the social desiderata; what was important was . . . for the
Republic to pass from the military to the industrial stage of
its development, and to make the passage quickly, for the
giant who was growing at our side was coming ever closer to

[9] Sierra, *Evolución política del pueblo mexicano* (ed. of 1940), p. 414.

us." [10] The United States would have, he insisted, a fatal tendency to absorb Mexico if it found her weak. Industry alone does not seem to him enough to guarantee strength, and he closes his history with an eloquent plea: "Thus we see our duty; to educate is to strengthen; liberty . . . has always been the property of the strong, whether individuals or societies; the weak have never been free. The whole evolution of Mexican society will have been abortive and frustrated if it does not eventuate in this final goal: Liberty." [11]

Francisco Bulnes (1849–1924)

Sierra's contemporary, the engineer, congressman, and publicist Francisco Bulnes, cannot be said to be a representative Mexican thinker. He throve on controversy, and no writer has provoked more refutations of his work. This fact, plus the unusual nature of his views on the problem of Latin-American civilization, justifies the analysis of at least one of his numerous writings, the book in which at the turn of the century he examined "The Future of the Hispanic-American Nations in the Face of the Recent Conquests of Europe and the United States."

The premise of this work recalls some of our current discussions of nutrition. History, if it proves anything, proves to Bulnes that the peoples that eat wheat are the only truly progressive ones.[12] These peoples have found the conquest of the corn-eaters easy, and it is comforting to have his assurance that the conquest of the rice-eaters is still easier, for theirs is the extreme of weakness.[13] The weakness of corn- and rice-eating peoples is not that their soldiers do not know how to die, but rather that they cannot kill in sufficient quan-

[10] *Id.* at 416.
[11] *Id.* at 458.
[12] Bulnes, *El porvenir de las naciones hispano-americanas ante las conquistas recientes de Europa y los Estados Unidos* (Mexico, 1899), p. 6.
[13] *Id.* at 7.

tities.[14] Knowing how to die may save the national honor at times, but often it leads to loss of country and honor at once. Thus far for the sake of truth and realism in our thinking, and without for a moment confusing militarism and civilization. Back of these facts lies food chemistry. Wheat-eaters get in their diet just the mineral materials they need, while the consumers of corn and rice suffer a grave deficiency of substances that are indispensable for their sustenance. The lack of phosphorus explains their low mental powers and "a sleepy, brutish appearance, as profoundly conservative as the mountains and as eminently melancholy as the graveyard." [15]

Bulnes passes from nutrition, which has been beneath the notice of most *pensadores* to considerations more in the tradition. "What service did the Conquest perform for humanity?" he asks. The reply is scathing:

The Spaniards introduced into America cattle, asses, pigs, sheep, horses, mules, all animals indispensable for civilization; wheat, the use of iron; voracious, licentious friars, the use of brandy; they extended the use of slavery, promulgated laws brutalizing in their effect, contributed ignorance laden with superstitious belief in miracles, a language laden with depreciatory attitudes toward conquered people, a religion full of hatred for progress, a patriotism that felt horror for the truth. . . . And instead of the irrigation which the country needed, they gave us thousands of churches and convents.[16]

If, during the centuries of the conquest, the country had enjoyed just as much freedom and good diet as Russian serfs got, it would have sufficed to transform the inhabitants into a great people. But when animals, vegetables, or human beings do not get the food which nature has meant for their conservation, biological law decrees their adaptation to inferior life conditions.[17] The result, Bulnes somewhat hastily

14 *Id.* at 8.
15 *Id.* at 12

16 *Id.* at 17.
17 *Id.* at 18–19.

assumes, is that the Indian and the man of Spanish blood are disappearing, both replaced by the mestizo. He embarks upon a survey of the value to society of each of these three types, and is no less severe than Bunge or Arguedas.

The Indian takes no interest in things, is stoical, unenlightened; death he scorns, and life as well, gold, morality, work, science, pain and hope. He loves seriously four things only: the idols of his old religion, the land that gives him his food, his personal freedom, and alcohol, to which last he owes such sad, mad deliriums as he knows. He does not laugh, nor speak nor sing, and hardly eats. The only great occasion he knows is the wake: the presence of a corpse seems to bring him joy, and make him dance. . . . The common mestizo has inherited a large share of the Spaniard's rapacity . . . he is boastful and brave as the Spanish are. The mestizo is in practice polygamous, faithless to all his women, as well as to his gods and his rulers. In his barbarous way he is a skeptic, and he has one great virtue, that nothing, no one, provokes his envy. As soon as he makes fifty cents a day, he will keep five households for as many affairs, and will not even know how many children he has; only a few of them will he know by sight. He adores the rights of man without knowing what justice is; he loves his country and thinks it is a great nation; he is to be trusted like an Arab when he promises to fight, and as little to be trusted as an astrologer when it is a question of paying his debts. In the matter of money, he neither collects, nor lends, nor pays; he hates usury, soap, the use of water either internally or externally . . . he is anticlerical . . . novelty, progress, audacity, civilization are words that arouse his enthusiasm. His mental qualities are in general, good . . . he is capable of civilization, provided he could learn to fight his alcoholism and follow the example of people with the instinct of workmanship.[18]

Along with purple passages like this one, Bulnes surprises the reader of Latin American thought with masses of statistics, tables on comparative production, and a determination to be realistic, let the ideals fall as they may.

Ideals for Latin Americans, he says, too often take the

[18] *Id.* at 30–31.

form of war-time patriotism, expressing itself in love of glory and hatred of the foreigner; he has little conception of what patriotism demands of the patriot in times of peace. The greatest lack in their peace-time patriotism is national unity.[19] How is unity to be achieved in a world where each man has a right to his opinon? Only by agreeing upon a very limited number of truths which are above discussion for all classes of society and freely accepted by all individuals can we achieve true unity. We will not achieve it unless we find truths which are solidly founded on the well-being and common economic interests of all. Anglo-Saxons have seen this, and have built upon the maxim "Society for the individual," while Latin Americans have floundered about with the idealistic and impractical formula, "The individual exists for society." [20] True national unity means mutual esteem among social classes, absolute recognition of the rights and duties of every individual, an altruism which includes the welfare of all inseparable from the welfare of each one, and the sharing of common beliefs about the past, present, and future of the nation. The question, Do the nations of Latin America possess these conditions of unity? is embarrassing.[21] The disunity of quarrelling parties is found everywhere. At the right, the conservative party continues everywhere to deserve the epigram that it never learns, never forgets.[22] Bulnes throws in his lot with the liberal party, derived from the middle class of professional people whose concern is intellectual progress, and who can therefore never conclude a truce with clericalism.[23] It is claimed that Catholicism does not now oppress us, he says, but that is only because we do not permit it. Restore to the Church the powers she once had to control society and education, and the right to gag her

[19] *Id.* at 67.
[20] *Id.* at 69.
[21] *Id.* at 70.
[22] *Id.* at 74.
[23] *Id.* at 76.

enemies, and she will again rule the world as in the Middle Ages.[24]

For the almost universal estheticism of Latin-American thinkers Bulnes has scant patience:

> The great Latin delusion is the belief that art is the highest, almost the only object of national life. Latins bend every effort to being artists in religion and turn out idolators; they strive to be artists in industry, and impoverish themselves; even in science they want to be artists, and they fail to understand scientific method. . . . Latins set themselves to be the great artists of politics, and the result is that a republic becomes for them a perfectly impossible system of government.[25]

We may comfort ourselves with the reflection that at least the clerical party can hardly become the controlling influence in America; the Indian is too much of a pagan, the mestizo too liberal and skeptical to allow that, and the only support the clergy can count upon is that of the upper-class women.[26] On the other hand, the economic basis for the kind of representative democracy achieved by the United States or Switzerland is not there; nor is there a numerous, enlightened, wealthy class on which to build a liberal plutocracy. The conclusion is that what fits the situation of countries in this stage is a liberal dictatorship, which will use the forms of democracy and will view its aims as essentially educational.[27]

If this seems at the same time a disappointing and a utopian conclusion, Bulnes would defend himself by pointing out the obvious lack of the qualities necessary to the successful functioning of democracy: truth, justice, foresight, coöperation. His land has not too much of any of these, although the government has tried to tell the truth in some of its own publications. In the absence of these qualities it does no good to shout our patriotism from the housetops; we do not have

---

[24] Id. at 80.
[25] Id. at 85.

[26] Id. at 94.
[27] Id. at 95.

the patriotism which implies enthusiasm for work; we are not patriots, or rather our patriotism is of that Spanish variety which consists in hating and looking down upon everything foreign, cherishing the absolute assurance that we will all be heroes in time of war, and acting in time of peace like the most cruel of *conquistadores*. "To what does Spain owe its ruin? To its patriotism." [28] If Latin America continues to worship this kind of patriotism, it has no future but a quick death, without glory or honor. And if some Latin-American nations have made considerable progress, it is because of the energy and merit of some real patriots who have not hesitated to show us our vices and mistakes. [29]

Opening our eyes to our defects and to our dangers is imperative, for the future will bring a struggle between races, and those who cannot hold their own with the Anglo-Saxon world will get from history only a sepulchre bearing an unmistakably condemnatory epitaph. [30]

The practical next step for countries like his own follows as the night the day. In view of the "violent" growth of the population of the United States, the danger lies in that quarter. So long as the Monroe Doctrine remains in force, backed by the tacit Anglo-American alliance, [31] Europe will not violate the sovereignty of Latin America. The single, formidable danger is that of the United States, and even it is not immediate, but rather probable and distant. Even if one admits, as Bulnes does, that "the United States, without having achieved perfection in its feeling for justice, occupies the highest moral level of present-day civilization," [32] still the commercial interests of the United States will imperatively require dividing the continent by a canal through Panama or Nicaragua. Somehow — peacefully, or if neces-

[28] *Id.* at 106.
[29] *Id.* at 109.
[30] *Id.* at 110.

[31] *Id.* at 114–115.
[32] *Id.* at 120.

sary by force — this will be accomplished, and the United States will possess more or less ceded, purchased, leased, or conquered territory. "No human force can withstand this need of the great republic." [33] By about the year 1980, the United States will have, he estimated, a population of some 250,000,000, and will be faced with a choice between very intensive cultivation and conquering the Latin-American land that lies outside the tropics. At present it does not have the conditions — excess population, need for land — which require expansion; by that time it will.[34] The strength that Latin America can oppose to this expansion is not military; it is a patriotism and a program for peace that must be developed. The Latin Americans must organize, not armies, but the national capacity for work and the upbuilding of domestic, social, and political virtues.[35]

Like Alberdi, the Mexican economist turns to European immigration. He has the none-too-happy experience of many decades to reflect upon, and it leads him to reflect that if one wishes to attract free men, one must be honest and frank with them. Past practice is ridiculed by pointing out the characteristic reticences and exaggerations of the usual books designed to attract immigrants. Such Chamber-of-Commerce literature has made itself so ludicrous with its "sociological flute-playing, whose highest note is the sublime, and lowest the admirable" that scarcely anyone pays any attention to it now.[36] Examining the future of various Latin-American countries, he concludes that of those that lie entirely or in large part in the tropics, only Brazil can hope to attract European immigration.[37] The problem of immigration is for Mexico, Chile, Argentina, and Brazil a question of life and death, for it is men that make a country, not formal

[33] *Id.* at 116.
[34] *Id.* at 122.
[35] *Id.* at 145–146.
[36] *Id.* at 202–203.
[37] *Id.* at 264.

political institutions, as Jacobins mistakenly believe.[38] Of the multitude of persons with more learning than himself, Bulnes asks with mock humility that they show him any other way, or demonstrate the existence of true democracy in Latin America, or even the possibility of its being achieved in a thousand years.[39] The thing that prevents it is in ourselves, he says. In a later work, "The Great Lies of Our History," Bulnes reduced North American principles to interests, and labeled the North American as essentially money-mad, with a greed that grows with success,[40] but he also impartially laid bare the failings of his own nation. He concludes his glance into the future with the observation that "it is not Europe or the United States with their ambitions that are the real enemies of the people of Latin America; there are no worse enemies of our welfare and independence than ourselves . . . their names are our tradition, our history, our morbid inheritance, our alcoholism, our education that fails to develop character." [41]

In a later work, in fact a series of articles from *La Tribuna* made into a book after his death, this clear and exact thinker examines "The Great Problems of Mexico." Indeed, in all his writing and speaking he has been concerned with nothing else than such problems and their origins.

He continues the same caustic analysis in his statement that "Mexico has taken eighty years to double her little population of 1820. And these seventy millions of inhabitants are not civilized citizens, but in their majority barbarians who spend less on their table than donkeys and have in their houses poorer furniture than stables do, and in their minds the same darkness that was there ten thousand years ago." [42] For nations so constituted he believes that the only

[38] *Id.* at 274.　　　　　　　　　　　　　　　　[39] *Id.* at 238.
[40] Bulnes, *Las grandes mentiras de nuestra historia* (Mexico, 1904), p. 114.
[41] Bulnes, *El porvenir*, pp. 281–282.
[42] Bulnes, *Los grandes problemas de México* (Mexico, 1926), p. 329.

way out is conciliation with the United States; even if they form a League, their combined strength will not be sufficient for any more.[43]

Bulnes was one of the five original *científicos* who held that there is a science of government, and that merely empirical government is bound to end in disaster. Whether his policy was essentially more scientific than others or not, he brought to its support the big guns of statistics.

José Vasconcelos (1871–   )

The twenty-odd volumes of Vasconcelos' writing fall naturally into three groups: the autobiographic, those that deal with the well-worn topic of anti-imperialism, and the development of his philosophic system. They are not unconnected, since the philosophy is not only a personal expression but the flowering of that culture which Vasconcelos wages endless war to protect against spiritual and material imperialism, and the life tells the story of the fight to embody the philosophy in educational and political institutions.

The tremendously voluminous autobiography has challenged comparison in certain respects with those of Rousseau and Saint Augustine, is highly interesting in itself, and indispensable to any student of the thought of this stormy and solitary figure. Since Bulnes there has been no success like this four-volume story of a Latin-American Ulysses; no other Mexican is so widely read inside and outside his own country as this Ramírez of our own day. It is no disrespect for the literary talents of Alfonso Reyes, brilliant director of the Colegio de México and of the admirable new *Cuadernos americanos*, and useful link between the Spain and the Mexico of the 1920's, nor for the solid sociological contributions of Manuel Gamio, that leads us to give first place among con-

[43] *Id.* at 331–332.

temporaries to the intensely dramatic and earnestly prophetic figure of José Vasconcelos.

That passage from geographic to biological and then to cultural explanation which is characteristic of the thought of the last hundred years in Latin-America and elsewhere is exhibited in Vasconcelos, who emphasizes now one, now another of these factors. Which is perhaps as it should be. The fusion of all three, when he attempts it in his Chicago or La Plata lectures, is something like this: Out of the response of races or people to the challenge of their physical environment there flowers a culture; the culture Vasconcelos, with his strong religious and esthetic undercurrent, defines as a movement toward the absolute, and as the poetry of conduct. Both expressions imply that it is much more than civilization; when he is most "prophetic" and least tolerant it would appear that civilization is for others, and a happy conjuncture of environment, race, and history has made true culture the property of Latin America. "All our past inclines us to prefer the cultural effort to that which is merely a matter of civilization." [44] Even if it be one culture among many, he says, it is our own, and to be defended. "No one in submission, and every one in his mission," [45] he exclaims (*sumisión* and *su misión* makes the play on words a bit better in Spanish). First and always an educator, he sees the defense of culture as the heart of the problem, rather than economics. As director of the Preparatory School, Rector of the University, Minister of Education, director of libraries, he fights for an education which will further Latin America's own type of culture, and laments as betrayal the encroachment of alien ideals. Dwight Morrow is the old danger in more insidious form. Protestantism works hand-in-glove with high capitalism. Cuba, in adopting Dewey and behaviorism, has volun-

[44] Vasconcelos, *La cultura en Hispano-América* (La Plata, 1934).
[45] *Id.*

tarily surrendered her soul to the same people who control
her sugar and manipulate her politics.[46] It is not the Caliban
in the influence of the United States that he fears, but the
dissolving force of our ideas. We would teach Latin America
to bow before the Golden Calf of technology; his message to
the Hispanic-American world is to recognize and magnify
their own Hispanic ideal of culture.[47] In this he is a true
follower of Rodó. What that ideal of culture is will emerge
from our study of his thought, but it may be said immediately that it is not a rejection of democracy, for he believes
that society exists for the individual, and that no other form
of government can carry out that ideal so well as democracy.
Its economic aspect will be socialism. For these he will work;
mystic as he is, he believes that the mystic is the most active
being in the world, and philosopher as he is, believes that the
possession of a philosophy alone confers the privilege and
the duty of public speech and action. He will condemn the
defects and injustices of our social life, the corruption of
politics, the dominion of technology, our collective greed, the
excess of alimentation (*sic*), political bossism, and the general lack of courage in civic life. But the elimination of all
these evils is not enough, and to hope for the disappearance
of the capitalist régime is not enough. At the root of our
troubles is empirical philosophy and utilitarian morality, and
the cure of our troubles is the rise of an aristocracy of the
spirit, no mere intelligentsia but an élite dedicated to his
twin ideals of the good and the beautiful. The basis for such
a culture has been inherited from Spain, so great in her colonial days, and the danger of North American peaceful penetration is precisely the attempt to spread anti-Spanish ideas
and institutions and to win masses away from Catholicism.

Vasconcelos, who had learned the necessity of cultural self-

[46] Vasconcelos, *El proconsulado* (Mexico, 1939), pp. 570–571.
[47] *Vasconcelos*, Pensamiento de América, no. 1 (Mexico, 1942), p. xxxi.

defense in a boyhood on the northern frontier, had learned the vital role of Catholicism in his culture from his adored mother. Nothing in his student experiences, bathed in the positivism of intellectual circles in the capital, had succeeded in making him an atheist. His Catholicism was never replaced. "I was not an unbeliever, but a heretic," he tells us. As time went on, the attractions of the traditional faith became stronger, his reservations less and less important; he became convinced that it was not possible to scrap the supernatural and at the same time inspire youth with great ideals. Justo Sierra had tried that and failed.

Hence his patriotic educational plan includes religion, just as it includes language, and blood, and if necessary the myth of Atlantis. His teaching program does not rest content with the utilitarian, but insists upon the dream. Robinson Crusoe becomes a symbol of the Anglo-Saxon mind, and *robinson-ismo* the merely problem-solving, *Ersatz*-finding faculty; Latins, perpetually inquiring why, endlessly dreaming dreams, demand another symbol, which he discovers in the prudent Ulysses, and the term *odiseismo*. Latin students naturally seek a general conception of the universe, and the teacher must be prepared to help them find it; he is one step farther on the road, and must accept the burden of authority; he socializes because he first is socialized. He communicates the norms, to the letter and even more to the spirit of which the student must adapt himself. So an education which may find a place for statistics, work, techniques, science, cannot be content with these, but must be crowned by ethics and esthetics.

But what of race in the thought of Vasconcelos? It is a subject that cannot be neglected in the case of an author who has called one of his books "The Universal Race," and invented for another the title *Indología*. Even in the latter there is no glorification of the Indian, no narrowly biological definition of the problem; culture is still in a sense the central consideration. He might have been thinking of the argument of this book when he wrote in an article that forms part of "What is the revolution?": "Our task is to demonstrate that mestizos and Indians are capable of assimilating and of equaling, at least of equaling, the culture of white men." [48]

The task of a philosopher in a country where Indians form a major part of the population is a task of synthesis, not of statistical statement. Synthesis means adding the heterogeneous to the homogeneous; it means the vision of the whole in which nothing is lost from the richness that variety gives, but all is transfigured and seen teleologically, seen as part of a process that ends in the eternal. [49] In such a vision all particulars take on something of the greatness of the whole, and move to the music of the whole. The last and final philosophy would be a philosophy of beauty, of the divine. It would be religion.

These are hard sayings for those of us who see all things through the glasses of our fragmentary specialties. But if we are patient we shall find Vasconcelos talking the same language, if not always expressing the same opinions as our specialists in race and race relations.

He does not intend by the term *Indología* to imply any favoring of the autochthonous tradition or the race native to American soil; he will give to each race its due, for each must play its fraternal part with the others in bringing in the new era of human history to which he looks forward. [50] Latin America is still indubitably far from such a new era. Lack of culture is still the rule; Latin America, with the exception of Brazil and Argentina, has not progressed or improved, but slipped backward. If we are to start, he says, it must be by

[48] Vasconcelos, *¿Qué es la revolución?* (Mexico, 1937), p. 218.
[49] Vasconcelos, *Indología* (Barcelona, n.d.), p. 6.
[50] *Id.* at 9.

taking thought as to the means at our disposal and the objects of our striving, and recognizing that we are "we," a people conscious of our unity and our separateness.[51] The difference of physical conditions would in itself almost explain the differences in development, temperament, and culture; almost, but not quite, for "spirit is richer, more flexible, more intense and many-sided than any mere physical reality." [52] The temperamental differences between North Americans and Latin Americans are summed up: the Yankee, hard-working, has stick-to-itiveness; Latin Americans are inconstant and indolent, but have a clear superiority in mental quickness. North America has achieved an enviable control over nature by the machine, but in the process the very essence of life has been strangled; Mexico and her sisters preserved a spiritual freedom they inherited from Spanish culture.[53] Unfortunately, relations with the mother country and the sister republics suffered with the coming of independence; the doctrine of nationalism and physical isolation in an environment beyond our poor powers to cope with have held us back.[54] Now at last that isolation has broken down, consciousness of Ibero-American unity is reviving; spiritual unity and political federation become possibilities. All these countries share a cultural tradition in which European and American elements, Spanish and Indian, play a part; all have sparsely inhabited but potentially rich territories; all are hybrid, representing not mere mixture of European bloods, but that of all known races, creating for the first time "the universal race." [55] How are such people to exploit such riches? In some cases, he admits, they will need abundance of foreign capital; in others law and interest will find an adjustment. Always the peril of foreign monopoly must be fought.[56]

[51] *Id.* at 11–12. [53] *Id.* at 15–16. [55] *Id.* at 26.

[52] *Id.* at 14. [54] *Id.* at 20. [56] *Id.* at 60.

Vasconcelos is forced to reconcile his unflattering picture of present racial realities in Latin America with the unbounded hope of the future by asserting that human raw material is extremely plastic; races can change, even in one generation; the Indian has as a matter of fact changed notably since the coming of European culture. We can set no bounds to what may happen in this first case of a sudden, large-scale hybridization.[57] To those who stigmatize the mestizo as an inferior and credit the Anglo-Saxon's success to his uncompromising ethnocentrism, Vasconcelos asserts that in the long run, mixture will be more productive, will do more for humanity than any previous race. The North American competitor need not be feared: "There is something unpleasing, almost suspect about so sudden and resounding a success" as he has had.[58] The mixed bloods of Mexico can reasonably claim to be descended from two aristocracies, both products of nature's severe selective process.[59] To be sure, immigrants will come and will be welcomed, too, for such is the destiny of the continent. If they find we are working for an ideal vaster and higher than any they have known, they too will coöperate loyally in its realization.[60] What the mestizo can accomplish can hardly be measured by the past; he had the misfortune to be born into a civilization that was becoming second-rate.[61] In the future we shall see: the hour of the man of mixed blood is approaching.[62] His civilization will flourish if it follows the norms Vasconcelos lays down: the yielding of the nationalistic ideal before this broader, more inclusive one of race, but not of race in any exclusive, purist sense; and the forging of a régime which offers justice and acceptance to all men of whatever kind.[63]

Out of this civilization will come thought and expression

[57] *Id.* at 72–73.
[58] *Id.* at 75.
[59] *Id.* at 76.
[60] *Id.* at 84.
[61] *Id.* at 87.
[62] *Id.* at 92.
[63] *Id.* at 100.

that will put to shame those of our past, hampered by aping of the foreign model, and that will be our own, distinct from the thought and writing of North America.[64] Our contribution will bear the imprint of mysticism both in religion and in the attitude toward beauty.[65] Some of this mysticism Latin America lost for a while when French and English ideas — to which we owe much in the social and political area — replaced in part the tradition of Andalusia and of Italy. For almost half a century the romanticism of Rousseau ruled, replacing the dying flame of Catholicism in eager souls.[66] Positivism flourished, particularly in Mexico, Santiago, and Brazil, and its story remains to be written in the last two places. Emerging from Positivism, Latin-American thought has tended to fall into two camps, both equally unfortunate according to Vasconcelos; a blind reaction toward the past on the one hand, and on the other a hasty acceptance of leftist materialism and a pragmatism even grosser and more abject than that of North America because less clearly defined and less nobly led.[67] He notes also in philosophy the vogue of Bergson, and recently the indispensable return to Kant.

Whether the confrontation of two ways of thinking and of living in the western hemisphere will be, as history teaches, destructive to both, is a question. Vasconcelos can only hope that history will discover a new way, and the struggle of ideals will turn creative. An earnest search for the causes of hate and their unmasking may deprive them of their power.[68] The policy he preaches up and down the length of Hispanic America is, then, one of integrating the race, raising the level of the indigenous peoples, populating unused land, warily combatting the smooth diplomacy of a Pan-Americanism

[64] *Id.* at 112, 118.
[65] *Id.* at 121.
[66] *Id.* at 128–129.

[67] *Id.* at 134–135.
[68] *Id.* at 192–193.

"more dangerous than the cannon of the old English pirates." [69] Within the Anglo-Saxon and Latin-American communities the better elements can fight the good fight against imperialism and *caudillismo*; it is the worst elements of each race that cause trouble, and there is hope that men of good will can be brought to work together.[70] There are still such men in North America, heirs of the spirit of a day before imperialism, when the United States was example and mentor to two continents; these men and their true democracy live under the menace of new and nefarious powers, and need all the help they can get. The ideal is clearly one of coöperation in the vast task that is America.[71] The fusion of races and cultures will permit forward movement through Vasconcelos' three stages of civilization: the material, the intellectual, and the esthetic.[72] Acceptance of all races in democracy will mark the supreme achievement of the intellectual period, in which all questions are solved by collective intelligence and wars become impossible.[73] The first two stages of civilization find their leaders in the soldier, then the lawyer, the economist, the engineer. Each gives place to his natural successor, and last to the philosopher.[74] In the last stage, problems are, as Toynbee would express it, etherialized and transferred to a higher level; the leaders of mankind, who will be educators and philosophers, will ennoble life; all that art and religion have hitherto been unable to compass, will come spontaneously. "The principal task of society will not then be to defend itself against each man doing that which is right in his own eyes, as in the second period; nor against social injustice, as in the third; nor will it be the task of insuring production adequate to meet the needs of all, as in the fourth. It will be to prepare the soul for its endless rising and transcending the

[69] *Id.* at 194–196.
[70] *Id.* at 197.
[71] *Id.* at 199–200.

[72] *Id.* at 206–207.
[73] *Id.* at 209.
[74] *Id.* at 210.

material." [75] He even speaks of uniting oneself to society in order to help society to die, to reach something beyond all sensate ideals. If we starve then, it will be not for lack of food, but from choice. Is this ideal of the natural finding its consummation in the spiritual too high? Who shall say that it is too high for that new race that is coming into being, or that we have not more resources in ourselves than other philosophies have dreamed of? No use of techniques to solve our minor problems must distract us from the highest ends of which man is capable. Is not our present plight due precisely to the lack of a great ideal? [76]

In thirty years of writing, a man may be permitted to contradict himself, or to learn; and North American readers will be glad to know that Vasconcelos by the time he wrote "What is the Revolution?" (1937) had learned to express kindlier feelings about the Colossus of the North than those that dot the pages of *Indología*. Pan-American Congresses are at last accomplishing something; Roosevelt is praised; our architecture is improving; more active work in scholarship and thought is going on in the United States than anywhere else; Americans are the most idealistic people of the time, and the most earnestly devoted to the solution of the religious problem. [77]

It is apparent that it is not only in the three thick volumes of his Metaphysics, Ethics, and Esthetics that one must seek Vasconcelos' philosophy. It is an integral part of Vasconcelos, the man of action and feeling, the man with a program. For his philosophy is no mere explanation of the puzzling; it is a plan of salvation. We have seen something of its application; it is time we followed its most formal exposition.

Introducing the "Treatise on Metaphysics," Vasconcelos

[75] *Id*. at 217.
[76] *Id*. at 220–230.
[77] Vasconcelos, *¿Qué es la revolución?* p. 213.

remarks: "I explain in this volume the first part of a system of philosophy entitled esthetic monism, which will be completed in an Ethics and an Esthetics composed of three parts: the apollonian, the dionysiac, and the mystic or religious." [78] To an age suspicious of all-embracing systems, Vasconcelos offers a defense of his constructive synthesis of all contemporary knowing: even a bad or incomplete system is a thousand times better than the absence of system, the complete lack of grasp shown by the fragmentary thinking of specialists. He dislikes them as much as Comte did, and they have no more place in his future society than in Comte's "Positive Polity." Better a system that tries to include all the elements of man's nature in its mystical intuition than the pseudo-philosophy of the rationalists who are content to banish from philosophy all that does not fit into their abstract scheme. The rationalistic temper is really anti-philosophical, and rationalism leads inevitably to scientificism. Genuine constructive synthesis requires the mystic impulse; we philosophize with the whole man, and with the play of all our faculties achieve unity.[79] Vasconcelos, says one of his admirers, "has thought all human thoughts, to achieve his own synthesis." [80] His own statement is to the effect that "there are not various syntheses, one for each culture, but only one common synthesis, vast and confused, in which all races, civilizations, and times have collaborated, and in which they will continue to collaborate." [81] The rejection of historic or cultural determination which shocks us here is further pointed in the judgment "that only an age incapable of true philosophic thought would invent a philosophy of history, or attempt to base philosophy on history. For everything really important is quite unrelated to history." [82]

[78] Vasconcelos, *Tratado de metafísica* (Mexico, 1929), title-page.
[79] *Id.* at 11–12.
[80] *Vasconcelos* (Pensamiento de América, no. 1), p. vii.
[81] Vasconcelos, *Tratado de metafísica*, p. 17.   [82] *Id.* at 27.

Neither the historian nor the scientist can grasp the reality that is more solid just because it is more spiritual and intangible as the philosopher can grasp it with the instruments of perception that have their roots in his very soul [83] and are so close to emotion that Vasconcelos is tempted to call his system an emotional philosophy.[84]

The point of departure for philosophy is the awareness of existence, of unity, of a particle of existence isolated in oneself, and of a universe "at the same time quiet and active, in repose and in emanation." [85]

Knowledge is, in the last analysis, a bringing of these existences into relation.[86] But knowledge is never a word with which Vasconcelos is long content; he approaches the esthetic monism which is the goal of his system when he stresses the value of music as a means of knowing realities, penetrating the mystery in a way that reason cannot do. For in music we do not merely apprehend, we impose our dynamism on the physical world, humanize it, and are fused with it.[87] Emotion is thus essentially monistic and leads us to unity and esthetics as fatally as intelligence does to dualism and science.[88] If a concept to account for the unity of existence is needed, it is found in energy, which is one in essence but various in the rhythms in which it presents itself.[89] This philosophy might also be called one of personality, for this procedure of uniting, synthesizing, is the property of personality. The road to unity is at the same time moral, for it creates ever new values. All of this has been most clearly recognized by Vedantic philosophy, with its insistence on the consubstantiality of the "I" and the "all." At the same time this reference to his "Hindustanic Studies" recalls Vasconcelos' attempt at a universal synthe-

[83] *Id.* at 23.
[84] *Id.* at 26.
[85] *Id.* at 33–35.
[86] *Id.* at 151.

[87] *Id.* at 149.
[88] *Id.* at 173.
[89] *Id.* at 237.

sis embracing the best of Brahmin, Buddhist, and Christian thought.[90]

Knowing falls into three classifications: that of physical science, which dissociates; that of ethics, which organizes; that of esthetics, which realizes. In the instant of heroic or saintly action, ethics is transfigured into esthetics, for the life of saint or hero is a work of art. Indeed, with esthetics we pass into a higher realm, for it is godlike of men to transcend the good and evil which narrowly concern them and turn to the disinterestedness of the beautiful. When art becomes liturgic, mystical, we take the final step to the highest kind of knowing, religion.[91]

General considerations introduce the volume in which the Ethics is set forth. The emphasis is almost utilitarian in its insistence that we can free ourselves only by freeing our thought first, that the world is full of unacceptable, naturalistic philosophies, and our achieving even a provisional synthesis of our own philosophy will act as a biologico-social defense for our culture. First the philosopher furnishes the orientation, then the statesman can undertake to carry out ideals in practice.[92] Phenomenology is rejected as a convenient weapon in the fight against pragmatism, but essentially just another specialization, and incapable of arriving at a synthesis of human values.[93] To hand over the reins to social science as George Lundberg pleads with us to do in his article, "What to do with the Humanities?" (Harper's, June 1943), is so completely unsatisfactory that Vasconcelos, we are sure, would not deign to discuss it. No science can be valid in more than its own narrow field of specialization, none can formulate truly general laws.[94]

[90] Id. at 316.
[91] Id. at 317.
[92] Vasconcelos, Ética (2a ed., 1940), pp. 31–35.
[93] Id. at 37.
[94] Id. at 54.

The language in which Vasconcelos makes his positive contribution is characteristic. "The road to the final order is given us by love, and the poet is love's interpreter." A philosopher may be defined as a poet with a system, for philosophy is born of a poetic inspiration and becomes orderly and rational through the organization the philosopher imposes upon it.[95] In opposition to the traditional emphasis on *cogitatio* which has misled us, Vasconcelos proposes a philosophy of emotion. Not all thought is apprehension, seizing the object. There is a poetic type which finds it enough to recognize a presence, to exchange influences, even at a distance. Our knowledge of the divine is the highest type, and the farthest removed from appetite. Loosely, emotion splits into two currents, ethics which pursues ends, and esthetics which limits itself to being with joy.[96] If the ends which morals pursue are not dictated by the emotion felt in the presence of the superior, ethics degenerates into mere utilitarianism, as all lay systems fatally have tended to do. The emotion that is directed toward the esthetically or mystically superior is the source and criterion of true morality.[97] "Good and beauty are found only on the road to God." [98] Historically, ideas, sentiments, and values arise as the fruits of personal or collective development, but if this development has no model or goal outside of itself, in God, all can end only in tragedy and suicide.[99]

Into the lengthy discussions of the categories of value we cannot venture. The reader will assume correctly that so-called intellectual values are only fictitious, and that ethical and esthetic values are real but properly preparatory to the real value, which is mystical and divine and provides the standard for all subsidiary values. To the Nietzschean cate-

[95] *Id.* at 55.
[96] *Id.* at 111–113.
[97] *Id.* at 175.
[98] *Id.* at 178.
[99] *Id.* at 238.

gories of apollonian (plastic), and dionysiac (rhythmic), Vasconcelos adds mysticism as an esthetic category and as transition to religion.[100]

The end of the "Ethics" descends from the heights to review a bit of history, in the light of the philosophical system. Colonial Hispanic America, he concludes, was culturally superior to the English colonies; the superiority was economic as well, and from a human point of view it is obvious to all. Both societies are decadent now; both lost their vision, North America that of equality, Latin America the divine breath of Saint Francis that blew through it. If geographic and technical causes contributed to make Nordic achievements for a while more striking, the decadence of North America has been the more rapid, and Nordic society is more difficult to set on the right track. Latin America's situation is of the two the more hopeful. Latin America can learn to produce, and to make of consumption and distribution matters of ethical concern.[101]

Of the three volumes, Vasconcelos confesses that he thought out the "Esthetics" first. The predominant role of esthetic considerations would be evident even without the name esthetic monism, which he gives to his system.

Intelligence distinguishes the forms of sensation; emotion when it enters into play, distinguishes intention.[102] It is concerned with persons and values. Knowing touched by emotion is "a continuous effort to lift the partial existence of isolated entities, things and persons, into participation in absolute existence. . . . Knowing goes beyond human ends, has a yearning for the divine end, the absolute tendency. At this point esthetics appears." [103] If, to some, emotional and

[100] *Id.* at 310.
[101] *Id.* at 612–614.
[102] Vasconcelos, *Estética* (2a ed., 1936), p. 107.
[103] *Id.* at 121.

esthetic knowing appears vague and confused, Vasconcelos
replies that its order is of that superior kind that is infused
in all the members; art orders its materials, or is not art; we
recognize its worth by form, line, and melody, or are Philis-
tines. In fact, of all the kinds of knowing, this alone deserves
the name; for "rational knowing constantly follows the process of converting the personal into the impersonal, and this
properly is not knowing, but its opposite. True knowledge
supposes the undiminished, in fact heightened presence of the
personal, standing in a clear relation with the surrounding
Universe in all its concreteness and many-sidedness." [104]

Esthetic knowing progresses through contemplation of
physical things and passional acts, to the mysticism in which
things and beings are seen as functions of the divine, all opposition between subject and object lost by means of purga-
tion, illumination, identification.[105] All mental process is a
kind of organization, but whereas empirical science organizes by induction, and logic by deduction, esthetics does so by
the process of identification, unification, or as he here calls
it, composition. The unity or composition is of three types:
the temple of Theseus is apollonian, the dancing Siva, dionysian; the crucifix is mystical.[106] The apollonian so arranges
the parts that without forsaking repose they simulate a life
that is not there.[107] Greek art is composed of the calm order-
ing of elements that in themselves are inferior. The loss of
this calm brings us to dionysian art with its passion. What
the Greeks did not know was the soul's passion. The highest
art learns through the story of a God made man to suffer pain
and redeem mankind from sin how to leave dionysian art behind, to purify it, and through mysticism to achieve that
true beauty which is conformity to the divine order.[108]

[104] *Id.* at 141.
[105] *Id.* at 171.   [107] *Id.* at 350.
[106] *Id.* at 340–347.   [108] *Id.* at 356–360.

"Mysticism is the belief in the intuition of the absolute, its method is an art which no longer manipulates forms, but content." [109] After insisting that in the dance there is a religious object which consists in the spiritualizing of a plastic art, Vasconcelos finds the peak of art in a true liturgy which has purified itself of estheticism and rationalism to become the trappings and the suits of salvation, and in the holy life which is itself a work of art.[110] All things lower have fallen into their proper place as determined by their relation to this highest end of living, feeling and willing.

We are left with a query. No mystic would be satisfied with mystical art alone. Is Vasconcelos going to stop with the garments in which the mystical experience clothes itself, and refer us to Revelation for its essence, or will he give us the Theodicy he mentions?

Antonio Caso (1883–   )

There is much less *Sturm und Drang* in Antonio Caso. We ask ourselves if it is not perhaps the more thoughtful and less passionate youth of Mexico and other Latin-American countries who find in this profoundly ethical philosopher their revered master.

For a long time, and in many eloquent books, Caso has been expounding his reasons for rejecting positivism, his concern with values and with the human personality, his anxiety lest Mexico forget these things. Except as they show where his own sympathies and leanings lie, we shall not be concerned with his essays on other philosophers. In "Moral Philosophers and Their Doctrines" (1915), he analyzed the French moralists whose influence has been so strong in Latin America, the more violent individualism of Stirner and Nietzsche, the social morality of Hostos, and the patriotism

[109] *Id.* at 365.   [110] *Id.* at 643, 721, 731.

of Sierra. In his "Philosophic Problems" (1915), he condemned positivism for giving an exaggerated value to some parts of experience and neglecting others. In his "Discourses to the Mexican Nation" (1922; a borrowed title which might well serve with appropriate change of the adjective for nearly all Latin-American thought), he speaks out the full, unflattering truth as he sees it.

"This idealism of which we talk in Hispanic America does not exist. Of all European or half-European peoples that history records, we are the most realistic." Beyond talk, what is there? Certainly, we have not put our hearts into cultural enterprises, still less into humanitarian labors.[111] Our innate, tropical, indolent realism found its justification in positivism, and so we are Sancho Panza realists, and Don Quijote idealists at the same time.[112] What Mexico needs is neither ideals that cannot be realized nor supine acceptance of an imperfect reality. He would agree with Vasconcelos (as he does not always do) in feeling that such acceptance is the vilest cowardice, and rebellion even for the sake of one knows not what, is better. What this people needs is strength to conquer the obstacles that stand in the way of our ideals, and ideals that are broad and human and can stand contact with life.[113] For the embodiment of this attitude he turns back to Sarmiento for "the plebeian impulsiveness, the generous if unorganized effort, the eternal youthful petulance" which he cannot find in his contemporaries.[114]

Latin America, Caso maintains, has scarcely known constitutional monarchy. It has had entirely too much of *caudillo* rule, outside, above, and even contrary to the law, but continuing by sufferance of the people.[115] If it is to rise permanently above this intolerable level it must be because

[111] Caso, *Discursos á la nación mexicana* (Mexico, 1922), p. 56.
[112] *Id.* at 65–66.
[113] *Id.* at 72.
[114] *Id.* at 86.
[115] *Id.* at 122.

Mexicans of good will accept as goals to be worked for "economic and social prosperity, justice, and improved education. So long as our people do not require of their rulers the practice of liberal institutions, the commands of the law will be an illusion, and our political life will suffer its characteristic defects."[116]

Turning from politics to the even more fundamental problem of education, Caso lays down as the supreme law of education, respect for the personality of the student; as its supreme aim, the development of the student's personality.[117] These aims are not being realized; Mexico's fear of new ideas will not permit the necessary individualism.[118] "People work little in Mexico; in the schools, hardly at all. . . . Our primary schools are the greatest of our national failures."[119] The fault lies in part at the door of the teachers, who should be philosophers, or at least should read the philosophers who have written the classics of education: Plato, Montaigne, Rousseau, Herbert Spencer, Ellen Key.[120]

It is when he addresses the nation on "Our Mission as Human Beings" that Caso becomes most inspiring. "The world is still unfinished," he preaches. "Morality is the effort to make the highest use of human nature. There are no weak virtues. . . . The virtuous man is the strong man."[121] We must call into play our hidden potentialities for good, must not accept the low aim of pleasure, but instead the pleasure of being good, of being courageous.[122] "The first vice is laziness, and the first virtue enthusiasm."[123] Dead rules are not morality, and are only a poor substitute for motives to virtuous action.[124] The imperfection of a perfectible world is the best of such motives, and this alone gives meaning to human life and action.[125]

[116] *Id.* at 130.
[117] *Id.* at 211.
[118] *Id.* at 213.
[119] *Id.* at 218-219.
[120] *Id.* at 221, 224.
[121] *Id.* at 231.
[122] *Id.* at 232.
[123] *Id.* at 239.
[124] *Id.* at 241.
[125] *Id.* at 244.

In the volume of essays entitled "Doctrines and Ideas," he returns to the subject of idealism. Unlike Ingenieros, he feels that one is first of all an idealist, then adopts ideals. There exist, paradoxically, idealists who have never found their ideals, who hunger and thirst after a satisfactory ideal. They have the basic quality of disdaining the real because of its imperfection, and loving the ideal, so distant and so fair, but they have been unable to choose a definite aim that convinces their minds and holds their allegiance. So restlessly they wait, and "suffer and love, affirm and deny, fight and are disappointed." Doubting the validity of their own reason, they are misologists. No symbols compel their loyalty; their hearts are in the right place, but Merriam's *miranda* and *credenda* are lacking.[126]

Surveying the philosophy of our time, Caso concludes that it is attempting a true synthesis. It is not ignorant of science, indeed bases itself on scientific data. There are, however, other data on which it does not turn its back, data from religion, art, and history. Philosophy (and he can speak with most assurance for Antonio Caso) assembles data from all sources, and only then sets about its final task.[127] The union of morals and esthetics we have met before appears in Caso's saying: "A clearly defined act of heroism, expressed artistically, assures its own continued life. . . . It enters into eternity." [128]

One must learn to expect the unexpected of Latin-American thinkers, for instance their high opinion of writers scorned in the United States. An example is Caso's praise of Gobineau, whom he considers one of the great political moralists. He admits that he is one-sided in his theory, but after all, he argues, the race theory has only the function of a Platonic myth.[129]

[126] Caso, *Doctrinas e ideas* (Mexico, 1924), pp. 41–43.
[127] *Id.* at 112.
[128] *Id.* at 119.
[129] *Id.* at 134.

Uncompromising hostility to certain features of North American policy and culture is less of a surprise. Living next door to the United States, "the greatest common divider" of Latin America, we must forever remind ourselves, he says, that we are part of a single father-land, "holy, an ideal that fails not, a reality immaterial but invincible." [130] The movies of Hollywood are a lie and a slander.[131] "The sources of the national wealth are not in the hands of our own citizens. Commerce, industry, and a part of agriculture belong to other races." Only the worst of all industries — politics, war and bureaucracy — are left for the Mexicans. Mexicans will be slaves until they give up the idea that they are lords and masters. These are days for work, not for war or politics. "When Mexico shall have become a nation of good workers, from top to bottom of society, she will have been saved forever. She will belong to herself." [132]

In the less technical parts of his "Esthetics," published in 1925, Caso attempts to strike a balance between individualism and a cultural approach, arriving at a synthesis which in its wisdom reminds us of Charles Horton Cooley. "A purely individualistic conception of art," he holds, "is false; but an esthetics which neglects the individual factor, and attempts to convey to us the whole secret of artistic production by means of collective causes and actions, is also false, and for even stronger reasons." [133] For art is both individual and collective, indissolubly so. Individual models are converted into laws and rule the taste of a whole period or century.[134]

The element in artistic production that is forever contingent and unpredictable is the personality of the creative artist.[135] Personality is the most individual, the most "different" thing there is in the world, and it reaches its highest

[130] *Id.* at 209.
[131] *Id.* at 218.
[132] *Id.* at 223-224.
[133] Caso, *Principios de estética* (Mexico, 1925), p. 206.
[134] *Id.* at 208.
[135] *Id.* at 209.

expression in art.[136] All the elements Taine teaches are causes of art — the race, environment, moment, schools, traditions, techniques — these only limit the possibilities of the artist. Without such common funds of ideas and sentiments, "the work of art would be a pure mystic state, hermetic, and ineffable." [137] He neglects to mention that such factors may open up new possibilities to the artist, as changes in the class structure, or psychoanalytic investigation have done, but he does admit that artists deal with the ideas of their time, their minds are filled by its preoccupations, and from it they even learn what objects *are* artistic, and proper themes for art.[138] In a vast and complicated culture, the artist is not limited but can pick and choose to an extent that enlarges the area of the "original." [139]

Art and morals, contemplation and action, are historic rivals. Can they be reconciled? He thinks so, especially in that most fruitful of historic events, the heroic act expressed artistically. In the last analysis, both art and heroism are supreme expressions of a kind of "superabundance" which amazes and confounds the observer.[140]

In "The Concept of Universal History and the Philosophy of Values" he addresses himself to the relation between history and science, art, and philosophy, a problem with which only moderns have concerned themselves.[141] No philosophy of history that makes progress its key word can stand; "for only intellectual, scientific and practical progress is a fact. Universal progress has not existed and does not exist. Belief in the all-round improvement of humanity is just a modern superstition." [142]

[136] *Id.* at 210.
[137] *Id.* at 209–210.
[138] *Id.* at 211.
[139] *Id.* at 214.
[140] *Id.* at 222–227.
[141] Caso, *El concepto de la historia y la filosofía de los valores* (Mexico, 1933), p. 12.
[142] *Id.* at 33.

What is the business of history? Certainly not to search
for general causes. "The state of things that are permanent
does not constitute history. Collective facts are not historical. The masses are only the substratum of history. History is never the science of the general. Not only is it difficult to discover the laws of history, it is contradictory to
hunt for them." [143] History is rather, as he called it in an
earlier book, "an intuition of that which was." [144]

History is a cultural science, that is, it deals with us who
are real beings, the essence of whose being is not *just* being,
but the values we embody and pursue. Philosophy cannot
take the position of naturalistic science, which is blind to
values.[145] Only a philosophy based on history can hope to
achieve a really philosophical point of view. For if it is concerned with the useful, the good, the beautiful, the true, the
holy, the valuable, it must remember that each of these is
good or useful or beautiful only because it is good, useful,
and beautiful to a society. Suppress society and with it culture, and where will value be? [146] The function of sociology
in a world of values is summed up in the statement: "Between the psychological world and the ontological is the
sociological." [147]

The realization of man's highest possibilities is not, however, collective; it happens in society, but to individuals.
Progress is not social, but individual; only a few men have
been its incarnation, their lives the most meaningful and
valuable things that history can show.[148] Among them are
the heroic figure that is the wise man, the saint that is a philosopher, the historian who is fundamentally poet.[149] So we
have come round the circle to answer our question, What is
history? It is "an act of creative imitation; not invention

[143] *Id.* at 58–59.
[144] Caso, *Problemas filosóficos*, p. 248.
[145] Caso, *El concepto de la historia*, pp. 73, 80.
[146] *Id.* at 84.

[147] *Id.* at 85.
[148] *Id.* at 111–112.
[149] *Id.* at 132.

like art, not abstract synthesis like science, not intuition of universal principles like philosophy." [150]

In the same year (1934) Caso addressed "New Discourses to the Mexican Nation," dealing with such pressing and practical matters as Marxism, historic materialism, and class struggle, and hailing with enthusiasm the same tendency expressed in National Socialism and in the Roosevelt administration. This was not his last word on the subject of totalitarianism, as we shall see later. There is strong emphasis here on aristocracy, for "the most aristocratic is at the same time the most revolutionary element in life, the most constructive and the most destructive." The great intellectual leaders of modern life have been inventors, who constitute an aristocracy of science. But instead of working to increase the number of such leaders, "Mexico stands out for its failure to understand the nature and function of universities, for its neglect of the aristocracy of science and its accompanying enthusiasm for the lie of popular education." [151]

A more philosophical book also published in 1934 is Caso's "The Act of Ideation: Essences and Values." After a brief historical review, Caso points out that Nietzsche, who preached the transvaluation of all values, did more preaching than defining.[152] The analysis of the concept of value is perhaps the most disquieting question before philosophers today; an immense amount of study and reflection is needed to clarify it and to complete the work of Nietzsche.[153] Reality is not only a matter of essences and existences; it is also a matter of value. Even if we knew all that is, we should not know all; we must find out what has value, and what makes it have value. Durkheim provides one answer: society creates values; they exist in society as ideal creations of the

[150] *Id.* at 141.
[151] Caso, *Nuevos discursos a la nación mexicana* (Mexico, 1934), p. 58.
[152] Caso, *El acto ideatorio: las esencias y los valores* (Mexico, 1934), p. 109.
[153] *Id.* at 119.

group, social realities rather than ontological ones.[154] Other philosophers, more objectivist in tendency, prefer to think of values as objects having value in themselves, a value which the human mind perceives or apprehends, but does in no way create.[155] This leads us only to a new form of the realist, conceptualist, nominalist argument, which Caso does not pretend to resolve. He is content to suggest that values are relations, and that they do not exist in isolation, "but tend to totality, incorporate themselves in persons, and in persons realize themselves." [156]

Caso, recognized as an authentic master of Latin-American thought, hailed on the twenty-fifth anniversary of his teaching career with spontaneous enthusiasm and reverence for his contribution to the spiritual formation of the continent, which lies in his wisdom and serenity, continues to publish more quiet but probing studies. Four of them are brought together under the title, "The Philosophy of Culture and Historical Materialism."

New ways of thinking are abroad in the world; naturalism, materialism, and empiricism are *passé*; progressive thought takes the form of the philosophy of spirit or of values, and of intuitionism.[157] A philosophy of that which exists is not enough, for "there are things which exist and are of no value, and there are things which do not exist but are important as values." [158] Caso seems never to see that values, too, exist, but as socio-psychological entities rather than physical ones. Instead, he puts it that there are two separate realms of investigation, the ontological and the axiological. For instance, "among Latin-American people — half way on the road to being peoples, with a civilization that must be measured in quarters — justice frequently does not exist" — but

154 *Id.* at 143.
155 *Id.* at 144.
156 *Id.* at 153–156.
157 Caso, *La filosofía de la cultura*, p. 13.   158 *Id.* at 14.

it is there as a value, as an ideal, perhaps all the more so for not being achieved.[159]

This is a point of view as far removed as possible from Marxian materialism. This once-popular theory fails to see that the material and the intellectual are always indissolubly united. "Human needs can be satisfied only by the use of intelligence; matter is manipulated socially, by a culture." [160] A brilliant North American economist, Walton Hamilton, has expressed the same idea unforgettably in the phrase, "Natural resources are not in the earth, they are in our heads." If even technique and economics are imbued with spirit, the Marxian talk of basic (economic) structure and added superstructure (ideologies) is quite unacceptable.[161] Men long committed the error of omitting economic facts from history; it is just as bad to go to the other extreme and try to explain everything in economic terms. Social life is more subtle than any such scheme.[162] To make law, religion, and culture mere epiphenomena is to fail to know them. It is only by premising the plurality of values that we can understand history. "Philosophic thought does not consist in the absurd attempt to unify, in the process losing true knowledge, but rather in an approach that respects difference where it exists, and recognizes the like for what it is, and the identical in its identity with itself." [163]

Values are not given in nature, they are found in history. They constitute its very texture, and what is material is not history, what is historical cannot by its nature be merely a part of the story of materialism.[164] Only in one sense is materialism historic, namely that it was a fact of the past, a part of intellectual history.[165] When it attempts to be more it falls into the absurdity of denying a part of reality, the

[159] *Id.* at 15.
[160] *Id.* at 22.
[161] *Id.* at 25.
[162] *Id.* at 29.
[163] *Id.* at 31.
[164] *Id.* at 33.
[165] *Id.* at 35.

reality we call ideal. With so false a simplification of reality it can never be an adequate philosophy.[166]

Thinking in another essay of the first quarter century of Mexico's national university, and of the mission of universities, Caso reflects on the proper attitude toward history. The past is always a part of us. How can we hope to deny the action of time, organizing and harmonizing the work of the generations? To be sure this work is modified and transformed, but the important thing to remember is that we cannot break with it. Those who try to do so destroy that unity of style which constitutes a culture, and end in barbarism. Mexico, unfortunately, has tried to make this kind of break with traditions. Do not misunderstand; Caso does not wish slavish adherence to all the heritage of the past. "The true conservative does not just repeat; he also creates, creates without destroying that which may be put to good use in making further progress." [167] We have without mentioning the word "university" defined its essential mission in these words. It can fulfill its function only if it has liberty to conserve and to create. "The University is at the same time Culture, Reason, and Tradition." [168] Given self-direction, freedom, and sufficient economic support it can live up to this program,[169] and make its country one of those happy ones that "think and work, create and educate, know and love." [170] Perhaps the verb "create" is not the right one, for creation is difficult, perhaps so uncommon as to be unheard of; let us say rather work, the kind of work that consists of research and teaching, not forgetting to see to it that the benefits of both reach the masses of the people.[171]

The final essay in this volume, on the Decline of Culture, treats Spengler and Lothrop Stoddard as if they belonged on

[166] *Id.* at 38.
[167] *Id.* at 88–89.
[168] *Id.* at 93, 96.

[169] *Id.* at 101.
[170] *Id.* at 108.
[171] *Id.* at 124.

the same level, ignores Toynbee, and finds the most acceptable solution in the work of Nicholas Berdiaeff, who success-
fully fuses the moral ideals of Christianity with the political
ideal of aristocracy, and inspired by both achieves that union
of social and personal ideals which communism is powerless
to achieve, for it confessedly moves toward no moral ideal,
and explains its own history as being necessary in a materialistic sense.[172]

It would take a superhuman effort not to be more interested in Caso's 1941 volume, "The Human Personality and
the Totalitarian State" than in his earlier work. In this he
has defined his political position and discussed the relation
of personality to community and the political framework of
society.

Social life, he begins, evolves between the poles of liberty
and law. "Life in society without liberty is inconceivable
from the moral point of view. Social life without law is
equally inconceivable. So all social life implies the necessary
combination of liberty and law." The aim is liberty within
a régime of law, and it can be achieved only by a third element, which looks toward both liberty and law; this is power,
authority.[173] "The abomination of power is anarchy; the
abomination of liberty is despotism." [174]

The final goal is sometimes forgotten, to our cost. Democracies are prone to confuse the means with the end, — to
erect an admirable means, liberty, into an end in itself, which
does not make sense. For man's conduct is explicable only
in terms of final goals. The means we employ only imper-
fectly realize the final end for which they were conceived,
which "cannot be other than that of attaining the happiness
of mankind, with the realization of the supreme values of

[172] *Id.* at 147–152.
[173] Caso, *La persona humana y el estado totalitario* (Mexico, 1941).
[174] *Id.* at 25.

culture: truth, beauty, justice, goodness, holiness. Between the final end and the beginning of human action there are established a whole series of subordinate ends, high and noble if you like, but which lead often to error if some political or social theory makes of them the ultimate norms of our activity." [175] Only a monstrous result can be expected if we subordinate culture to democracy and liberty, advancing that precious gift, liberty, an indispensable condition of human perfection, to the place of supreme end. We desire liberty and democracy for the good, the true, for justice, beauty, and holiness.[176] It is man's freedom to think that seems important to Caso. Freedom and thought are inseparable, and only man possesses them. The greatest tyrannies of history have been those that have crushed the spirit of man and put shackles on his free thinking.[177] The soul of the world, the intelligence that has created our cultural values and given us progress, is our thinkers who have used their freedom to solve problems, to invent. Their right to do so is as natural and inalienable as their power.[178] The cumulated, corrected residue of their thought is Science, foundation of human progress, the only thing that has progress as its law. "It made the primitive horde into the modern city, and will remake present society in ways we cannot imagine. The true creators of humanity are the inventors." [179]

There is another liberty essential in the life of nations, that of political association, and in forms other than those provided by the State itself, for it is not the only social form. Totalitarianism fails to recognize this. "The danger of the totalitarian states is that they provoke and incite to anarchism. If the State declares itself absolute, unjustly, above all principles, all laws, then the individual also can declare him-

[175] *Id*. at 28.
[176] *Id*. at 29.
[177] *Id*. at 50.

[178] *Id*. at 109.
[179] *Id*. at 114.

self absolute, above all principles and laws." [180] We must protect the principle of personality, and yet not let it run wild. It may be different in the Orient, which is all quietude, but personalism is a necessary part of the Occident; God is personal for us.

Both individualism and communism lower the dignity of the person. Person and culture are concomitants. The person implies the society in his development. Society in turn needs the person to *be*. . . . The human person is being in its highest form. Or rather, the qualities which our highest geniuses reveal are still below our ideal. Man's ideal can never be satisfied, save by postulating a Person who while active is at the same time omnipotent; loving, is yet absolutely disinterested; intelligent, but embraces all knowing in a single thought; free, but autonomous; holy, is holiness itself. This person which our ideals call for is the synthesis of being and the ideal, is God.[181]

On the mundane level, the ideal is justice, which is neither excessive individualism nor the intensive community, but rather "a moral union of men, respecting values." We are persons, not biological entities, and no community should allow itself to forget that fact, and tyrannize over spiritual centers of action. Nor should the individual set himself over against the community and forget that "above individuality is human culture, a perpetually renewed synthesis of values. These values were not worked out by the individual, nor by the present community. They reflect the historic continuity of many generations, the moral solidarity of many peoples."[182]

The human person at his best does not need to reject the rule of law as individualism and communism both do. Within law he is free to satisfy his natural ambition, which is not to have more, but to be more.[183] The political and social should not interfere with his nature, but in a sense he transcends

[180] *Id.* at 142–143.
[181] *Id.* at 190.
[182] *Id.* at 192.
[183] *Id.* at 193.

both, and finds his fulfillment on the plane of absolute spirituality.[184]

Bourgeois individualism thinks only of guaranteeing the individual his right to be, of the right of each one to be according to his essence and without infringing the equal right of every other. While having is necessary, it is the mistake of our civilization to have allowed being to be obscured by having, to have despised being, and glorified having.[185] Nietzsche, to be sure, defended vigorously the rights of the person, but he totally mistook the nature of Christianity, which is as far as may be from love for weakness. "The Christian is the strong soul who loves the weak but only so that he may cease to be weak. . . . Charity is not love for weakness, for decadence; it is strength to conquer them." [186] "Humanity has forgotten love." [187]

If Nietzsche was wrong in eliminating Christians from his outstanding personalities, we may agree with him that there is more to the definition of great personality than Christian virtue. Societies are always producing culture, and culture is simply the synthesis of accepted values. The genius is the personality that sums up in his own person the values of his time or his nation. This does not mean that he is a mere product of history. To be an historic person, he must first of all be a person, and unique. He gives to history more than he has gotten from the society in which he was born. History is more than the biography of great men, but it is meaningless without them. Both the pure collectivism of positivistic sociology and the pure Carlylean individualism are false. "History is personalism and collectivism, indissolubly bound together." [188]

Adopting as title a phrase that had been used in a review

[184] *Id.* at 200.
[185] *Id.* at 201–202.
[186] *Id.* at 237–238.
[187] *Id.* at 243.
[188] *Id.* at 251–253.

of his previous book, Caso continues the same discussion in "Man's Danger." "A Personalist Looks at the Political Process" might have served as a more descriptive title.[189]

As Caso looks at government, every form of it that has existed rests upon some legal fiction, but he does not conclude that the political problem is therefore insoluble. It is a fiction that England really possesses the liberty that is her aim, or France the equality that she puts first, while the United States, which seeks both at once, is threatened in its attempt by the strong internal force of capitalism.[190] But their failure to achieve is still far from the régime of totalitarianism, for which liberty is the enemy; and whether we look at the economic or the moral aspect, we find that "the Anglo-Saxon peoples are the best endowed in the world." [191]

The error of the totalitarian states is their deification of the State, and their failure to recognize that above it is the spirit of man, manifesting itself in religion, art, science, philosophy, morality, and law. It is by his participation in these cultural forms that man fulfills his function of being "the medium between eternal values and their historic realization." [192] Their crime is their lack of respect for the human personality. Caso is led to define his personalist position: "Personalism, yes, for it is spirituality and affirmation; individualism, no, for the individual as such fails to recognize the moral law, that each human person should realize his personality to the full, playing his part within society, which carries on the seamless web of a spiritual tradition which traverses the ages." [193]

Personalism stands for every one's being recognized for what he is: a human person. "The idea of person imposes —

[189] Caso, El peligro del hombre (Mexico, 1942), pp. 21–23.
[190] Id. at 29.
[191] Id. at 31.
[192] Id. at 42.
[193] Id. at 50.

because it implies — respect." [194] It is because he respects *every* human person that Caso is a feminist, of a kind far removed from the follies that often parade under the name of feminism. He is not willing that personalism should be kidnapped by any single social panacea like feminism. It offers a cure for the great disease of our times, the lack of respect for the person which is shown in our talk of "biological entities," "masses," and other terms referring to the anonymous and collective. It is to be noted that Caso speaks of the characteristics of "our period" and does not refer merely to Mexico or Latin America; he speaks of all Western Culture, and he speaks with authority.

In good Aristotelian terms, man should realize his essence, which is to act as a personality, as a creator of values. One should like a little more explanation of how men create values if the values are eternal, but instead of tackling this difficult problem, Caso descends to a lower level, to teach us that the bases of respect for personality are freedom of worship, private property, and political liberty; where these exist the individual is still recognized as having some rights *vis-à-vis* the State; where they have disappeared, such authority as holds sway must be illegitimate.[195]

If one feels for the thread that runs through the works of Caso, it will be found in his growing insistence on values, on personality, and the corollaries of these emphases for politics. He becomes less the commentator on other men's work, more profoundly himself, although in this most recent work there is high praise for the Russian, Berdiaeff, who has been extensively translated into Spanish, and in sympathy with him an ever closer approximation of the orthodox Christian position.

[194] *Id.* at 71.
[195] *Id.* at 96.

Samuel Ramos

Many of the same problems trouble the younger Mexican professor of philosophy, Samuel Ramos, as may be seen by a brief incursion into his "Toward a New Humanism." Humanism is the key word, rather than personalism, and his attitude toward science is perhaps less friendly than that of Caso, but the two men move in the same universe of discourse.

There are psychological factors which explain why modern man needs a spiritual reform if he is to recover his inner balance. The trouble is rooted in a "schism of the soul," to use Toynbee's term, and when introspection has revealed the trouble, reform will be possible.[196] Man's age-long struggle to plant and build has surrounded him with an artificial jungle in which in vain he tries to make his way; he bows under the weight of a world grown too complicated for him.[197]

No easy solution for these difficulties will be found by thinking of them as social problems inhering in the externals of social organization. We must think of the totality of human aspirations and must combat the sub-humanity engendered by bourgeois capitalism and materialism, must rally generous-spirited youth behind the values of humanism.[198]

Philosophy can define these values for us and help man to recover his spiritual world, for its business is not just with empirical man, but with man as idea, man as he ought to be. Its intuitive investigation meets all the prejudices which science has built up against such direct procedures. The only course to follow is to throw off boldly the burden of acquired knowledge and come to grips with reality immediately, by intuition.[199] The discipline that is to deal with the question

[196] Ramos, *Hacia un nuevo humanismo: programa de un antropologia filosófica* (Mexico, 1940), p. 18.
[197] *Id.* at 26.
[198] *Id.* at 27.   [199] *Id.* at 44–45.

"What is man?" he calls philosophical anthropology, although perhaps philosophical psychology would more nearly
have expressed his meaning. It will answer that man is a being who has not only a consciousness of his being, but of
thoughts and values. The essence of man is his spirit, which,
self-enriching, progresses through the world adding unto itself ever new values, moving toward a goal that is supra-
individual.[200] Artists and moral reformers, with their greater
sensitivity, are those who more perfectly fulfill the function
of value-discovery, but all of us can project onto value-
objects a kind of mirage which will move us more ardently
to seek them; all of us can seek that true estimate and rank-
ing of values which is the foundation of morality. For morality is tested by renunciation of the lower for the sake of the
higher, by a free act of the will. We are free to reject as well
as to follow the values of our culture, and without that freedom we could not be moral. We are ourselves values, to be
respected by others, to be realized by ourselves.[201] A heavier
responsibility rests upon men who have it in them to be
great; their "non-conformity toward current values pre-
destines them to be the creators of new ones." The vulgar-
ization of old values dooms them to be unsatisfactory, and
new problems demand new solutions. Without mentioning
either, Ramos approaches the theories of Ingenieros about
idealists, and of Toynbee on the creative minority.[202]

[200] *Id.* at 81–82.
[201] *Id.* at 134–135.
[202] *Id.* at 135.

CHAPTER X

Conclusion

H ERE, THEN, in the lyric prose of some thirty-five Latin-American thinkers and spiritual leaders, we find the source of much that is puzzling in the social and political as well as the cultural life of the "other Americas." We have seen the great importance that is attached to the form in which the thought is clothed. Facts are not enough; indeed, as many travelers have found, an assemblage of facts marshaled in an effort to substantiate some claim or other about the artistic or social life of our people in North America is often as not met with a cool incredulity by Latins. So accustomed are they to being swayed by what we consider unduly sweeping generalizations, couched in glowing periods that sway the mind and emotions, rather than being convinced by methodical, logical steps, that the North American who is attempting to bring about a closer understanding overshoots his mark, and leaves his audience more convinced than before of the gulf that lies between us. Positivism, so characteristic of our thinking, presents few attractions to most Latin Americans, except in a country like Argentina, where the thinking of Alvarez seems more similar to ours than that of most Latin philosophers and where the racial composition of the country and its geographical advantages have provided the physical energy and the natural resources to build a civilization as dynamic and aggressive as our own.

To understand the power of the Spanish Falange we need to trace the attitude of South Americans toward the mother country, and in the works of Gálvez we see the tie at its strongest. We cannot fail to realize its strength when we perceive how the soul of Spain pervades the writings of even the most anti-clerical and Hispanophobe. José Luis Romero feels that the European tradition is so strong that it is foolish to speak of a "national" literature at all: "National literatures have no meaning in America. In every country there are merely figures in one great movement of thought originating in Europe and FELT in an American way. So it is absurd to attempt to group literature according to national schools."

Whatever may be the case with literature, one cannot fail to observe the importance of the national spirit in the thought of the great patriot-thinkers, like Sarmiento, Lastarria, González, Gálvez, Rojas, Freyre, Varona, Martí, and Hostos. It is interesting to note that of the ten or more thinkers whose patriotism was unusually strong, at least half are from the Argentine. The background of the attitude of the Argentine nation today is clearly seen in the writings and influence of these men.

In many of the works mentioned in this book we find a tolerant, if not an actively sympathetic, attitude toward the United States. Many of the writers find much to admire in our social institutions and our political framework, as well as in our famous standard of living. If we are told that the civilizations of North and South America must complement each other, we can seek the contribution of Latin America in the works of these thinkers. It is a platitude to say that true international friendship must be mutual, must be based on an exchange of some kind, either of commodities or of ideas. Much has been written of the contribution that the United States could make to the industrial, economic, and scientific progress of Latin America. Less attention has been devoted to a consideration of the contribution that she stands ready to make to us of her rich philosophical heritage, her interest in the thought process, and her custom of appealing to the intellectual élite among the youth to help achieve the high destiny of their country. Perhaps Latin America, with her series of great educators like Sarmiento, Bello, Letelier, Alvarez, González, and others, can show us how to become more conscious of the drives that underlie our constant activity, how to become more articulate and more inspired in the appeal we make to youth in the United States to help solve the difficult social and political and economic problems that are before us.

The "universal" man has been less conspicuous in our national life than in that of South America. Our neighbors reproach us constantly for our tendency to specialize and thus fail to see life whole, like their great figures, known for the breadth of their culture — Rodó, Ingenieros, Rojas, or Hostos. This is not the place to debate that question, but the writings of those men throw some light upon the whole problem of what knowledge and what ideas are basic and must be included in any plans for changing education in the post-war world.

The effort of this book has been throughout to give an honest account of the thinking of the men who have been regarded as most able by Latin Americans themselves, and who have had the greatest influence in shaping the intellectual currents of their own countries or of all Latin America. None has been excluded because of the character of his views. Some like the United States and some hate us; some are enthusiastic Hispanophiles, and some abominate Spain; there are Catholics and atheists, and at least one communist and one fascist. But there have been omissions. We must mention them and apologize, at the same time accepting responsibility for the decision as to inclusion or exclusion. In some cases, a passing reference will at least put anyone eager to track down more *pensadores* on a promising trail.

From the Central American republics we have included no one; the same is true of Paraguay. Haiti has been treated as negligently as she and her three million French-speaking people generally are in Latin-American discussions, and we can only apologize and direct a deep bow to Dantes Bellegarde and other distinguished Haitians.

Colombia has had a fame for its intellectual life which renders it even more embarrassing to give it no representation in a book of this character. It is the poorest of amends to send the inquiring reader on a probably fruitless quest to the nearest library for the works of José Maria Sámper, Carlos Arturo Torres, and Baldomero Sanín Cano.

If we choose not to learn, but merely to understand how our friends came to be our friends, and our enemies our enemies, we can do so very quickly by reading the exuberant praises or the violent denunciations of our country in the always poetic and oratorical prose of certain *pensadores*. It is to be hoped that soon the North American, stereotyped as the man of action, and the South American man of thought may one day fuse into The American and march forward on the road to progress of which Vasconcelos so glowingly spoke: "From thought alone are derived the humblest as well as the highest forms of progress; by thought alone can we hope for redemption, meaning by 'thought,' obviously, not only cold reasoning, but the whole mystical notion of existence with all its anguish, its delights and its splendor."

Bibliography

CHAPTER I. INTRODUCTION

GAOS, JOSÉ, "Localización histórica del pensamiento hispano-americano," *Cuadernos americanos* (Mexico), no. 4 (1942), pp. 63–86.

—— "Caracterización formal y material del pensamiento hispano-americano," *Cuadernos americanos*, no. 6 (1942), pp. 59–88.

—— "Significación filosófica del pensamiento hispano-americano," *Cuadernos americanos*, II (1943), 63–86.

GARCÍA CALDERÓN, FRANCISCO, *Ideas e impresiones* (Madrid, 1919). Contains "Las corrientas filosóficas en la América latina" and "La originalidad intelectual de América."

HENRÍQUEZ UREÑA, PEDRO, *Seis ensayos en busca de nuestra expresión* (Buenos Aires, 1923), "El descontento y la promesa," pp. 1–41.

SÁNCHEZ, LUIS ALBERTO, *Breve historia de la literatura americana (desde los orígenes hasta nuestros días)*, 3a edición, reformada (Santiago, 1940).

CHAPTER II. INDEPENDENCE AND NATIONHOOD

ECHEVERRÍA, ESTEBAN

Obras completas, 5 vols. (Buenos Aires, 1871–1874): I, *Poemas varios*; II, *El ángel caído*; III, *Poesías varias*; IV, *Escritos en prosa*; V, *Escritos en prosa con notas y esplicaciones por Don Juan María Gutiérrez*.

Dogma socialista, edición crítica y documentada, prólogo de Alberto Palcos (La Plata, 1940). This edition includes the biography by Gutiérrez and many related documents.

BOGLIOLO, RÓMULO, *Las ideas democráticas y socialistas de Esteban Echeverría* (Buenos Aires, 1937).

BUCICH, ANTONIO J., *Esteban Echeverría y su tiempo* (Buenos Aires, 1938).

ECHAGÜE, JUAN PABLO, *Seis figuras del Plata* (Buenos Aires, 1838).

FURT, JORGE M., *Esteban Echeverría* (1936).

ORGAZ, RAÚL A., *Echeverría y el saintsimonismo* (Buenos Aires, 1934).

PALCOS, ALBERTO, *Echeverría y la democracia argentina* (Buenos Aires, 1941).

ALBERDI, JUAN BAUTISTA

Obras completas, 8 vols. (Buenos Aires, 1886–1887).

Escritos postumos, 16 vols. (Buenos Aires, 1895–1901).

Obras selectas, 18 vols. (Buenos Aires, 1920).

Autobiografía: la evolución de su pensamiento, serie, Grandes escritores argentinos, vol. II (1928).

BUCICH, ANTONIO J., *Homenaje á Juan Bautista Alberdi* (Buenos Aires, 1935).

BUCICH ESCOBAR, ISMAEL, *El Retorno de Alberdi* (Buenos Aires, 1930).

CAROCANO, MIGUEL ANGEL, *Alberdi, su doctrina economica* (Buenos Aires, 1934).

Colmo, Alfredo, *Principios sociologicos* (Buenos Aires, 1905).

Garcia Mérou, Martín, *Alberdi, Ensayo critico* (Buenos Aires, 1890).

Hidalgo, Alberto, *Alberdi, aspectos de una vida de luchas y pesares* (Buenos Aires, 1941).

Ingenieros, José, "Sociologia argentina," *Obras,* VIII, 331–469, on Echeverría, Alberdi, and Sarmiento.

Mijares, Augusto, *Hombres e ideas en América: Ensayos* (Caracas, 1940), pp. 29–50.

Mujica, Adolfo S., "La personalidad de Alberdi," *Revista de filosofía,* XII (1920), 179–191.

Orgaz, Raúl A., *Alberdi y el historicismo* (Cordoba, 1937).

Peña, David, "Alberdi, Sarmiento y Mitre," *Revista de filosofía,* VIII (1918), 321–365, and IX (1919), 332–357.

Quesada, Ernesto, *La figura histórica de Alberdi* (Buenos Aires, 1919).

Rojas Paz, Pablo, *Alberdi, el ciudadano de la soledad* (Buenos Aires, 1941), bibliography.

Toledo, Antonio B., *Alberdi y la cultura espiritual* (Buenos Aires, 1935).

SARMIENTO, DOMINGO FAUSTINO

Obras, 52 vols. (Santiago and Buenos Aires, 1885–1903).

Facundo, o civilización y barbarie en las pampas argentinas. Many editions. The first edition (Santiago, 1845) had the title *Civilización i barbarie.* . . . An English translation, by Mrs. Horace Mann, *Life in the Argentine Republic in the Days of the Tyrants, or Civilization and Barbarism,* was published in 1868.

Viajes por Europa, África y América (1850).

Recuerdos de provincia (1850).

Cuatro conferencias, Grandes escritores argentinos, vol. VI (1928).

Los caudillos, Grandes escritores argentinos, vol. XVIII (1928).

Contra Rosas, Grandes escritores argentinos, vol. XLIX (1934).

El pensamiento vivo de Sarmiento, prólogo y selección de Ricardo Rojas.

Blanco-Fombona, Rufino, *Grandes escritores de América, Siglo XIX* (Madrid, 1917), pp. 77–171.

Bunge, Carlos Octavio, *Sarmiento, estudio biográfico y crítico* (Madrid, 1926).

Echague, Juan Pablo, *Seis figuras del Plata* (Buenos Aires, 1938), pp. 9–51.

Lugones, Leopoldo, *Historia de Sarmiento* (Buenos Aires, 1911), 2a ed. 1931.

Mijares, Augusto, *Hombres e ideas en América* (Caracas, 1930), pp. 19–28, 41–50.

Nichols, Madaline W., *Sarmiento: A Chronicle of Inter-American Friendship* (Washington, 1940), with bibliography.

Ponce, Anibal, *Sarmiento, constructor de la nueva Argentina* (Buenos Aires, 1938).

Santovenia y Echaïde, Emeterio S., *Genio y acción: Sarmiento y Martí* (La Habana, 1938).

Comisión Nacional de Homenaje a Sarmiento, *Sarmiento: cincuentenario de su muerte,* 5 vols. (Buenos Aires, 1939): I, *Discursos y escritos (en la Argentina)*; II, *Discursos y escritos (en el exterior)*; III, *Páginas selectas*; IV, *Páginas selectas, sobre bibliotecas populares*; V, *El homenaje a Sarmiento, programa.*

CHAPTER III. THE GENERATION OF '42 AND AFTER

BELLO, ANDRÉS

Obras completas, 15 vols. (Santiago, 1881–1893).
AMUNÁTEGUI, MIGUEL LUIS, *Vida de don Andrés Bello* (Santiago, 1882).
BLANCO-FOMBONA, RUFINO, *Grandes escritores de América, siglo XIX* (Madrid, 1917), pp. 11–75.
CALDERA, RODRÍGUEZ RAFAEL, *Andrés Bello* (Caracas, 1935).
MIJARES, AUGUSTO, *Hombres e ideas en América: Ensayos* (Caracas, 1940), pp. 51–76.
ORREGO VICUÑA, EUGENIO, *Don Andrés Bello* (3a edición, Santiago, 1940).

LASTARRIA, JOSÉ VICTORINO

Obras completas de Don J. V. Lastarria, 14 vols. (Santiago, 1906–1934).
La América (Santiago, 1867).
FUENZALIDA GRANDÓN, ALEJANDRO, *Lastarria i su tiempo: su vida, obras e influencia en el desarrollo político e intelectual de Chile* (Santiago, 1893).
MELFI, DOMINGO, *Dos hombres: Portales y Lastarria* (Santiago, 1937).
ZAÑARTU, SADY, *Lastarria, el hombre solo*. Prólogo de Ricardo A. Latcham. Bibliography. (Santiago, 1938).

COLMO, ALFREDO

Principios sociológicos (Buenos Aires, 1905).
Los países de la América latina (Madrid, 1915).
Política cultural de los países latino-americanos (Buenos Aires, 1925).
La revolución en la América latina (Buenos Aires, 1932).

GARCÍA CALDERÓN, FRANCISCO

Hombres e ideas de nuestra tiempo (Valencia, 1907).
Le Pérou contemporain (Paris, 1907; London, 1913).
Latin America, Its Rise and Progress, English translation [1913] of *Les démocraties latino-américaines* (Paris, 1912).
La creación de un continente (Paris, 1913).
CARRIÓN, BENJAMÍN, *Los creadores de la nueva América*, prólogo de Gabriela Mistral [1928], pp. 119–164.
GARCÍA GODOY, FEDERICO, *Americanismo literario* (Madrid, 1917), pp. 153–195.

BILBAO, FRANCISCO

Obras, 2 vols. (Santiago, 1865).
Obras completas. Edición hecha por Manuel Bilbao, 2 vols. (Buenos Aires, 1866).
Obras completas. Editadas i con una introducción por Pedro Pablo Figueroa, 4 vols. (Santiago, 1897–98).
La América en peligro, prólogo y notas de Luís Alberto Sánchez (Santiago, 1941). Includes other writings.
El pensamiento vivo de Francisco Bilbao. Prólogo y selección de Armando Donoso (6a ed., Santiago, 1940).

Donoso, Armando, *Bilbao y su tiempo* (Santiago, 1913).
——, "Or Ensayo sobre Francisco Bilbao," *Revista de filosofía*, III (1916), 204–265, 401–411; IV (1916), 203–248.

LETELIER, VALENTÍN

La lucha por la cultura, miscelánea de artículos políticos i estudios pedagógicos (Santiago, 1895).
Evolución de la historia, 2 vols., 2a edición, aumentada (Santiago, 1900), first published as *Por qué se rehace la historia* (Santiago, 1888).
Galdames, Luis, *Valentín Letelier y su obra, 1852–1919* (Santiago, 1937).

Chapter IV. A REACTION — RODÓ

RODÓ, JOSÉ ENRIQUE

El Mirador de Próspero (Montevideo, 1913).
Hombres de América (Barcelona, 1920).
Ariel, first published as vol. III of *La Vida Nueva* (Montevideo, 1900). Edition used, the third (1926). English translation by F. J. Stimson (Boston, 1922).
Los últimos motivos de Proteo: manuscritos hallados en la mesa de trabajo del maestro (Montevideo and Buenos Aires, 1932).
Motivos de Proteo (Montevideo, 1909; 2a ed., Montevideo, 1941). English translation by Angel Flores, *The Motives of Proteus*, with introduction by Havelock Ellis and bibliography (New York, 1928).
Rodó, serie Pensamiento de America, vol. IV (Mexico, 1943), prólogo y selección de Samuel Ramos.
Arias, Alejandro C., *Ideario de Rodó*, Salto, Uruguay.
Berrien, William, "Rodó" (unpublished dissertation).
García Calderón, Ventura, *Semblanzas de América* (Madrid, 1919), pp. 7–25.
Gil Salguero, Luis, "Ideario de Rodó" (to be published).
González-Blanco, Andrés, *Escritores representativos de América* (Madrid, 1917).
Henríquez Ureña, Max, *Rodó y Rubén Darío* (La Habana, 1918), pp. 1–75, bibliography.
Henríquez Ureña, Pedro, *La obra de José Enrique Rodó* (Mexico, 1810).
Marasso Rocca, Arturo, *Estudios literarios* (Buenos Aires, 1920), pp. 93–122.
Pérez Petit, Victor, *Rodó, su vida, su obra* (Montevideo, 1818).
Sánchez, Luis Alberto, *Balance y liquidación del novecientos* (Santiago, 1940).
Scarone, Arturo, *Bibliografía de Rodó*, 2 vols. (Montevideo, 1930).
Zaldumbide, Gonzalo, *Montalvo y Rodó* (Instituto de las Españas, New York, 1938).
Zum Felde, Alberto, *Proceso intelectual del Uruguay* (Montevideo, 1941), pp. 223–250.

VAZ FERREIRA, CARLOS

Lógica viva (Montevideo, 1910; 2a ed. 1920).
Sobre feminismo (Montevideo, 1933). Contains (pp. 11–55) "Estudio preliminar: límites de lo humano," by Luís Gil Salguero.
Fermentario (Buenos Aires, 1938; Montevideo, 1940).
Sobre los problemas sociales (Buenos Aires, 1939).
Moral para intelectuales.

La actual crisis del mundo desde el punto de vista racional (Buenos Aires, 1940).

CERUTI CROSA, PEDRO, *Crítica de Vaz Ferreira* (Montevideo, 1933).

FERNÁNDEZ ARTUCIO, HUGO, "Ubicación de la persona humana," *Revista hispánica moderna*, VI (1940), 109–112.

REYES, ALFONSO, "La filosofía social de Vaz Ferreira," *Repertorio americano*, vol. 37, no. 9, pp. 137–138 (abril 16, 1940).

ZUM FELDE, ALBERTO, *Proceso intelectual del Uruguay* (Montevideo, 1941), pp. 274–291.

CHAPTER V. POSITIVISM AND IDEALISM IN ARGENTINA

ALVAREZ, AGUSTÍN

South America, historia natural de la razón (Buenos Aires, 1894). English translation, WPA, 1938.

La transformación de las razas en América (Barcelona, 1906).

Historia de las instituciones libres (Barcelona-Madrid, 1909).

La creación del mundo moral (Madrid, 1913).

¿A dónde vamos? (Buenos Aires, 1915).

Manual de patología política (Buenos Aires, 1899); second ed. (1916), with biography by Evar Méndez.

Educación moral; tres repiques (Re-edición, Buenos Aires, 1917).

La herencia moral de los pueblos hispano-americanos (Buenos Aires, 1919). Prólogo de Félix Icasate-Larios.

INGENIEROS, JOSÉ, "Un moralista argentino," *Revista de filosofía*, IV (1916), 464–470.

BUNGE, CARLOS OCTAVIO

Obras, 13 vols. (Madrid, 1926–1928).

Nuestra América (Barcelona, 1903). The 2nd ed. (1905) adds the subtitle, *Ensayo de psicología social*. The edition used is that of 1926, with prologue by Ingenieros.

ARGUEDAS, ALCIDES

Un pueblo enfermo: Contribución a la psicología de los pueblos hispanoamericanos (Barcelona, 1910; 3rd ed. Santiago, 1937).

Historia de Bolivia, each volume with a separate title:
 La fundación de la República (La Paz and Madrid, 1920).
 Los caudillos letrados, 1828–1848 (Barcelona, 1923).
 La plebe en acción, 1848–1857 (Barcelona, 1924).
 La dictadura y la anarquía 1857–1864 (Barcelona, 1926).
 Los caudillos bárbaros 1864–1872 (Barcelona, 1929).
 La guerra injusta 1872–1880 (projected).
 La política conservadora 1880–1898 (projected).
 La política liberal 1898–1920 (projected).

La danza de las sombras, apuntes sobre cosas, gentes y gentezuelas de la América española. 2 vols. (Barcelona, 1934).
 I. *Literatura y viajes.*
 II. *Política y la guerra.*

CARRIÓN, BENJAMÍN, *Los creadores de la nueva América* (Buenos Aires, 1925), pp. 165–217.

GONZÁLEZ, JOAQUÍN V.

Obras, 25 vols. (Buenos Aires, 1936–1937). Contains valuable articles, biographical and critical, by Alfredo Palacios (I, 13), Ricardo Levene (I, 91), de Vedia (X, 11), Arrieta (XV, 11), Posada (XV, 229), Ricardo Rojas, and others.

Ideario, 2 vols. (Buenos Aires, 1938).

MERCANTE, VICTOR, "Joaquín González," *Revista de Filosofía*, XXI (1925), 226–249.

ROJAS, RICARDO, *Elogia de González* (Buenos Aires, 1925), p. 124.

INGENIEROS, JOSÉ

Obras, 23 vols. (Buenos Aires, 1904–1940).

BAGÚ, SERGIO, *La vida exemplar de José Ingenieros* (Buenos Aires, 1936).

BERMANN, GREGORIO, *José Ingenieros* (Buenos Aires, 1926).

PONCE, ANIBAL, "Para una historia de Ingenieros," in Ingenieros, *Obras*, I, 1–101.

Revista de filosofía, enero de 1926, vol. XXIII, entire number devoted to Ingenieros.

RIAÑO JUAMA, J., *Ingenieros y su obra literaria* (La Habana, 1933). Prólogo de Juan J. Remos.

KORN, ALEJANDRO

Obras, 3 vols. (La Plata, 1938–1940). Introducción de Francisco Romero.

BARJA, CÉSAR, "Alejandro Korn," *Revista iberoamericana*, II (1940), 359–382.

REYES, ALFONSO, "Korn y la filosofía argentina," *Repertorio americano*, año 21, no. 882, pp. 24, 26 (1940).

UGARTE, MANUEL

Destiny of a Continent, introduction by J. Fred Rippy (New York, 1925).

CARRIÓN, BENJAMÍN, *Los creadores de la nueva América* (Madrid, 1928), pp. 77–117.

GÁLVEZ, MANUEL

Crítica e ideología:

El diario de Gabriel Quiroga (Buenos Aires, 1910).

El solar de la raza (Buenos Aires, 1913; new edition, 1936).

La vida multiple: arte y literatura 1910–1916 (Buenos Aires, 1916).

El espíritu de aristocracia y otros ensayos (Buenos Aires, 1924).

Este pueblo necesita (Buenos Aires, 1934).

La Argentina en nuestros libros (Santiago, 1935).

Novels:

El mal metafísico (1917).

La sombra del convento (1917).

La maestra normal (1918).

La tragedia de un hombre fuerte (1922).

GREEN, OTIS H., "Manuel Gálvez, 'Gabriel Quiroga' and La maestra normal," *Hispanic Review*, July 1943, and subsequent articles.

ROJAS, RICARDO

Obras, 20 vols. (Buenos Aires, 1922–1930; incomplete).

La obra de Rojas, collected criticisms (Buenos Aires, 1928).

La restauración nacionalista: crítica de la educación argentina y bases para una reforma en el estudio de las humanidades modernas (1909), *Obras*, vol. IV.

Blasón de Plata (1910), *Obras*, vol. I.

La Argentinidad: ensayo histórico sobre nuestra conciencia nacional en la gesta de la emancipación, 1810–1816 (1922), *Obras*, vol. III.

Eurindia: ensayo de estética fundado en la experiencia histórica de las culturas americanas (Buenos Aires, 1924), *Obras*, vol. V.

COVIELLO, ALFREDO, "Semblanza del príncipe de las letras argentinas (o la personalidad viviente de Ricardo Rojas)," *Revista Ibero-americana*, febrero de 1943, pp. 47–75.

CHAPTER VI. REBELLION ON THE WEST COAST

MONTALVO, JUAN

Geometría Moral (Madrid, 1902).

Capítulos que se le olvidaron á Cervantes (1895).

Siete Tratados (Paris, 1912).

Mercurial Eclesiástica (Madrid, 1918?).

El Cosmopolita, 2 vols. (Paris, 1923).

El Espectador (Paris, 1927).

El Regenerador, 2 vols. (Paris, 1927).

Ideario de Montalvo (1932).

Montalvo, serie Pensamiento de América, vol. III (Mexico, 1943), prólogo y selección de Manuel Moreno Sánchez.

BLANCO-FOMBONA, RUFINO, *Grandes escritores de América, siglo XIX* (Madrid, 1917), pp. 223–265.

CHECA DROUET, BENIGNO, *Vida de Montalvo* (Lima, 1933).

GARCÍA CALDERÓN, VENTURA, *Semblanzas de América* [1920?], pp. 201–206.

JARAMILLO ALVARADO, PÍO, *Montalvo, político* (Anales, Quito, 1932).

MERCHÁN, RAFAEL MARÍA, *Estudios críticos* (Bogotá, 1886; Madrid, 1917), pp. 69–130.

REYES, ALFONSO, *Simpatías y diferencias* (Madrid, 1921), pp. 169–175.

REYES, OSCAR EFREN, *Vida de Montalvo* (Quito, 1935).

RODÓ, JOSÉ E., *Hombres de América* (Barcelona, 1920).

ZALDUMBIDE, GONZALO, *Montalvo y Rodó* (Instituto de las Españas, New York, 1938).

GONZÁLEZ PRADA, MANUEL

Páginas libres (1894).

Horas de lucha (1902; 2a edición, Callao, 1924).

González Prada, por los más notables escritores del Perú y América (Cuzco, 1924).

Nuevas páginas libres (1931).

Bajo el oprobio (Paris, 1933).

Propaganda y ataque (Buenos Aires, 1939).

Anarquía (3a edición, Santiago, 1940), bibliography.

Prosa menuda (Buenos Aires, 1941).

BLANCO-FOMBONA, RUFINO, *Grandes escritores de América, siglo XIX* (Madrid, 1917), pp. 267–325.

GARCÍA CALDERÓN, VENTURA, *Semblanzas de América* [1920?], pp. 175–183.

GARRO, J. E., "Manuel González Prada," *Revista hispánica moderna*, julio y octubre, 1941, pp. 195–214.

INSTITUTO DE LAS ESPAÑAS, *Gonzáles Prada*, serie, Literatura contemporánea, or in *Revista hispánica moderna*.

SÁNCHEZ, LUIS ALBERTO, *Don Manuel, revisado* (Santiago, 1937).

MARIÁTEGUI, JOSÉ CARLOS

La escena contemporánea (Lima, 1925).

7 ensayos de interpretación de la realidad peruana: escritos de Mundial y Amauta (Lima, 1928).

"La revolución y la inteligencia," pp. 36–64; "Biología del fascismo," pp. 327–347; "Hechos e ideas de la revolución rusa," pp. 410–430, *Revista de filosofía*, vol. XXIII (1926).

Defensa del marxismo; la emoción de nuestro tiempo, y otros temas (Santiago, 1934).

Mariátegui, serie Pensadores de América, universidad nacional de Mexico, notas de Manuel Moreno Sánchez (Mexico, 1937).

BAZÁN, ARMANDO, *José Carlos Mariátegui* (Santiago, 1939).

CARRIÓN, BENJAMÍN, *Mapa de América* (Madrid, 1930), pp. 195–225.

MIROSHEVSKY, V., "El populismo en el Perú: papel de Mariátegui en la historia del pensamiento social latino-americano," *Dialéctica* (La Habana, Cuba), año I, num. 1 (mayo-junio, 1942), pp. 41–59.

VARGAS, J., "En defensa de José Carlos Mariátegui, marxista," *Claridad* (Buenos Aires) vol. XIII, num. 280 (1934).

HAYA DE LA TORRE, VICTOR RAÚL

Por la emancipación de América latina: Artículos, mensajes, discursos (1923–1927).

Política aprista (Lima, 1933).

¿A dónde va Indoamérica? (Santiago, 2nd ed. 1935).

El antimperialismo y el Apra (Santiago, 1936).

COSSIO DEL POMAR, F., *Haya de la Torre, el indoamericano* (Mexico, 1939).

SÁNCHEZ, LUIS ALBERTO, *Raul Haya de la Torre o el político, crónica de una vida sin tregua* (Santiago, 1934).

SANIN CANO, BALDOMERO

La civilización manual y otros ensayos (1925).

Indagaciones y imágenes (Bogotá, 1926): I, *Sociales y históricas;* II, *Críticas.*

CHAPTER VII. THREE THINKERS OF BRAZIL

DA CUNHA, EUCLYDES

Os sertões: Campanha de Canudos (Rio, 1902; 15th ed. 1940). English translation by Samuel Putnam (University of Chicago Press, 1943).

À marjem da historia (Porto, 1909).

Contrastes e confrontos da Cunha a seus amigos.

BELLO, JOSÉ MARIA, *Inteligência do Brasil* (Rio, 1940).

FREYRE, GILBERTO, *Atualidade de Euclydes da Cunha* (Rio, 1941).

PONTES, ELOY, *A vida dramática de Euclydes da Cunha* (Rio, 1940).

VENANCIO, FRANCISCO, *A glória de Euclydes da Cunha* (Sao Paulo, 1940).

MANOEL BOMFIM, JOSÉ DO

A América latina: males de origem; estudo de parasitismo social (Rio, 1905).
O Brazil na America, caracterização da formação brazileira (Rio, 1909).
O Brazil na historia: deturpação das tradições, degradação politica (Rio, 1930).
O Brazil nação; realidade da soberania brazileira (Rio, 1931).

FREYRE, GILBERTO

Casa-grande e senzala, Formação da família brasileira sob o regimem de economia patriarchal (Rio, 1933; 3rd ed. 1938).
Sobrados e mucambos, Decadência do patriarchado rural no Brasil (1936).
Nordeste. Aspectos da influencia da canna sobre a vida e a paizagem do nordeste do Brasil (Rio, 1937).
O mundo que o portuguêz criou. Aspectos das relações sociaes e de cultura do Brasil com Portugal e as colonias portuguesas (Rio, 1940).
Um engenheiro francês no Brasil (Rio, 1940).
Região e tradição, Prefacio de José Lins do Rego (Rio, 1941).
HANKE, LEWIS, "Gilberto Freyre: historiador social brasileño," *Revista hispánica moderna*, vol. VI, no. 2 (abril, 1939), pp. 97–120.
—— "Gilberto Freyre: Brazilian Social Historian," *Quarterly Journal of Inter-American Relations*, July 1939, pp. 24–44.
WERNECK SODRÉ, NELSON, *Orientações do pensamento brasileiro* (Rio, 1942), pp. 41–58.

CHAPTER VIII. THE CUBANS AND HOSTOS

VITIER, MEDARDO

Las ideas en Cuba: proceso del pensamiento político, filosófico y crítico en Cuba, principalmente durante el siglo XIX, 2 vols. (La Habana, Cuba, 1938).

VARELA, FÉLIX

Lecciones de filosofía, Biblioteca de la revista de la universidad de La Habana, La Habana, Cuba, n.d. [1940?]. Earlier editions are more accurate.
AGRAMONTE, ROBERTO, *El padre Varela*, Universidad de la Habana, June–July, pp. 64–87.
CUEVAS ZEQUEIRA, SERGIO, "Para la historia de la filosofía en Cuba," *Revista de filosofía*, XIII (1921), 438–453.
GONZÁLEZ DEL VALLE Y RAMÍREZ, FRANCISCO, *El padre Varela y la independencia de la América hispana* (La Habana, 1936).
HERNÁNDEZ TRAVIESO, A., *Félix Varela y la reforma filosófica en Cuba* (La Habana, 1942).

LUZ Y CABALLERO, JOSÉ DE

GONZÁLEZ DEL VALLE, FRANCISCO, *José de La luz y Caballero como educador; recopilación de sus escritos e introducción de Francisco González del Valle* (La Habana, 1931).
RODRIGUEZ, J. I., *Vida de Don José de la Luz y Caballero* (New York, 1874).

SACO, JOSÉ ANTONIO

Obras, 2 vols., New York, 1853.

Colección póstuma (La Habana, 1881).

Ideario reformista (La Habana, 1935).

CAMACHO, PÁNFILO D., *José Antonio Saco, aspectos de su vida* (La Habana, 1930).

ORTIZ, FERNANDO, *José Antonio Saco y sus ideas cubanas* (La Habana, 1929).

—— "Valoración cubana de José A. Saco," *Revista de filosofía,* XXX (1929), 361–392.

PONTE DOMÍNGUEZ, FRANCISCO J., *La personalidad política de José Antonio Saco* (La Habana, Cuba, 1931).

SOTO PAZ, RAFAEL, *La falsa cubanidad de Saco* (Luz y del Monte, La Habana, 1941).

VALVERDE, ANTONIO L., *José Antonio Saco, estudio biográfico* (La Habana, 1930).

VARONA, ENRIQUE JOSÉ

Obras, 4 vols., incomplete (La Habana, Cuba, 1936–1938).

I. *Varona, su vida, su obra, y su influencia,* por Elias Entralgo, Medardo Vitier, Roberto Agramonte.

II. *Estudios y conferencias.*

III. *Desde mi belvedere.*

IV. *Violetas y Ortigas.*

Conferencias filosóficas (La Habana, 1880).

Estudios literarios y filosóficos, Colección de trabajos independientes (La Habana, 1883).

Artículos y discursos; literatura, política, sociología (La Habana, 1891).

Por Cuba (Discursos) (La Habana, 1918).

Con el eslabón (San José, Costa Rica, 1918).

De la colonia a la república; selección de trabajos políticos, ordenada por su autor (La Habana, 1919).

Homenaje a José Enrique Varona en el cincuentenario de su primer curso de filosofía, 1880–1930, miscelánea de estudios literarios, históricos y filosóficos, Secretaría de Educación: Dirección de Cultura (La Habana, 1935), bibliography.

Páginas Cubanas (La Habana, 1936).

AGUAYO, A. M., *Tres grandes educadores cubanos: Varona* (La Habana, 1937).

CUEVAS ZEQUEIRA, SERGIO, "José Enrique Varona, pensador y filosófo," *Revista de filosofía,* XI (1920), 370–376.

ENTRALGO, ELIAS, *El ideario de Varona en la filosofía social,* Publicaciones de la biblioteca municipal de la Habana, cultura popular (1937).

PERAZA Y SARAUSA, FERMÍN, *Bibliografía de Varona* (La Habana, 1932).

VITIER, MEDARDO, *Varona, maestro de juventudes* (La Habana, 1937).

ZEQUEIRA, JOSÉ, *La figura de Varona* (La Habana, 1937).

MARTÍ, JOSÉ

Obras, 42 vols. (La Habana, 1939–40).

Ideario, ordenado por M. Isidro Méndez (La Habana, 1930).

Martí, serie, Pensamiento de América, prólogo y selección de Mauricio Magdaleno (Mexico, 1942).

CARBONELL, NESTOR, *Martí, su vida, su obra* (La Habana, 1923).
GARCÍA GODOY, FEDERICO, *Americanismo literario*, pp. 25–72 (Madrid, 1917).
GARCÍA MARTÍ, RAÚL, *Martí, biografía familiar* (La Habana, 1938).
IRÁIZOZ Y DE VILLAR, ANTONIO, *Las ideas pedagógicas de Martí* (La Habana, 1920).
ISIDRO MÉNDEZ, M., *Martí* (La Habana, 1941).
LAZO, RAIMUNDO, *Martí y su obra literaria* (La Habana, 1929).
LIZASO, FÉLIX, *Martí, el místico del deber* (Buenos Aires, 1940).
LIZASO, FÉLIX, *Martí y la Utopía de América* (La Habana, Cuba, 1941).
MAGDALENO, MAURICIO, *Fulgor de Martí* (La Habana, Cuba, 1941).
MAÑACH, JORGE, *Martí, el apóstol* (Madrid, 1933).
MARTÍNEZ BELLO, ANTONIO, *Ideas sociales y económicas de José Martí* (La Habana, Cuba, 1940).
MARQUEZ STERLING, CARLOS, *Martí, maestro y apóstol* (La Habana, Cuba, 1942).
MIJARES, AUGUSTO, *Hombres e ideas en América: Ensayos* (Caracas, 1940), Martí, pp. 77–112.
RODRÍGUEZ-EMBIL, LUIS, *José Martí, el santo de América* (La Habana, 1941), bibliography.
SANTOVENIA Y ECHAÏDE, EMETERIO S., *Dos creadores, Mazzini y Martí* (1936).
—— *Genio y acción: Sarmiento y Martí* (1938).
QUESADA Y MIRANDA, GONZALO DE, *Martí, hombre* (La Habana, 1940).
—— *Martí, periodista* (La Habana, 1929).

ACOSTA, CECILIO

Obras, 5 vols. (Caracas, 1907–1909).
Cartas venezolanas (Madrid, n.d.).
Páginas escogidas, prólogo de José Martí (Caracas, 1940).
DESOLA, RENÉ, *Al encuentro de Cecilio Acosta*, Academia venezolana, No. 31 (1941), pp. 272–290.

HOSTOS Y BONILLA, EUGENIO MARÍA DE

Obras, 20 vols. Additional bibliographical volume (1939).
América y Hostos, 1839–1939, 2 vols. (La Habana, 1940).
BLANCO-FOMBONA, RUFINO, *Grandes escritores de América, siglo XIX* (Madrid, 1917), Hostos, pp. 173–221.
—— "Hostos, filósofo moralista," *Revista de filosofía*, XIX (1924), 203–209.
BOSCH, JUAN, *Hostos, el sembrador* (La Habana, 1939).
PEDREIRA, ANTONIO S., *Hostos, ciudadano de América, Bibliography* (Madrid, 1932).
—— *Revista iberoamericana*, I (1939), 297–305.
Revista hispánica moderna, vol. V (octubre, 1939). Also bibliographies in this volume.

CHAPTER IX. THE MEXICANS

MORA, JOSÉ MARÍA LUIS

Obras sueltas, 2 vols. (Paris, 1837).
Mora—Ensayos, Ideas y Retratos, Biblioteca del estudiante universitario, No. 25 (Mexico, 1941). Prólogo de Arturo Arnáiz y Freg.
El Dr. José María Luis Mora, 1794–1850, Homenaje de la universidad nacional de México (1934).

Toscano, Salvador, *Vida del Dr. Mora*, Biografías populares, no. 1 (Mexico, 1936).
Zea, Leopold, *El positivismo en México* (Mexico, 1942).

RAMÍREZ, IGNACIO

Obras, 2 vols. (Mexico, 1889). Vol. I includes life by Altamirano.

ALTAMIRANO, MANUEL IGNACIO

Discursos (Mexico, 1934).
Aires de México: Prosas de Altamirano, Biblioteca del estudiante universitario, no. 18 (Mexico, 1940). Prólogo de Antonio Acevedo Escobedo.
González Ramírez, Manuel, *Vida de Altamirano*, Biografías populares, No. 5, Mexico, 1936.

SIERRA, JUSTO

Prosas, Biblioteca del estudiante universitario, No. 10 (Mexico, 1939). Prológo de Antonio Caso.
Evolución política del pueblo mexicano (1910), republished by Casa de España en Mexico (1940).

BULNES, FRANCISCO

El porvenir de las naciones hispano-americanas ante las conquistas recientes de Europa y los Estados Unidos (Mexico, 1899).
Las grandes mentiras de nuestra historia (Mexico, 1904).
Los grandes problemas de México (Mexico, 1926).

VASCONCELOS, JOSÉ

La raza cósmica: misión de la raza iberoamericana. Notas de viajes a la América del Sur (Paris, n.d.).
Hispano-américa frente a los nacionalismos agresivos de Europo y Estados Unidos (La Plata, 1934).
La cultura en hispano-américa, conferencias y escritos, No. 15 (La Plata, 1934–35).
¿Qué es el comunismo? (Mexico, 1936).
Estética, Mexico, 1936, 2a ed.
¿Qué es la revolución? (Mexico, 1937).
Ética (Mexico, 2a ed., 1939).
Páginas escogidas, prólogo de Antonio Castro Leal (Mexico, 1940).
Vasconcelos, serie Pensamiento de America, No. 1 (Mexico, 1942). Prólogo de Genaro Fernández MacGregor.
Indología, una interpretación de la cultura iberoamericana (Barcelona, n.d.): *Ulises criollo, I; La tormenta, II; El desastre, III; Proconsulado, IV* (all parts of autobiography).
Carrión, Benjamín, *Los creadores de la nueva América* (Madrid, 1928), pp. 23–76.
Nano Lottero, Rómulo, *Palabras para América: El caso Vasconcelos* (Uruguay, 1931), pp. 21–77.
Sánchez Villaseñor, José, *El sistema filosófico de Vasconcelos: ensayo de crítica filosófica* (Mexico, 1939).

CASO, ANTONIO

Filósofos y doctrinas morales (Mexico, 1915).
Problemas filosóficos (Mexico, 1915).
Discursos a la nación mexicana (Mexico, 1922).
Doctrinas e ideas (Mexico, 1924).
Principios de estética (Mexico, 1925).
El concepto de la historia y la filosofía de los valores (Mexico, 1933).
Nuevos discursos a la nación mexicana (Mexico, 1934).
El acto ideatorio (las esencias y los valores) (Mexico, 1934).
La persona humana y el estado totalitario (Mexico, 1941).
El peligro del hombre (Mexico, 1942).
La filosofía de la cultura (Mexico, 1936).

RAMOS, SAMUEL

El perfil del hombre y de la cultura en México (Mexico, 1938).
Hacia un nuevo humanismo: programa de un antropología filosófica (Mexico, 1940).
Historia del pensamiento filosófico en México (Mexico, 1943).

Index

Index